WITHDRAWN

TOWARDS A THEORY OF COGNITION AND COMPUTING

For Marianne, Daniel, Esther and Mum, with my love.

**ELLIS HORWOOD SERIES IN ARTIFICIAL INTELLIGENCE
FOUNDATIONS AND CONCEPTS**
Series Editor: Dr AJIT NARAYANAN, Department of Computer Science, University of Exeter

ARTIFICIAL INTELLIGENCE AND INTELLIGENT SYSTEMS: The Implications
D. ANDERSON
ARTIFICIAL INTELLIGENCE TERMINOLOGY: A Reference Guide
C. BEARDON (available in Library Edn and Paperback)
AI AND PHILOSOPHY OF LANGUAGE
B. CARR
**ARTIFICIAL INTELLIGENCE AND EXPERT SYSTEMS:
Case Studies in the Knowledge Domain of Archaeology**
J.-C. GARDIN
FORMALISM IN AI AND COMPUTER SCIENCE
P. LEITH
**ON BEING A MACHINE, Volume 1: Formal Aspects of Artificial Intelligence
ON BEING A MACHINE, Volume 2: Philosophy of Artificial Intelligence**
A. NARAYANAN
ARTIFICIAL INTELLIGENCE: A Handbook of Professionalism
B. WHITBY
TOWARDS A THEORY OF COGNITION AND COMPUTING
J. G. WOLFF

TOWARDS A THEORY OF COGNITION AND COMPUTING

J. GERARD WOLFF B.A., Ph.D.
School of Electronic Engineering Science
University of Wales, Bangor

STAFFORD LIBRARY
COLUMBIA COLLEGE
1001 ROGERS STREET
COLUMBIA, MO 65216

ELLIS HORWOOD
NEW YORK LONDON TORONTO SYDNEY TOKYO SINGAPORE

006.3
W833t

First published in 1991 by
ELLIS HORWOOD LIMITED
Market Cross House, Cooper Street,
Chichester, West Sussex, PO19 1EB, England

A division of
Simon & Schuster International Group
A Paramount Communications Company

© Ellis Horwood Limited, 1991

All rights reserved. No part of this publication may be reproduced, stored in a retrieval system, or transmitted, in any form, or by any means, electronic, mechanical, photocopying, recording or otherwise, without the prior permission, in writing, of the publisher

Typeset in Times by Ellis Horwood Limited
Printed and bound in Great Britain
by Hartnolls, Bodmin, Cornwall

British Library Cataloguing in Publication Data

Wolff, Gerard J.
Towards a theory of cognition and computing. —
(Ellis Horwood series in artificial intelligence foundations and concepts)
I. Title   II. Series
006.3
ISBN 0–13–925025–5

Library of Congress Cataloging-in-Publication Data available

Table of contents

ACKNOWLEDGEMENTS 7

1. INTRODUCTION 9
   Language learning and cognitive development 10
   Computing 20
   Context 25
   Information and redundancy in computing and cognition 27
   Conclusion 29
   References 29

2. LEARNING A FIRST LANGUAGE 31
   LEARNING SYNTAX AND MEANINGS THROUGH
   OPTIMIZATION AND DISTRIBUTIONAL ANALYSIS 32
   Introduction 32
   Presuppositions of the theory 32
   Outline of the theory 33
   Empirical evidence 43
   Conclusion 60
   Summary 62
   References 62

3. THE SNPR MODEL 66
   LANGUAGE ACQUISITION, DATA COMPRESSION AND
   GENERALIZATION 67
   Introduction 67
   Efficiency and data compression 71
   Generalization 76
   Program SNPR 79
   Illustrative results 86
   Discussion 91
   Concluding remarks 95
   References 96

4. THE SP THEORY 100
   SIMPLICITY AND POWER — SOME UNIFYING IDEAS IN
   COMPUTING 100
   Abstract 100
   1. Introduction 101

  2. Simplicity and power in grammars and computing systems 102
  3. Organizing principles 111
  4. The SP language 114
  5. Applications 119
  6. Conclusion 133
  References 134
  Appendix: The calculation of size, power and efficiency of grammars 135

5. A PROTOTYPE OF THE SP SYSTEM 136
 The SP theory 136
 SP6 142
 Examples 147
 Conclusion 159

6. THE EXPECTED BENEFITS OF A MATURE SP SYSTEM 162
 The potential benefits of SP 163
 Conclusion 172
 References 172

7. THE SP LANGUAGE IN PROJECT MANAGEMENT 173
 THE MANAGEMENT OF RISK IN SYSTEM DEVELOPMENT:
 'PROJECT SP' AND THE 'NEW SPIRAL MODEL' 173
 Abstract 173
 1. Introduction 174
 2. Models of system development 174
 3. The PCIS project 177
 4. 'Project SP' and the 'New Spiral Model' 180
 5. Related issues 190
 6. Conclusion 191
 7. Acknowledgements 191
 8. References 191

INDEX 193

Acknowledgements

The ideas described in this book have been developed mainly while I have been employed in research and academic positions over a period of several years. I am very grateful for the opportunities which have been provided for me to pursue this work and for the support which has been given me by:

- Alun Thomas and colleagues in the Department of Audiology, The Heath Hospital, Cardiff (1971–76).
- Alan Kennedy and colleagues in the Department of Psychology, University of Dundee (1976–83).
- John O'Reilly, Peter Fleming and other colleagues in the School of Electronic Engineering Science, University of Wales, Bangor (from 1988).

My thanks also to:

- The Jane Hodge Foundation which paid for the first year of my employment at Cardiff.
- The South Glamorgan Area Health Authority which granted me one year's leave with pay from my post in Cardiff to enable me to complete my Ph.D. thesis.
- The British Social Science Research Council (now the Economic and Social Research Council) which provided a Personal Research Grant (HRP8240/1(A)) to release me from teaching and administration duties for the academic year 1982–83.

IBM UK Ltd gave me a one-year research fellowship (for work on the synthesis of speech from text) and I was employed with Praxis Systems plc for four years in software engineering and project management. Although they did not provide direct support for the research, I am grateful to IBM and Praxis for these opportunities which gave me some understanding of computing in a commercial environment and stimulated me to new thinking about cognition and computing.

During the time which I have been doing this research, many individual people (other than those already mentioned) have assisted the work in various ways. I am very grateful for all this help.

Donald Broadbent of the Department of Experimental Psychology, University of Oxford, took the trouble to give me detailed and constructive criticism of one of my early attempts at a journal article and has subsequently provided much needed moral support for the research programme.

8 ACKNOWLEDGEMENTS

Godfrey Harrison, formerly of the Department of Psychology, University College Cardiff, and now in the Department of Linguistics, University of Hong Kong, gave very useful advice and encouragement as supervisor for my Ph.D. degree, despite initial scepticism about the proposed programme of research.

Pat Langley at NASA Ames Research Centre in California has provided the stimulus of discussions and exchange of information about learning processes over the years. He has also given me very useful advice about recent (and not so recent) work in machine learning while I have been preparing the book.

Much of the early thinking about SP in relation to computing has benefited from lunch-time discussions I have had with Simon Tait of Praxis Systems plc.

The following people have also been helpful with discussion or comment, in providing information or in other ways:

- Jim Baldwin, Department of Engineering Mathematics, University of Bristol.
- Bob Borsley, Department of Linguistics, University of Wales, Bangor.
- John Campbell, Department of Computer Science, University College London.
- Frank Gooding, Department of Linguistics, University of Wales, Bangor.
- Geoffrey Hunter, Department of Philosophy, University of Wales, Bangor.
- Alan Hutchinson, Department of Computer Science, Kings College, London.
- Simon Jones, Department of Electrical and Electronic Engineering, University of Nottingham.
- Mark Lawson, Department of Mathematics, University of Wales, Bangor.
- Tim Porter, Department of Mathematics, University of Wales, Bangor.
- Derek Sleeman, Department of Computer Science, University of Aberdeen.
- Chris Thornton, Department of Artificial Intelligence, University of Edinburgh.
- Roger Young, Department of Philosophy, University of Dundee.

The research has benefited from the work of research students — Philip Quinlan at Dundee, Paul Mather and Andy Chipperfield at Bangor — and from extensive discussions we have had.

Other acknowledgements are given in the articles reproduced in the book.

The following people have taken the trouble to read drafts of the book or parts of it and to make constructive comments:

- Gordon Brown, Department of Psychology, University of Wales, Bangor.
- Andy Duller, School of Electronic Engineering, University of Wales, Bangor.
- Richard Forsyth, Department of Psychology, University of Nottingham.
- Marianne Jones, Japanese Resources Centre, Mackworth College, Derbyshire.

Special thanks to Ajit Narayanan of the Department of Computer Science, University of Exeter (Series Editor for AI Foundations and Concepts), who has edited the book and has made many useful suggestions for improving the text.

Of course, I am responsible for all errors of fact or judgement which may remain in the book.

Thanks also to the many other people, too numerous to list, even if I knew all their names, who have made comments and suggestions about the SP ideas after talks that I have given or on other occasions.

Finally, my thanks to Sue Horwood and her colleagues at Ellis Horwood with whom it has been a pleasure to work in the production of this book.

1
Introduction

This is a book about some ideas which I have been developing intermittently for nearly twenty years. For about half that time, the main focus of the research was trying to understand how a child learns his or her first language and, more generally, trying to understand how people learn new knowledge, organize what they know and use it. When I moved from this research to work in computing, I discovered, with some surprise, that ideas about language learning and cognition which had come out of this research were relevant to a wide range of issues in my new field. This realization led to the second phase of the research, which is still in progress, in which the ideas are being applied to concepts and issues in computing. A new kind of computing system is being developed which is based on this thinking.

As a convenient shorthand throughout this book, I will refer to these ideas about cognition and computing as 'the theory' as if they were a complete and encapsulated entity. The reality is that the theory — called 'SP' — is not complete, and there are problems still to be solved in this programme of research. Hence the use of the word 'towards' in the title of the book.

What sort of research is this? It started out as 'cognitive psychology' with the main focus on human information processing. The later work may be classified as 'computer science'. But because the overall aim now is to integrate these two areas, the book as a whole is probably best classified as 'cognitive science' in the original broad meaning of that term.

The book is composed mainly of articles which have already been published plus three other chapters (including this one) and some linking material. Although the articles have been published before, they have been scattered in a variety of journals and books. A purpose of this book is to bring together the more important publications from the research programme, for easy reference and so that the themes of the research and the evolution of the ideas may be more clearly seen.

Like any conscientious researcher, I have always tried to keep abreast of related work — as far as that is possible when the volume of published material is so large — and to acknowledge it appropriately. The articles which form the bulk of this book contain many references to other people's work. But in this chapter I take a more personal view of the research and describe the research programme in terms of my own thinking and my sometimes haphazard progress to new insights. Here is a short history of how the ideas developed.

LANGUAGE LEARNING AND COGNITIVE DEVELOPMENT
Getting started

In 1971 I was working as a research psychologist at the Heath Hospital in Cardiff and writing a book about how people use language, how children learn their first language and the language problems of deaf people (Wolff, 1973). The question which caught my attention as I was writing about language learning was how a child learning, say, English, comes to recognize the way in which the language is divided into words and other discrete segments like phrases and sentences. Just in case children do not actually recognize this kind of segmental structure, I checked the relevant literature and found that there is plenty of evidence that they do — and well before the age when they might have picked up ideas about the segmental structure of language by learning to read.

Possible clues to words and other segments in language include pauses between segments, intonation patterns including patterns of stress in language, meanings and the statistical structure of the language. For phrases and sentences it is easy enough to believe that children get enough clues from pauses between segments and from regular patterns of intonation which mark these units in ordinary speech (although the other clues which were mentioned may also make a contribution). But with words it is not obvious that there are enough clues from pauses or from intonation patterns to enable a child to learn where each word begins and ends in a stream of speech; sound spectrograms of speech — which provide a visual 'picture' of speech — show that people usually talk in 'ribbons' of sound with few pauses between words and no other systematic physical clues to where each word begins and ends. Although meanings may possibly help a child to learn the segmental structure of language it is not at all obvious how this could happen.

The superficially implausible idea that language learning may be based on statistics has been the central idea in this programme of research. The research strategy has not been to 'prove' this idea or to disprove alternative ideas about how language learning could occur. Rather, the aim of the research has been to explore how far it is possible to go in developing a language learning theory which is based on the statistical structure of language.

Obviously, children do not know explicitly about the 'chi square' test or multiple regression analysis but they seem to be sensitive to the statistical regularities which exist in language. To see these regularities, try playing the guessing game described here.

Ask a friend to think of a sentence but not to tell you what it is. Try guessing the first letter in the sentence and record how many guesses are needed before you get the right answer. Then do the same for the second letter and the third and all the subsequent letters. The number of guesses needed for any given letter is usually highest for the first letter in the sentence. The next letter is easier because knowing the first letter gives a clue to what may come next. The third and subsequent letters are even easier until you get to the end of the first word. Suddenly, the first letter of the second word is harder than the last few letters of the first word. Each time you reach the end of one word and start on the next there is usually a sharp increase in the number of guesses needed. In the same way that the number of guesses per letter tends to decrease towards the end of each word, letters get progressively easier to guess as you proceed through the sentence. And if you start a new sentence, letters at the beginning are unpredictable again. Although it is easiest to play this game using letters and the ordinary spellings of language, it should be clear that the same kinds of regularities exist in language in its spoken form.

Computer models

The guessing game shows how there is something in the statistical structure of language which could enable a child to infer what the segments are in language. But there is a big gap between a general idea of this sort and a detailed understanding of exactly *how* the learning process could work. If this is really how children learn the segmental structure of language, children must be doing some kind of statistical analysis — and the necessary 'processing' is likely to be quite complicated. It seemed that a useful way to understand what kind of processing would work was to develop computer models and to test them out with more or less realistic 'data'.

The method I used was to prepare a 'text' resembling natural language in some way and then try to develop a computer model which, without any prior knowledge of segments or structure in the text, and without any assistance from a human or non-human 'teacher', could analyse the text and reveal whatever structure was there.

The simplest kind of text was a sequence of words, drawn at random from a set of, say, ten, and assembled as an unbroken stream of characters without any punctuation or spaces between the words. Texts were also prepared from real language with all punctuation removed and without any spaces between the words. The main criterion of success for the computer models with these kinds of texts was an ability to discover what the words were in the text, given only the text as data and no prior knowledge of any words.

In later work, where computer models (described later in this chapter) were designed to discover grammatical structure, texts were constructed using simple grammars to control the sequences of words. As before, there were no markers of segment boundaries in these texts. The main criterion of success for these programs was an ability to discover or reconstruct from this kind of text what grammar was used to prepare the text.

In developing the discovery programs, several different statistical ideas were tried: using transition probabilities between symbols, using measures based on conventional statistics, and others. They all gave results which showed that the general approach was plausible. The early models showed that the segmental structure of artificial language-like texts could be discovered using only the statistical regularities in the material. But the best results by far — the most accurate discovery of segments — were obtained with the simplest idea. Model MK10 (Wolff, 1975) used a simple measure of conjoint frequency of symbols to sift out 'good' groupings from all the many possible 'bad' ones.

This model gave good results not only with artificial texts but with real language too. I tried running it on texts prepared as extracts from books with all punctuation removed and no spaces between words. The program, equipped initially only with a knowledge of the non-punctuation character set used in the text (normally, just the twenty-six letters of the alphabet but phonemic texts have also been used) could build up a knowledge of the word structure of the texts and, with most material, could develop a remarkably accurate parsing (analysis) of the text into its constituent words (Wolff, 1977).

If the program is allowed to run for long enough it will join words into larger groupings. An obvious question was whether these larger groupings would correspond to the phrase segments and clause segments which are conventionally recognized in language. Running on plain text, MK10 does not do very well at this level. The reason is almost certainly because it does not have any concept of *classes* of words — nouns, verbs, adjectives etc. If a text is transcribed by hand into a sequence of word class symbols and MK10 is used to process the unsegmented stream of symbols, it does quite a good job with most material at identifying the phrase groupings and clause groupings which we normally recognize (Wolff, 1980).

Levels of abstraction in the theory
This is, perhaps, an appropriate place to make some comments about the uses of computer models in this kind of work and the relationship between computer models and 'theory'. In developing a theory of a complex process (and the process by which a child learns his or her first language is undoubtedly complex), creating a computer model brings two major benefits:

- Writing a program which is explicit enough and precise enough to be run on a computer is a very useful way of reducing vagueness and ambiguity in a theory.
- Running the model on varied examples is an invaluable way of understanding the often complex and ramifying implications of a theory and seeing clearly whether or not a proposed theory can meet the facts which it has been designed to explain.

In developing computer models of language learning, and in the work I have been doing more recently, I have often found that initial 'armchair' thoughts about how some process might behave turn out to be wrong when they are tested in this way.

In this programme of research I have found it convenient to distinguish two main levels of abstraction in the theory:

- At the highest level are ideas, to be described later, like 'efficiency', 'power', 'size', 'pattern matching', 'unification' and 'hill-climbing search'.
- At a second, more concrete, level of abstraction are the knowledge structures and the methods which are needed to realize the most abstract concepts in a working model.

A computer model may be regarded as a relatively 'concrete' expression of a theory. It contains the information needed to make a theory fully explicit and unambiguous. It may also contain 'programming' details which are not part of the theory but which are needed to make the model run with the available technology. If a suitable modelling language is used with capabilities for 'information hiding' and abstraction, these implementation details can be hidden from view.

Learning non-verbal concepts
Right from the beginning it seemed possible that the ideas about the learning of segments in language would generalize. The kind of statistical analysis which can

lead to a recognition of discrete segments in speech may also enable a child to learn non-verbal concepts — the 'meanings' which lie behind the words of language — and also to learn the association between words and their meanings.

For example, it is possible to see ordinary objects in the world — tables, chairs, cars etc. — as 'segments' of the visual world comparable with words and other segments in a stream of speech. Visual objects and words can both be understood as coherent clusters of features which appear in a variety of contexts. The contrast between the relative stability of features within a segment and the variety of contexts in which it may appear marks the segment as discrete even when there are no other clues to the boundary between the segment and what lies outside it.

This kind of 'statistical' notion of how we see the world may be extended to more abstract concepts. *Classes* and *sub-classes* of objects may also be understood as coherent clusters of features but at a higher level of abstraction than individual objects. The process of learning non-verbal concepts, including structures of classes and sub-classes, may be seen as a kind of 'cluster analysis' or 'numerical taxonomy' of the kind commonly used by biologists and social scientists.

At an early stage of the research programme I tried to develop a 'statistical' model of how non-verbal concepts may be learned. Rather than simply produce another clustering program (hundreds of different clustering programs have been written), I aimed for a model which would create conceptual structures like those which people seem to create — which are similar to but by no means identical with the relatively artificial structures generated by ordinary clustering programs. Six features were targeted:

- *Salience*. Certain categories of object or other perceptual entity are widely used by people (and perhaps animals too) because they are salient or natural groupings. Of the many possible ways of classifying people, say, such groupings as 'male' and 'female' are employed in preference to arbitrary or bizarre categories such as 'people who have fair hair and a handspan greater than seven inches'.
- *Hierarchy*. One concept or class may include another, e.g. 'woman' and 'mother'.
- *Overlap*. A given entity may be assigned to two or more conceptual classes which are not hierarchically related, e.g. 'woman' and 'doctor'.
- *Fuzziness of conceptual boundaries*. The boundaries of conceptual categories are not usually sharply defined. Another way of expressing this is to say that the confidence with which objects may be assigned to a given category varies. For example, 'cottage' is a category which shades into 'house' or 'hut'; it may be difficult to decide in which of the three categories a given building belongs.
- *Polythesis*. Most human concepts are polythetic which means that no particular attribute or combination of attributes need necessarily be present (or absent) for an object to belong to a given category.
- *Weighting of attributes*. Intuitively, some attributes are more significant in the development of classes than others. The attributes 'fur', 'four legs' and 'tail' are weak determiners of the concept 'cat' while 'retractile claws' and 'purring' are relatively strong.

The model which I developed at that time (Wolff, 1976) was fairly successful in capturing most of these features but was relatively weak on polythesis. Probably the main value of this exercise was in identifying the target features to be captured by a model and demonstrating how the statistical approach to learning could be extended to the domain of non-verbal concepts.

The SNPR model which was developed later as a model of how syntax may be learned (and which is described below and in Chapter 3) can also be seen as a model of how non-verbal concepts may be learned. It fits all six criteria rather well and, in particular, it demonstrates how polythetic categories may be learned. These points are discussed in Chapter 2.

Grammatical rules
There is more to the organization of a language than simple patterns of words, phrases and sentences. It is not possible to define any natural language as a finite set of 'utterances'; it is very clear that in all natural languages there is an infinite set of possible utterances and it is likely that the majority of spoken or written sentences are new combinations of words which have never been produced before. In most languages, words and other structures fall into classes such as nouns, verbs and adjectives. Any definition of the organization of the language — a 'grammar' — must also contain a set of abstract 'rules'. Rules — with classes — should have a capability to create or recognize the infinite set of acceptable utterances and exclude the (even larger) infinite set of utterances which native speakers of the language would reject as being in some sense wrong or forbidden for that language.

As with non-verbal concepts, it seemed possible that the statistical approach might generalize to the learning of grammatical rules. This kind of idea is not new. It was pursued for several years by Z. S. Harris and other 'taxonomic' linguists before Chomsky's influential criticisms (e.g. 1959) brought most of the research in this tradition to an end.

One of the questions to be answered in developing this idea is, "What kinds of rules are needed in a grammatical system to describe a natural language accurately?" Chomsky's critique of taxonomic methods was based partly on the (correct) belief that taxonomic notions of 'rule' were too simple and partly on the (false) belief that 'transformational' rules were an essential part of grammatical systems for natural language.

It was (and is) very difficult to see how transformational rules could be learned by statistical learning techniques and this difficulty led to the widely held belief that the taxonomic tradition was doomed and that children must be born with much of the structure of language already established in their heads.

More recent research and discussion has established that some kinds of non-transformational system (e.g. Definite Clause Grammars described by Pereira & Warren (1980)) are almost certainly as powerful as transformational grammar but at the time that I was working on this problem I was ready to settle on one of the simple non-transformational systems ('Context-Free Phrase Structure Grammar' — CF-PSG) merely as a sub-set of what is needed in a grammatical system for natural language and a reasonable preliminary test-bed for taxonomic ideas.

As described earlier, the general idea was to prepare an unsegmented text according to the rules of a simple grammar and then try to develop a program which, given only the text as data and no other knowledge of grammatical structure, could re-create the grammar used to construct the text.

My first attempt at a program to learn grammatical rules (1978b) was good enough to show that the idea was feasible. In this model, the text is first analysed by MK10 and the segments identified by that program are treated as prototype rules. A second program was written ('GRAM15') which analyses the set of segments identified by MK10 to find *classes* of syntactically equivalent segments and then modifies the segments so that they include these classes at appropriate positions within the segments. The modified segments are essentially grammatical rules for the text. For example, from two segments such as MARYRUNS and MARYWALKS, the program infers that {RUNS, WALKS} is a class of syntactically equivalent segments (because they both share the context 'MARY'). Once this class is identified, MARYRUNS and MARYWALKS is collapsed into MARY{RUNS, WALKS}, which with an appropriate tag (e.g. 'r1') becomes a simple rule (r1→MARY{RUNS, WALKS}) describing part of the structure of the original text.

The MK10/GRAM15 model is capable of discovering a grammar for an artificial text, given only the text and no prior knowledge of its structure. And the grammar which it discovers is usually the same as or reasonably close to the grammar used to construct the text.

SNPR: a more realistic model
The main weakness of the MK10/GRAM15 model is that it is unrealistic from a psychological point of view. It is obvious that children do not spend half their childhoods learning segments in language and the other half learning word classes and creating grammatical rules. It is much more likely that these two processes are integrated.

A lot of effort was put into developing a new model for the learning of grammatical rules, called SNPR, which was designed to remedy this weakness and solve some other problems (described below). This model builds up its knowledge of basic segments, classes of segments and grammatical rules in an integrated way from the earliest stages (Wolff, 1982; see Chapter 3). For artificial language-like texts, at least, this model is remarkably successful both in inferring plausible rules from unsegmented text and in the way it integrates the learning of segmental structure with the learning of classes of structure.

This integration is the key to two other problems: a long-standing objection to the taxonomic idea that word classes may be inferred from shared context and the 'generalization' problem described in the next sub-section. These points are explained more fully in Chapter 2 and the introduction to Chapter 3.

Generalizations, overgeneralizations and the correction of overgeneralizations
One of the aims in developing the SNPR model, in addition to integrating the learning of segmental structures with the learning of class structures, was solving a set of problems related to 'generalization'.

One of the significant facts of language learning is that, from the finite (albeit large) sample of language we have heard since birth, we infer a set of rules which can create or analyse an *infinite* range of sentences and can exclude all the many possible non-sentences. In Fig. 2.1 (Chapter 2, page 36) the finite sample of language we have heard since birth is represented by the smallest balloon, the infinite set of 'legal' sentences is represented by the middle-sized balloon while the even larger infinite set of possible utterances is represented by the largest balloon; the difference between the largest balloon and the middle-sized balloon is the set of 'illegal' utterances which do not belong in the given language.

The problem to be solved in any theory of language learning is how to generalize from the finite sample to create a grammar which can generate all and only the legal sentences without overgeneralizing and creating rules which generate illegal forms. The problem is an awkward one because both types of generalization — legal and illegal — have zero frequency in the learner's experience. The problem is awkward, too, because available evidence suggests that children can discriminate correct and incorrect generalizations without the need for explicit correction by a 'teacher', without the provision of 'negative' samples of language (samples marked as 'wrong') and without any other explicit marking of overgeneralizations.

The SNPR model provides a mechanism — described in Chapter 3 — which appears to work well, at least with artificial texts. The success of the mechanism is qualified with the words 'appears to' because it depends on intuitive judgements of which generalizations are 'correct' and which are 'incorrect'. However, these intuitions are strong: the generalizations which the model makes and which it allows to persist are strikingly more 'natural' and appropriate than the many other generalizations which the model makes and which it subsequently weeds out from its grammatical structures.

As far as I know, this solution to the problem of distinguishing correct generalizations from incorrect ones without negative information or explicit correction of errors had not been proposed before and, as far as I know, more recent work on machine learning by other researchers has not produced anything equivalent†.

An abstract view of cognitive development
It is often said that developments in science are not as tidy and logical as they appear to be in journal articles and textbooks. This is not to say that scientists necessarily have any sinister motive for hiding the unplanned nature of new insights. It is more likely that tidiness is needed in presenting new ideas to ensure that they are understood.

In developing the MK10, MK10/GRAM15 and SNPR models, I was attempting to understand how selected features of the language learning process could be explained in terms of statistical analysis. Much of the effort was directed towards the creation of concrete mechanisms which could imitate aspects of language learning in a reasonably clean, simple and general way without ad hoc features.

In the course of devising these mechanisms, it became clear gradually that the more successful ones could be understood in more abstract terms than those in which they had been originally designed. In general terms, all three models can be seen as mechanisms which create a succinct description of a language from raw linguistic data. In the case of MK10, the compact description is the set of segments created by

---

† I am grateful to Pat Langley and Richard Forsyth, who are much more closely in touch with the literature on machine learning than I now am, for confirming that they have not seen any equivalent mechanism described anywhere. Models have been proposed which correct overgeneralizations but they use mechanisms which are distinct from the purely 'statistical' mechanisms in SNPR. These points are discussed in Chapter 2.

the program. In the case of MK10/GRAM15 and SNPR the compact description is a grammar.

Could it be that language learning is nothing but a process of data compression, essentially the same as the compression techniques which are used in ordinary computer applications to reduce the costs of storing or transmitting data? The three models do resemble standard compression techniques in some respects but there are also significant differences. The MK10 model actually provides a method of developing codes for data compression which has some advantages compared with standard methods (Wolff, 1978a).

It became apparent that the three models, like mainstream compression methods, are designed to identify *redundancy* in data and to remove it wherever possible. (Redundancy, in this context, means redundancy in the technical sense of Shannon's information theory (Shannon & Weaver, 1949) and is close in meaning to 'unnecessary repetition of information'.)

The main difference between the learning models and most compression techniques (the 'lossless' techniques, at least) is that non-redundant information is deliberately omitted from the knowledge structures which the models create. A grammar is, typically, *less* than a compressed version of raw linguistic data; it is a compressed version of raw data with non-redundant information missing.

What is the use of all this? If this is really the kind of processing which is going on when a child learns his or her first language, what is its purpose or function? In what way does this kind of view of language learning help us to understand the things we see happening as children learn? The answer which emerged at this stage in the research program (which I first described in Wolff (1982), reproduced in Chapter 3, and which is described more fully in Chapter 2) is that the kind of long-term structure of knowledge ('grammar') which we create as we learn a language can be seen as a means of encoding new information in an economical way and thus increasing the efficiency with which we manipulate and use information. This view of grammatical function is distinct from, but also compatible with, the more conventional view of a grammar as system of rules for creating or analysing sentences.

In its simplest form, economical encoding of information can be done by assigning a short identifier or tag to a relatively large body of information. If, for example, the cliché phrase 'How do you do?' has been given a tag '1' then '1' may replace 'How do you do?' in all the contexts in which it occurs, thus saving on storage space and facilitating the transmission or manipulation of information.

When a grammar is seen in these terms, its effectiveness as a means of encoding new information economically may be measured in terms of the difference between the size of a given body of information in its raw state and the size of the same information after it has been encoded by the grammar. This expressive *power* of the grammar (also termed 'compression capacity' or CC in Chapter 2) generally varies with the *size* of the grammar: big grammars usually have a higher power than small ones. (The concept of size of a grammar was termed S_g in the articles reproduced in Chapters 2 and 3.)

Learning a grammar may be seen as a process of adding new structures in such a way that the *efficiency* of the grammar — the ratio of power to size — is maximized. At all stages, the learning process seeks to maximize power for any given size or minimize size for a given power. At no stage is the grammar a full description of the raw language from which it was derived: there is always non-redundant information missing.

Generalization fits naturally into this abstract view of language learning. In this view, generalizations correspond to the missing information just mentioned. A grammar is more general than the raw data from which it is derived to the extent that non-redundant information which is present in the raw data is missing from the grammar.

The mechanism in SNPR which distinguishes 'correct' generalizations from overgeneralizations may also be seen in these abstract terms. On the abstract view, generalizations are formed only to the extent that they raise the ratio of power to size. Overgeneralizations are those generalizations which have the effect of lowering this ratio. The balance between generalization and overgeneralization corresponds to a peak in the ratio of power to size.

Learning more realistic grammars
In parallel with developing this abstract view of learning, I was trying to progress beyond the confines of simple CF-PSGs to understand how more realistic types of grammatical system could be used in the learning process. Thanks to a Personal Research Grant from the British Social Science Research Council (now the Economic and Social Research Council), I was able to concentrate on this problem in the year 1982–83, free from teaching and administration.

The main weaknesses of CF-PSGs for representing natural language are:

- They cannot represent 'discontinuous dependencies' in the syntax of natural language in an efficient way. (Discontinuous dependencies are dependencies or associations between parts of a sentence which are not contiguous within the sentence. For example, a singular subject for a sentence must be matched by a singular verb (and likewise for plurals) even though there may be many words (e.g. qualifying clauses) between the subject and the verb.)
- They cannot easily be used to represent the meanings (semantics) of language or to integrate syntax with semantics.

When I first chose CF-PSGs as an approximation to what is needed to represent structures of natural language, the main contenders for the title of 'realistic system' were Chomsky's Transformational Grammar (TG) and variants of it. The main shortcomings of TG for my purposes were:

- It is hard to see how transformations can be learned.
- It is not clear how meanings should be represented in TG and integrated with syntax.
- It is not clear how TG can be incorporated within a model of cognition which supports the interpretation (understanding) of natural language (although TG lends itself quite well to the production of language).

Fortunately, during the time that I had been developing SNPR, there were new insights into how natural language could be represented and new models had been proposed, some of which fitted into my framework of ideas much more naturally than did TG. The most attractive of these new systems, from my point of view, was the Definite Clause Grammar (DCG) formalism described by Pereira & Warren (1980). The DCG system, based closely on the Prolog computer language, was attractive for four main reasons:

- It appears to be powerful enough to represent the subtleties of natural language structure in an efficient way, including discontinuous dependencies in syntax.
- Syntax and semantics may be integrated in the one uniform formalism.
- It is relatively easy to see how both interpretation and production of language may be modelled with the system.
- Because DCGs are like CF-PSGs but with some extra mechanism, there seemed to be a good chance of generalizing the processes in the SNPR model to work with DCGs.

No new learning model resulted from this phase of research but a number of useful insights were achieved. In Wolff (1987), I have described the kind of way in which a learning system for DCGs might be organized. Understanding the relevance of DCGs to the overall problem and understanding the possible ways in which the kinds of mechanisms in SNPR might be generalized and applied to the learning of DCGs was a useful step forward. But I now believe that DCGs are not the best target and that the ideas described later in this chapter and in the later parts of this book are likely to be a better way to go.

Is this really how children learn to talk?
The main thrust of the work which I have described so far was to explore how far it was possible to go in developing learning models based on 'statistical' principles and to understand relevant theoretical issues. But does a child really learn his or her first language in the same way as the models? Are the models psychologically 'true' or are they just interesting mechanisms?

The models were designed to meet the broad facts of language learning (that children evidently learn some kind of 'grammar'). In creating the models, I tried to avoid developing mechanisms which were clearly at odds with the way children learn. And I used observational facts of how children learn language (from many studies published by other researchers) as a source of ideas about possible mechanisms. But, in general, the models were shaped by the internal 'logic' of the statistical approach and there was no attempt to model detailed features of language learning directly.

The models demonstrated the capability of certain mechanisms and suggested their potential for further development, but the models in themselves do not in any way prove that children really learn a first language in that kind of way. Of course, there is no proof in a strict sense of any scientific theory but it is still pertinent to ask how good the fit is between what the models do and observations of what children do when they learn to talk.

The MK10 and SNPR models have several properties which fit remarkably well with observed features of language learning by children. Some of these properties — the ability to abstract plausible structures from raw linguistic data, for example — were targeted in the design of the models. But many of the properties which match observations of what children do in the course of language learning are by-products of the way the models were designed. The existence of these several correspondences, especially the ones which were not targeted in the design of the models — and the lack of any serious mismatch between properties of the models and observational data — strengthens the belief that the models are more than mere 'feasible mechanisms' and may capture some of the essentials of real language learning by children.

All the relevant evidence that I have been able to find is described quite fully in Wolff (1988). That article is reproduced in this volume in Chapter 2.

COMPUTING

Since 1983, my interests have been focused more on computing than psychology, first on a one-year IBM Research Fellowship at the IBM Science Centre in Winchester, then, for four years, in software engineering with Praxis Systems plc in Bath and now in computer systems engineering at the School of Electronic Engineering Science, University of Wales, Bangor.

Seeing connections

I first began to see possible connections between language learning and computing when I was looking at DCGs and the Prolog computer language on which they are based.

A large part of the processing in the MK10 and SNPR models is devoted to a search for redundancy in linguistic data and the extraction of that redundancy wherever it is found. Since, informally, redundancy means 'unnecessary repetition of information', redundancy can be detected by looking for the repetition of patterns in data and this can be done by comparing or 'matching' patterns to find sets of patterns which are the same. Wherever a pattern repeats more often than other patterns of the same size, there is redundancy. And redundancy can be reduced by the merging or 'unification' of identical patterns to replace multiple instances with one.

MK10 and SNPR are, in large part, dedicated to comparing (matching) patterns and unifying patterns which are the same. But the same is true of Prolog! The two models for autonomous inductive learning turn out to be similar, in a fundamental way, to a system which in its original and still important purpose is the representation of logical propositions and the drawing of logical inferences. This was my first insight which suggested a possible integration of areas which are not normally regarded as having much similarity[†] and the possible generalization of ideas developed originally to understand the learning of a first language.

Other insights came when I was working on a project at Praxis to develop an 'Integrated Project Support Environment' (IPSE). The basic purpose of an IPSE is to increase productivity in software development. The basic strategy to meet this goal is providing software engineers with a supportive and easy-to-use computing environment which is, in some sense, 'integrated'. The precise meaning of 'integ-

---

[†] There is quite a lot of research on the learning of logical structures but relatively attention has been given to the integration of learning processes with processes for logical inference. A notable example of the latter type of study is Muggleton & Buntine (1988). They describe how an 'inversion' of Robinson's (1965) resolution mechanism can serve as a mechanism for learning in a model which uses error correction by a human teacher.

ration' in this context is still a subject of discussion, but removing unnecessary or artificial barriers between different kinds of knowledge is widely accepted as an important part of its meaning.

The types of knowledge used in a typical software development project include 'project plan', 'budget', 'time sheet', 'definition of requirements', 'data model', 'data flow diagram', 'formal specification', 'high level design', 'low level design', 'source code', 'object code' and others. An IPSE should be able to store these different kinds of knowledge, it should provide the means of linking them into whatever groupings are needed in each project and it should provide tools which can be used on a variety of types of knowledge with a minimum of arbitrary restrictions or barriers.

Integration of different kinds of knowledge would be made easier if we could find some kind of 'universal' formalism. If different types of knowledge are all expressed in one language it is easier to create tools which can be applied flexibly across the range and it is easier to combine diverse items in whatever groupings are needed.

At a trivial level, this universal language already exists: all kinds of knowledge may be expressed as a stream of binary digits ('bits'). At the other end of the scale, a universal language could be made by simply adding together the different notations and languages already in use to make one giant, general-purpose language. What is needed is a language which has more expressive power than an unstructured stream of bits but which is less cumbersome than an unrationalized combination of existing languages. In the terms which have already been mentioned, a universal language for integrating different kinds of knowledge should combine *simplicity* in its organization with the expressive *power* needed to represent diverse kinds of knowledge in an economical way.

The problem is similar to the problem I had previously in finding a formalism which could express both the syntax and the semantics of a natural language in an efficient way and which could allow them to be integrated flexibly in whatever combinations are needed in the given language. Could it be that DCGs, which provided an answer to the natural language problem, would be a suitable formalism to represent the different kinds of knowledge to be stored and used in an IPSE?

The main weakness of the DCG system in this connection (and this is also a weakness of the formalism as a system for representing the semantics of a natural language) is that it lacks any proper mechanism for representing structures of *classes* and *sub-classes* of objects and it lacks the useful capability — provided now in several 'object-oriented' programming languages — for a class at any level to *inherit* attributes from higher levels. Although it is possible to contrive this kind of thing using DCGs (I gave examples in the 1987 article), the formalism does not lend itself well to representing semantic structures in this kind of way.

The SP language and system
The proposals for the SP language and the SP system of which it is a part first arose from trying to see how this weakness of DCGs could be overcome without losing the good features of the formalism. It became apparent gradually that processes of pattern matching, unification and search similar to those used in the MK10 and SNPR models could be the basis of a simple but powerful language which might solve this problem and which might have something useful to say about several other problems and issues in computing. In general, the SP theory could be the basis of a

new kind of computing system with potential advantages compared with existing systems.

This is not the place to describe the SP concepts in any detail — they are covered in Chapters 4 to 7. Here is a summary of the main ideas:

- The basic conjecture is that all kinds of computing and formal reasoning may usefully be seen as a search for *efficiency* in a body of information where efficiency is defined as:

    $$efficiency = power/size$$

    In the article reproduced in Chapter 4, the concept of *power* is defined as the 'expressive power' of the body of information, meaning its usefulness for describing new information. This definition has now been replaced, in Chapter 5, by the related but simpler notion that the power of a body of information is the non-redundant information it contains. *Size* is simply the number of 'bits' in the given body of information.
- A search for efficiency means, for the most part, searching for redundancy in information and removing it wherever it is found. As noted earlier in this chapter and explained more fully in Chapters 4 and 5, this can be achieved by comparing or 'matching' patterns, and merging or 'unifying' patterns which are the same, combined with a search through the space of possible unifications to find the set or sets giving the best overall gains in efficiency. Because the search space is usually large, it will be necessary to use 'hill-climbing' techniques or something equivalent.
- The SP computing system will be dedicated to this kind of pattern matching, unification and hill-climbing search.
- A central feature of the SP system will be the SP language. This is intended to be a 'universal' language combining simplicity in its organization with high expressive power. Its semantics will be provided by the processes of pattern matching, unification and search in the SP system.
- In versions of the SP system designed to make a thorough search of the space of possible unifications (which I have termed 'broad' SP), it is likely that high levels of parallelism will be needed to meet the heavy computational demands of the search process.

Solving problems

Despite its very simple syntax, the SP language can represent class hierarchies with inheritance of attributes. It has the additional advantage in this connection that, unlike most other 'object-oriented' languages, hierarchical structures of classes may be *integrated* with 'part-whole hierarchies' — the latter term referring to the way most objects naturally divide into parts, sub-parts, sub-sub-parts, and so on. The integration of class hierarchies with part–whole hierarchies is explained more fully in Chapters 4 and 5.

An important aim in designing the SP language and system has been that it should be at least as good as DCGs in areas where DCGs are strong: representing discontinuous dependencies in syntax in an efficient way and integrating syntax with semantics. There is work still to be done in the area of discontinuous dependencies but it looks as if the SP language can provide a mechanism which is simpler and more elegant than the mechanisms in DCGs. This is described in Chapters 4 and 5.

The SP language aims to be a 'universal' language which is capable of expressing a wide variety of kinds of knowledge in an efficient way — including the syntax and semantics of natural languages — and which will allow different kinds of knowledge to be integrated flexibly in whatever combinations are needed for a given application.

The language shows promise in this direction but more work is needed to explore the range of possible applications of the language. One thing, however, is clear: if the language is to be used to represent two-dimensional objects like maps or diagrams, or objects with three or more dimensions, then the current definition of the language will need to be generalized to accommodate these things.

Part of the motivation for doing this work are the practical benefits and advantages of the SP system which we anticipate when the system is mature. The range of potential benefits of the system is described in Chapter 6. To give readers an idea of where this research may lead, I include a summary here of the main points (including the features just described):

- *Knowledge management.*
  - As a system for storing and retrieving knowledge, I expect the mature SP system to integrate the functions of a database and an expert system providing a means of storing and retrieving knowledge in a flexible way and providing the kind of 'intelligence' described below.
  - There is the possibility that one simple language can replace the several relatively complicated languages used in conventional systems for storing and retrieving knowledge.
  - The SP language has the potential to express a wide variety of kinds of knowledge in succinct form and to integrate different kinds of knowledge using 'object-oriented' principles. Class hierarchies and part–whole hierarchies may be integrated.
  - The SP system has the potential to learn new concepts from experience and to normalize a knowledge base automatically.
- *Software engineering.* As a vehicle for software development, the SP system has several potential advantages over existing systems:
  - It has the potential to provide one simple language and one model of computing for all purposes: requirements capture (including data modelling), systems analysis, formal specification, 'programming' and others. This can simplify software development and can save confusion and wasted effort.
  - The system may be the basis of a conceptually simple and highly integrated IPSE, storing the several kinds of knowledge used in a development project, including the knowledge associated with project management, and providing appropriate tools.
  - The SP language has the potential to be used as an executable specification language. This would eliminate all processes of translation, refinement, verification and compiling, thus saving costs and removing a major source of errors.

- The system has potential advantages over existing systems in the re-use of software.
- Software written in the SP language should be easier to modify than conventional software.
- There should be advantages in the design of the user interface making applications easier to learn and to use than in conventional systems.
- There should be advantages in 'configuration management', meaning the control of 'versions' or 'variants' of development products and the associations between them.
- SP's ability to organize its knowledge and learn new structures means that it has potential for 'automatic programming', meaning the automatic structuring of software into modules ('objects') and class hierarchies.

- *Artificial intelligence.* The SP system should have several of the capabilities associated with the term 'artificial intelligence':
  - The ability, already noted, to learn and to organize knowledge structures automatically.
  - An ability to reason logically when sufficient information is available.
  - An ability to make probabilistic inferences when information is uncertain or incomplete.
  - The SP language should provide an efficient medium for representing and using the syntax and semantics of any natural language.
  - The system should have a capability for 'fuzzy' pattern recognition — an ability to recognize patterns despite errors and omissions.
  - There seems to be potential in the system for problem solving and for the automatic generation of plans.

I stress again that these points represent a view of future possibilities which provides much of the motivation for developing the system. Some of these expectations and claims may seem tendentious for a system which does not yet exist. But there is a prototype of the system which demonstrates several of these capabilities, at least in primitive form. The prototype is described in Chapter 5 with examples of the kinds of things it can do.

Developing the system
Since September 1988, I have been at the School of Electronic Engineering Science, University of Wales, Bangor. Thanks to the support of Professor John O'Reilly, Professor Peter Fleming and my other colleagues in the School, the appointment has been a valuable opportunity to pursue these ideas. I have been fortunate to have the assistance of two research students, Paul Mather and Andrew Chipperfield. We have developed prototypes of the SP system as software simulations on a Sun workstation. The most successful of these, SP6, is described in Chapter 5. Currently, we are working on a new and improved version of the simulation and looking at a range of relevant issues:

- Techniques for pattern matching, unification and searching the space of alternative unifications are being explored.

- We are looking at the ways in which SP concepts relate to existing concepts in computing and cognition. What is the relation between the elements of an SP machine and those of a Turing machine? Can arithmetic operations and concepts of number be accommodated within the SP framework of ideas and, if so, how? Can logic and logical inference be accommodated within the SP framework? And so on.

In keeping with the earlier remarks about the relation between computer models and the theory, I regard the SP system as a concrete expression of the SP theory. Developing the SP system is a valuable forcing ground for the SP theory and running the system on appropriate examples is a valuable means of understanding and demonstrating the implications of the theory and its relation to existing concepts in computing and cognition. Development of the system is planned in three phases:

(1) At present, we are developing the system as software simulations on a conventional computer — a Sun workstation — and clarifying the ways in which pattern matching, unification and search can be done.
(2) When these ideas have matured, we plan to develop the system as software simulations on existing high-parallel computing machines — the AMT DAP or a multi-transputer system. The underlying machine should provide enough power to make the SP system in this form usable for practical purposes.
(3) At some stage, there is likely to be a case for developing new hardware dedicated to the basic operations in SP. It is likely that high levels of parallelism will be used.

CONTEXT

The previous section brings the story of this research programme up to date. In this section, I briefly discuss the relationship between the SP ideas and some other areas of research which deserve comment. There is a more comprehensive summary of related work in Chapter 5.

'Neural' computing and cluster analysis

Some research in 'neural' computing (which, for readers unfamiliar with the field, is research to understand and exploit the properties of networks of artificial nerve cells) includes the idea of searching for minimum 'entropy' in a system using a search process based on 'simulated annealing' or related technique (see, for example, Campbell *et al.* (1989) and Hinton & Sejnowski (1986)). Similar ideas have been part of research on cluster analysis and numerical taxonomy for many years (see, for example, Boulton & Wallace (1970)).

Searching for minimum entropy in neural computing or cluster analysis is obviously similar to the SP idea of searching for efficiency in a body of information. The main differences between the SP programme of research and the other two fields are these:

- Unlike research on cluster analysis which focuses on one area of application, the

SP programme aims to develop a comprehensive theory of cognition and computing.
- Unlike research in neural computing, the SP programme is not tied to any one type of computer architecture. The aim of the SP research is to understand computing processes in terms which are independent of any particular type of hardware.
- Much research in neural computing assumes a 'connectionist' paradigm which focuses on patterns of connections in neural networks and dispenses with many of the ideas in the more traditional 'symbolic' view of computing. By contrast, the SP programme is attempting to interpret and integrate 'symbolic' ideas from such fields as logic, object-oriented design and theoretical linguistics. The SP theory may provide a bridge between the connectionist and symbolic views of computing.

The concept of *abstraction* fits easily into the SP framework and the SP theory is itself a fairly abstract view of cognition and computing. In this respect, the SP view conflicts with the view held by some people with connectionist leanings that there is no sensible level of description for computing systems other than what happens in computing hardware. At the same time, if the SP view fulfils its promise, it should be possible to recognize SP principles at work at more than one level: both in the workings of computing hardware and in the manipulation of 'symbols'.

Recent work (Elman, 1990) has shown how an appropriately designed neural net can, from language-like text, develop a sensitivity to segment boundaries and (with the aid of a conventional clustering algorithm) classes of segment too. There seems to be still some way to go before neural nets can match what the MK10 and SNPR models can do, although a direct comparison is difficult because of differences in the aims and philosophy of the two kinds of research.

Algorithmic information theory
The SP theory is based most directly on Shannon's (Shannon & Weaver, 1949) ideas about the nature of information and, in particular, on his concept of *redundancy*. But there is now a newer view of the nature of information in the relatively new field of 'algorithmic information theory' (AIT) which has been developed by Chaitin (1987, 1988) and others.

In AIT, which is concerned mainly with issues of completeness and decidability in computing, randomness in a body of information is *defined* as incompressibility. If a body of information cannot be generated by any computer program which is shorter than that body of information then, by definition, the information is random. Correspondingly, if a computer program can be written to generate the information which is shorter than the information, then it is not random and contains redundancy.

The AIT view of information appears to enrich rather than displace older ideas. Shannon's view of redundancy as unbalanced frequencies of symbols or groups of symbols in a body of information seems to be entirely compatible with the AIT view of redundancy as compressibility of a body of information. And the ideas in the SP theory about how redundancy in a body of information may be discovered and reduced appear to be compatible with both views.

INFORMATION AND REDUNDANCY IN COMPUTING AND COGNITION†

In this section, I offer some thoughts about the broader significance of information and redundancy in understanding natural and artificial information processing systems.

The SP theory means stepping back from the concepts we normally use in thinking about cognition and computing — 'rules', 'data', 'programs', 'classes', 'symbols', 'schemata', 'grammars', 'semantics', 'automata' and so on — and seeing them all as *information* containing greater or lesser amounts of *redundancy*. But if you open any textbook called '*Computer Science*' or something similar, or any textbook on '*Artificial Intelligence*', you are unlikely to find any section in the table of contents about Shannon's information theory or, for that matter, algorithmic information theory. There is not likely to be any entry in the index on those topics either. In cognitive psychology, there has been some interest in information theory intermittently over a period of years — associated with the idea of 'cognitive economy' — but it either does not feature in current textbooks on this subject or, if it does, it is not treated in any depth.

The neglect of information theory in these areas is odd, because computing and cognition is all about information: storing it, retrieving it and using it in various ways. It is not as if the validity of information theory were in dispute: the theory is firmly established in fields like telephony and data communications where it is considered relevant. The idea of a 'bit', which is a basic concept in information theory, is very familiar in computing. But information theory itself gets little or no attention in most current treatments of computing theory, artificial intelligence or cognitive science.

Information and meaning

One possible reason why information theory has been neglected in computer science, in research on artificial intelligence and, to a lesser extent, in cognitive psychology is the idea that information theory is all about measuring quantities of information and does not have anything to say about what the information *means*.

This idea does seem plausible if you think of information as a mass of bits, much as it would appear in, say, a binary dump of a computer program. It is certainly hard to see meaning in a mass of bits like this, but that is not really the point. The stream of bits which is the object code of a computer program is indeed meaningless in itself. It requires *interpretation* by other structures, those parts of the computer which respond to instructions (bit patterns) like 'add', 'jump', 'rotate' and so on.

The point is that the organization of the computer can itself be represented in binary code. The parts of the computer which respond to bit patterns in the object code and thus give them meaning, are themselves patterns of information just like the program.

The meaning of any given piece of information is another piece of information which is associated with it. 'Association' means regular co-occurrence. Regular co-occurrence means redundancy. In short, the notion of 'meaning' can be seen as just one of many kinds of regularity or redundancy which can be found in information.

---

† Some of the text in this section is taken, with modifications, from the article with the same title by J. G. Wolff, Spring 1989, *AISB Quarterly* **68**, pp. 14–17. Copyright 1989 by the Society for the Study of Artificial Intelligence and Simulation of Behaviour. Adapted with permission.

Redundancy, cognition, computing and inductive reasoning
There is a biological argument for taking the SP view in thinking about how brains and nervous systems work: natural selection must put a premium on efficiency in the processing of information; therefore, we should expect to find mechanisms in brains and nervous systems which promote efficiency in information processing; and efficiency in the processing of any given body of information can only be achieved by exploiting whatever redundancy may exist in that information.

This kind of argument was a main motivation for research under the banner of 'cognitive economy' and there is a lot of evidence to support it. Apart from well-documented neurophysiological evidence for economical coding in the nervous system, there are the previously mentioned phenomena in the way children learn their first language which can be explained in terms of efficiency in cognition. These are reviewed in Chapter 2.

But there is another kind of argument which may persuade us to take the concept of redundancy seriously in thinking about systems for processing information. The previous argument depends on the assumption that information is useful. But why is it useful? Why should natural information processing systems (brains and nervous systems) have evolved at all? Why should there be multi-million pound industries for producing artificial systems for storing and processing information?

There are, of course, lots of particular reasons. Leaving aside art and entertainment and similar things which are, perhaps, only indirectly to do with survival, a brain enables us to find food more effectively, to avoid dangerous situations, to invent useful things like computers and so on. A computer helps us to control machinery, manage accounts, diagnose diseases and many other more or less useful things.

But, arguably, all, or at least many, of these particular reasons depend on a more general idea: that storing and manipulating information enables us to predict the future and predicting the future enables us to keep out of trouble and get the things we need for living.

Predicting the future on the basis of stored information depends on the principle of inductive reasoning: the future will be like the past. More accurately, the principle of inductive reasoning is that patterns of events which have occurred relatively frequently in the past will tend to recur in the future.

But frequent recurrence of patterns means redundancy! Thus, inductive reasoning, which provides the rationale for storing and using information in brains and computers, depends on the assumption that the patterns of information in the world contain redundancy. This is the second reason why the concept of redundancy should be regarded as significant in thinking about natural and artificial cognition.

Why should we assume that the future will be like the past?
We can, of course, go on to ask, as philosophers have done for many years: 'What is the rational basis for inductive reasoning?' Why do most people have this strong intuition that because the sun has always risen every morning it will do it again tomorrow or because every paving stone in a path has held our weight so far, the next one will too? None of these conclusions can be proved logically.

It is no good arguing that inductive reasoning is rational because it has always worked in the past. This argument eats its own tail. Here is an argument why inductive reasoning is rational which does not depend on the principle which it is trying to justify:

> If we assume that the world, in the future, will contain redundancy in the form of recurring patterns of events, then brains and computers which store information and make inductive inferences will be useful in enabling us to anticipate events. If it turns out that the world, in the future, does indeed contain redundancy then our investment in the means of storing and processing information will pay off. If it turns out that the world, in the future, does not contain redundancy then we are dead anyway — reduced to a pulp of total chaos!

This kind of reasoning made fortunes for speculators after World War II: it was rational to buy up London bomb-sites during the war because, if the war were won, they would become valuable. If the war were to be lost, the money saved by not making the investment would, in an uncomfortable and uncertain future, probably not be much use anyway.

CONCLUSION

In this introductory chapter, I have described the history of the research programme and some related ideas without attempting a detailed description of the theory. The chapters which follow provide that fuller picture. Here is a summary of what they are about:

- Chapter 2 summarizes the results of the research on language learning including a fairly full review of relevant empirical evidence.
- Chapter 3 gives a detailed description of the SNPR model with details of the kinds of results it can produce.
- Chapter 4 describes the SP theory and discusses how it may be applied to several issues in computing. This chapter also sketches the proposed SP system and SP language.
- Chapter 5 is mainly about the SP6 prototype of the SP system with examples of the kinds of things it can do.
- Chapter 6 describes the practical benefits which I expect from a mature SP system.
- Chapter 7 is mainly about project management but it includes a description of how an informal version of the SP language may be used as a knowledge base for software development projects.

REFERENCES

Boulton, D. M., & Wallace, C. S. (1970). A program for numerical classification. *Computer Journal* **13**, 63–69.

Campbell, C., Sherrington, D., & Wong, K. Y. M. (1989). Statistical mechanics and neural networks. In I. Aleksander (Ed.), *Neural Computing Architectures*, London: North Oxford Academic.

Chaitin, G. J. (1987). *Algorithmic Information Theory*. Cambridge: Cambridge University Press.
Chaitin, G. J. (1988). Randomness in arithmetic. *Scientific American* **259**(1), 80–85.
Chomsky, N. (1959). A review of B. F. Skinner's '*Verbal Behaviour*'. *Language* **35**(1), 26–58.
Elman, J. L. (1990). Finding structure in time. *Cognitive Science* **14**, 179–211.
Hinton, G. E., & Sejnowski, T. J. (1986). Learning and relearning in Boltzmann machines. Chapter 7 in D. E. Rumelhart and J. L. McClelland (Eds), *Parallel Distributed Processing*, Vol I, Cambridge, MA: MIT Press, pp. 282–317.
Muggleton, S., & Buntine, W. (1988). Machine invention of first order predicates by inverting resolution. *Proceedings of the Fifth International Conference on Machine Learning, Michigan*, San Mateo: Morgan Kaufmann, pp. 339–352.
Pereira, F. C. N., & Warren, D. H. D. (1980). Definite clause grammars for language analysis — a survey of the formalism and a comparison with augmented transition networks. *Artificial Intelligence* **13**, 231–278.
Robinson, J. A. (1965). A machine-oriented logic based on the resolution principle. *Journal of the ACM* **12**(1), 23–41.
Shannon, C. E., & Weaver, W. (1949). *The Mathematical Theory of Communication*. Urbana: University of Illinois Press.
Wolff, J. G. (1973). *Language, Brain and Hearing*. London: Methuen.
Wolff, J. G. (1975). An algorithm for the segmentation of an artificial language analogue. *British Journal of Psychology* **66**, 79–90.
Wolff, J. G. (1976). Frequency, conceptual structure and pattern recognition. *British Journal of Psychology* **67**, 377–390.
Wolff, J. G. (1977). The discovery of segments in natural language. *British Journal of Psychology* **68**, 97–106.
Wolff, J. G. (1978a). Recoding of natural language for economy of transmission or storage. *Computer Journal* **21**, 42–44.
Wolff, J. G. (1978b). The discovery of syntagmatic and paradigmatic classes. *Bulletin of the Association for Literary and Linguistic Computing* **6**(2), 141–158.
Wolff, J. G. (1980). Language acquisition and the discovery of phrase structure. *Language & Speech* **23**, 255–269.
Wolff, J. G. (1982). Language acquisition, data compression and generalization. *Language & Communication* **2**, 57–89.
Wolff, J. G. (1987). Cognitive development as optimization. In L. Bolc (Ed.), *Computational Models of Learning*. Heidelberg: Springer-Verlag.
Wolff, J. G. (1988). Learning syntax and meanings through optimization and distributional analysis. In Y. Levy, I. M. Schlesinger and M. D. S. Braine (Eds), *Categories and Processes in Language Acquisition*, Hillsdale, NJ: Lawrence Erlbaum.

2
Learning a first language

The article reproduced here summarizes the results of the research programme which I pursued between 1972 and 1983. It describes the theory of language learning which I developed during that period both in its abstract form and in its more concrete realization in the MK10 and SNPR computer models. The bulk of the article is a review of the empirical evidence which is relevant to the theory — mainly data gathered by other researchers in studies of children learning a first language.

As I described in Chapter 1, the main features of this work are:

- The MK10 model (which is a sub-set of the SNPR model) demonstrates how the segmental structure of natural language (words, phrases etc.) may be discovered by statistical analysis alone without the aid of 'negative' samples or correction by a human or non-human 'teacher'.
- The SNPR model demonstrates how un-augmented CF-PSGs may be discovered by statistical analysis alone without negative samples or a teacher. Unlike many other models for grammar discovery, SNPR is designed to work with language samples containing no markers of segment boundaries. It discovers segmental structure in the language sample and classes of contextually equivalent segments. And it integrates the two kinds of learning so that segments may contain classes and classes may contain segments at any level, in whatever combinations are used in the grammar.
- The SNPR model generalizes grammatical rules so that it can learn grammars which go beyond the data on which they are based — something which children clearly do. The model includes mechanisms for correcting overgeneralizations which do not depend on 'negative' samples or correction of errors by a 'teacher' or the 'grading' of language samples in any way. As noted in Chapter 1, these mechanisms were apparently new when they were proposed and no other equivalent mechanisms have apparently been proposed subsequently.
- There is quite a lot of evidence that children really do learn language by processes like those proposed in the MK10 and SNPR models. Much of this article is a review of that evidence.
- It is possible to understand the processes in the MK10 and SNPR models at an abstract level as an attempt to maximize *efficiency* in a knowledge structure where efficiency is the ratio of the *power* of the knowledge structure to its *size*. 'Correct' generalizations may be understood as generalizations which increase this ratio while 'incorrect' generalizations may be seen as ones which reduce the ratio.

I believe the points made in this last item (which I first described in the 1982 article reproduced in Chapter 3) are sound but I was not able to complete the quantitative studies needed to test them fully before I moved into other work.

LEARNING SYNTAX AND MEANINGS THROUGH OPTIMIZATION AND DISTRIBUTIONAL ANALYSIS†

INTRODUCTION

It is perhaps misleading to use the word *theory* to describe the view of language acquisition and cognitive development which is the subject of this chapter. This word is used as a matter of convenience; it applies here to what is best characterized as a partially completed program of research — a jigsaw puzzle in which certain pieces have been positioned with reasonable confidence, while others have been placed tentatively and many have not been placed at all. The most recent exposition of these ideas is developed in two papers: Wolff (1982) and Wolff (1987). Earlier papers in this program of research include Wolff (1975, 1976, 1977, 1980).

Wolff (1982) describes a computer model of linguistic/cognitive development and some associated theory. Wolff (1987) describes extensions to the ideas in the first paper. These papers and previous publications are somewhat narrow in scope, concentrating on detailed discussion of aspects of the theory. The intention here is to provide a broader perspective on the set of ideas.

The chapter begins with a brief summary of the presuppositions of the theory. Then the theory is described in outline: first a brief description of the computer model which is the main subject of Wolff (1982) and then a more abstract account, including the developments described in Wolff (1987). The body of the chapter reviews the empirical support for the theory.

PRESUPPOSITIONS OF THE THEORY

There is space here only for a rather bald statement of theoretical and empirical assumptions on which the theory is based. I will make no attempt to justify these ideas.

(1) The theory belongs in the *empiricist* rather than the *nativist* tradition: it seems that language acquisition may very well be a process of abstracting *structure* from linguistic and other sensory inputs where the innate knowledge which the child brings to the task is largely composed of perceptual primitives, structure-abstracting routines, and procedures for analysing and creating language. A *triggering*, nativist view cannot be ruled out *a priori* but the other view is plausible enough to deserve exploration.

(2) It seems clear that, while children may be helped by explicit instruction in language forms, by reward for uttering correct forms, by correction of errors,

† From *Categories and Processes in Language Acquisition* (Chapter 7, pp. 179–215) edited by Y. Levy, I. M. Schlesinger and M. D. S. Braine. 1988. Hillsdale, New Jersey: Lawrence Erlbaum. Copyright 1988 by Lawrence Erlbaum. Reprinted by permission.

and by other *training* features of their linguistic environment, including the grading of language samples, they probably do not need any of these aids. It seems prudent, as a matter of research strategy, to think in terms of learning processes which can operate without them but which can take advantage of them when they are available.
(3) In a similar way it seems prudent to develop a theory in which learning does not depend on prelinguistic communicative interaction between mother and child but which is at the same time compatible with the fact that such interactions clearly do occur.
(4) Although semantic knowledge may develop earlier than syntactic knowledge (or make itself apparent to the observer at an earlier age) it seems that the learning of both kinds of knowledge is integrated in a subtle way. One kind of knowledge is not a prerequisite for the learning of the other.
(5) Mainly for reasons of parsimony in theorizing, it has been assumed that a uniform set of learning principles may be found to apply across all domains of knowledge — which is not to deny that differences may also exist. The mechanisms proposed in the theory appear to have a wide range of application.
(6) It is assumed that there is a core of knowledge which serves both comprehension and production processes. The theory is framed so that the representation of this core knowledge and the posited processes for learning it are broadly compatible with current notions about processes of comprehension and production.

OUTLINE OF THE THEORY

As already indicated, the theory is based on the kinds of empiricist ideas of associationism and distributional analysis which were so heavily criticized by Chomsky (1965). Those earlier ideas have been extended and refined in two main ways:

- A series of computer models have been built and tested to provide detailed insights into the nature of the proposed mechanisms and their adequacy or otherwise to explain observed phenomena.
- The early ideas are now embedded within a broader theoretical perspective: learning may be seen as a process of optimization of cognitive structures for the several functions they must serve.

This section of the chapter will describe the theory in two stages:

(1) A relatively concrete description in terms of the most recent of the computer models in which the theory is embodied: program SNPR.
(2) A more abstract or 'conceptual' view which includes ideas not yet incorporated in any computer model.

Program SNPR

Table 2.1 summarizes the processing performed by the SNPR model. The *sample of language* is a stream of letter symbols or phoneme symbols without any kind of segmentation markers (spaces between words, etc.). The main reason for leaving out

Table 2.1 — Outline of processing in the SNPR model

1. Read in a *sample of language*.
2. Set up a data structure of *elements* (grammatical rules) containing at this stage, only the *primitive* elements of the system.
3. While there are not enough elements formed, do the following sequence of operations repeatedly:

   BEGIN
   - 3.1 Using the current structure of elements, *parse* the language sample, *recording* the *frequencies* of all pairs of contiguous elements and the frequencies of individual elements.

     During the parsing, *monitor* the use of PAR elements to gather data for later use in rebuilding of elements.
   - 3.2 When the sample has been parsed, *rebuild* any elements that require it.
   - 3.3 Search amongst the current set of elements for *shared contexts* and *fold* the data structures in the way explained in the text.
   - 3.4 *Generalize* the grammatical rules.
   - 3.5 The most frequent pair of contiguous elements recorded under 3.1 is formed into a single new *SYN* element and added to the data structure. All frequency information is then discarded.

   END

---

all segmentation markers is to explore what can be achieved without them, given that they are not reliably present in natural language. The letter or phoneme symbols represent *perceptual primitives* and should not be construed as letters or phonemes *per se*. If the model is seen as a model of syntax learning then the symbols may be seen as perceptual primitives like formant ratios and transitions. If the model is seen as a model of the learning of nonsyntactic cognitive structures (discussed later) then the symbols may be seen as standing for analysers for colours, lines, luminance levels, and the like.

Elements in the data structure are of three main types:

- Minimal (M) elements. These are primitives (i.e. letter or phoneme symbols).
- Syntagmatic (SYN) elements. These are sequences of elements (SYN, PAR, or M).
- Paradigmatic (PAR) elements. These represent a choice of one and only one amongst a set of two or more elements (SYN, PAR, or M).

The whole data structure has the form of a phrase-structure grammar; each element is a *rule* in the grammar. Although it starts as a set of simple rules corresponding to the set of primitives, it may grow to be an arbitrarily complex combination of primitives, sequencing rules (SYN elements), and selection rules (PAR elements). This grammar controls the parsing process.

The general effect of the repeated application of operations 3.1 (parsing and recording the frequencies of pairs) and 3.5 (concatenation of the most frequent pair of contiguous elements) is to build SYN elements of progressively increasing size. Early structures are typically fragments of words; word fragments are built into words, words into phrases and phrases into sentences.

The effect of operation 3.3 (sometimes called *folding*) is to create *complex* SYN elements, meaning SYN elements which contain PAR elements as constituents. For example, if the current set of elements contains 1→ ABC† and 2→ ADC, then a new PAR element is formed: 3→ B|D‡ and the two original SYN elements are replaced by a new SYN element: 4→ A(3)C. Notice that A, B, C, and D may be arbitrarily complex structures. Notice also how the context(s) of any element is defined by the SYN element(s) in which it appears as a constituent.

Operation 3.4 creates *generalizations* by using the newly formed PAR elements. For example, element 3, just described, would replace B or D in other contexts: 5→ EB would become 6→ E(3), and so on. Generalizations may also be produced by operation 3.5 as explained in Wolff (1982).

Operations 3.3 (folding) and 3.4 (generalization) do not come into play until enough SYN elements have been built up for shared contexts to appear. Likewise, operation 3.2 (rebuilding) will not play a part in the learning process until some (over)generalizations have been formed.

Correction of overgeneralizations

The *monitoring* and *rebuilding* processes shown in Table 2.1 are designed to solve the problem of *overgeneralizations*. If it is true that children can learn a first language *without explicit error correction* (and there is significant evidence that this is so), how can a child learn to distinguish erroneous overgeneralizations from the many *correct generalizations* that must be retained in his or her cognitive system?

Fig. 2.1 illustrates the problem. The smallest envelope represents the finite, albeit large, sample of language on which a child's learning is based. The middle-sized envelope represents the (infinite) set of utterances in the language being learned. The largest envelope represents the even larger infinite set of all possible utterances. The difference between the middle-sized envelope and the largest one is the set of all utterances which are not in the language being learned.

To learn the language, the child must generalize from the sample to the language without overgeneralizing into the area of utterances which are not in the language. *What makes the problem tricky is that both kinds of generalization, by definition, have zero frequency in the child's experience.*

Notice in Fig. 2.1 that the sample from which the child learns actually overlaps the area of utterances not in the language. This area of overlap, marked 'dirty data', and the associated problem for the learning system, is discussed later in the chapter.

To correct overgeneralizations, the monitoring process in SNPR keeps track of the usage of all constituents of all PAR elements in all the contexts in which they occur (remember that contexts are defined in terms of the elements built by SNPR).

---

† The notation '1→ ABC' means 'the symbol "1" may be rewritten as ABC' or 'the symbol "1" is a label for the structure ABC'. To aid understanding in this and later examples, integer numbers have been used for references (labels) to structures ('nonterminal symbols' in grammatical jargon) while capital letters are used to represent the material described in the grammar ('terminal symbols').
‡ Read this as 'the symbol "2" may be rewritten as B or D'.

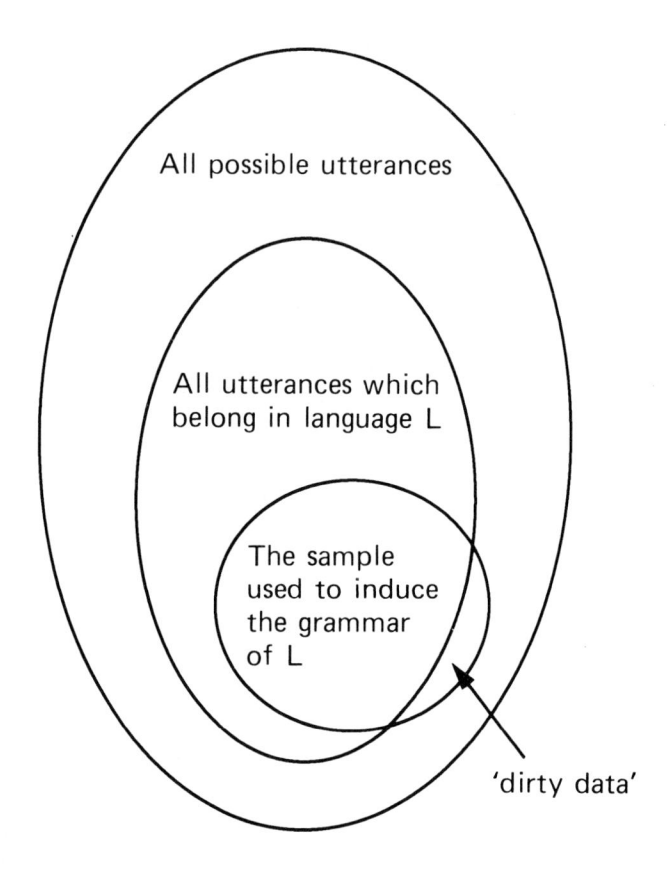

Fig. 2.1 — Kinds of utterance in language learning.

If any PAR element fails to use all its constituents in any context then it is *rebuilt* for that context (and only that context) so that the unused constituent(s) is removed. As a hypothetical example, a PAR element 1→ P|Q|R may fail to use R in the context 2→ A(1)B. In such a case it becomes 3→ P|Q and 2 is rebuilt as 2→ A(3)B. The structure 1→ P|Q|R may still be used in other contexts.

This mechanism, in which structures are eliminated if they fail to occur in a given context within a finite sample of language, is an approximation to what one imagines is a more realistic mechanism which would allow the *strength* of structures to vary with their contextual probability.

This kind of mechanism will allow a child to observe that 'mouses', for example, is vanishingly rare in adult speech and will cause the speech pattern for 'mous' to be removed (or *weakened*) in the structure which generates 'mouses', 'houses', 'roses', etc. The correct form ('mice') will be learned independently.

Preserving correct generalizations
What is special about the mechanism in SNPR for correcting overgeneralizations is that certain kinds of generalization cannot be removed by it. The mechanism thus

offers an explanation of how children can differentiate *correct* and *incorrect* generalizations without explicit error correction.

To see how it is that the rebuilding mechanism cannot touch some generalizations, consider the following example. From a text containing these three sentences:

> John sings
> Mary sings
> John dances

it is possible to induce a fragment of grammar like this:

> 1→ (2)(3)
> 2→ John|Mary
> 3→ sings|dances

Notice that there is a generalization: the grammar generates 'Mary dances' even though this was not in the original sample.

Notice, in particular, that the monitoring and rebuilding mechanism cannot remove this generalization. The reason is that, in the sample from which the grammar was induced, 'sings', 'dances', 'John', and 'Mary' are *all* used in the context of the structure '1'.

In running SNPR, many examples have been observed like this where generalizations are preserved and distinguished from other generalizations which are eliminated.

Other mechanisms
There is no space here for a full discussion of the problem of correcting overgeneralizations without external error correction. The mechanisms in SNPR are one of only a few proposals that have been put forward. Braine (1971) has proposed a mechanism but I have not been able to understand from the description how it can remove overgeneralizations without at the same time eliminating correct generalizations. The proposal by Coulon & Kayser (1978) apparently fails because, judging by the sample results they give, wrong generalizations are allowed through the net. The 'discrimination' mechanism in Anderson (1981) seems to depend on the provision of explicit *negative* information to the model.

Other mechanisms that have been proposed (e.g. Langley, 1982) use covert error correction; to do this they need to make what I believe are unwarranted assumptions:

- that a child's knowledge of meanings may be used to correct overgeneralizations. If the learning process has to bootstrap semantic structures as well as syntactic structures (as children apparently do), then some other mechanism is needed for the correction of overgeneralizations;
- that there is a one-to-one relation between syntax and meanings. This is quite clearly false for natural language.

The process in SNPR depends on *relative contextual probabilities* of structures and does not employ any notion of falsification of hypotheses or the like.

The notion that a child may learn by creating hypotheses and observing whether they are confirmed or falsified is unsound for much the same reasons that scientific hypotheses cannot be either confirmed or falsified (Lakatos, 1978). A full discussion of this interesting issue is not possible here.

Summary

To summarize the outline of SNPR's functioning, the overall behaviour of the program is to build up cognitive structures by concatenation, using frequency as a heuristic to select appropriate structures. Interwoven with the building process are processes to form disjunctive groups, to form generalizations and to correct overgeneralizations. The structures built by the program have the form of unaugmented phrase structure grammars.

The abstract view of the theory

Program SNPR embodies most but not all of the ideas in the theory. This section describes the model in more abstract terms than in the previous section and incorporates ideas from the most recent phase of research (described in Wolff, 1987).

Taking the abstract view, the central idea in the theory is that language acquisition and other areas of cognitive development are, in large part, processes of building cognitive structures which are in some sense *optimal* for the several functions they have to perform. This view is a development of notions of 'cognitive economy' which were in vogue in the 1950s and which have attracted intermittent attention subsequently.

This abstract view fits well with and in a sense grows from a recognition that human cognitive systems are products of natural selection and are therefore likely to be conditioned by principles of efficiency.

Compressing cognitive structures

One of the functions of a cognitive system is to be a store of knowledge. It seems clear that, *other things being equal*, storage demands of cognitive structures should be minimized. The brain's storage capacity is large, no doubt, but it is not infinite and it seems reasonable to suppose that natural selection would have favoured compact storage.

There are at least six ways of reducing the storage demands of a body of data:

(1) A pattern (a sequence of elements) which is repeated in a variety of contexts may be stored just once and then accessed via pointers from several contexts. A sequence like

　　ABCDPQRABCDABCDPQRABCDPQRPQR

may be reduced to 12112122, where $1 \rightarrow$ ABCD and $2 \rightarrow$ PQR. This is *chunking*. It is also like the use of subroutines in computer programs.
(2) Two or more patterns sharing the same context may be placed in a disjunctive group which is accessed via a reference or pointer from the given context. This saves repeated storage of the context pattern. For example ABCPQRDEF and ABCXYZDEF may be reduced to ABC(1)DEF where $1 \rightarrow$ PQR|XYZ. This is *folding*.
(3) *Frequent, large* patterns in 1 will clearly produce a bigger saving than rare small

patterns. For reasons spelled out in Wolff (1982) it is best to concentrate on frequency in searching for repeating patterns. There is here a clear theoretical justification for regarding frequency as an important variable in learning. The importance of frequency was recognized in associationist psychology (e.g. Carr, 1931), mainly for intuitive reasons, but it fell out of favour when associationism went out of fashion.

(4) Repeating contiguous instances of a pattern may be recorded just once and marked for repetition. For example, AAAAAAAAAA may be reduced to A+ or A[11].† This is *iteration*. A device with similar effect is *recursion*.

(5) Storage space may be saved by simple *deletion* of information or *not recording it*. As discussed in Wolff (1982), there is a close connection between this mode of economy and the phenomenon of *generalization*. This point is amplified below in discussing the tradeoff between the size of a knowledge structure and its usefulness.

(6) The last technique in this list is the principle of *schema-plus-correction*; this is described and discussed in Wolff (1987). The idea here, of course, is that a pattern may be recorded by a reference to a class or schema of which it is an example, together with the details (corrections) that are specific to the given item. 'Tibs' may be described as 'cat [tabby, 5-years-old, one-leg-missing]'.

Five of these techniques for reducing storage (or transmission) costs of data (items (1), (2), (3), (4), and (6)) may be described as techniques for *data compression*: They exploit any *redundancy* that may exist in a body of data; in general, they do not result in a loss of information. The fifth principle is different because information is lost or never recorded.

Using cognitive structures as codes

A second major function of a cognitive system is to provide a set of codes for patterns of information: afferent patterns coming from the senses, efferent patterns transmitted to the organism's motor system, information patterns transmitted in the course of the brain's internal data manipulations (i.e. thinking), and also the patterns of information to be stored in the cognitive system itself.

An obvious and relatively simple example is the use of words as codes for perceptual/conceptual complexes: words certainly are not the only codes employed in the nervous system and need not, of course, be employed at all. As before, we are assuming that, *other things being equal*, codes that minimize the amount of information to be used for a given purpose will be preferred over other less efficient codes. Precisely the same compression principles may be applied to minimizing required storage space and maximizing the efficiency of codes.

Tradeoff

There is a tradeoff between the *size* of a knowledge structure and its *power* for encoding knowledge. At one extreme there is a very compact grammar like this:

$$1 \rightarrow 2^*$$
$$2 \rightarrow A|B|C|\ldots|Z$$

† '+' means 'repeat one or more times'. '[11]' means 'repeat 11 times'.

This small grammar generates any (alphabetic) text of any size; but it achieves no compression because the text is encoded in the conventional way as a stream of characters.

At the other extreme is a 'grammar' with one rule like this:

1 → 'the complete sample of language observed to date'

This grammar is not at all compact but it provides a very efficient code: Given the existence of the grammar, one small reference ('1') may be used to represent the whole sample.

Between these two extremes lies a spectrum of grammars.

It is perhaps useful to remark in passing that there is a close connection between this spectrum and the phenomenon of *generalization*. The first grammar, above, is extremely general; the second is extremely specific. In between are grammars which, in varying degrees, are more general than any specific language sample.

The connection between generality in grammars and the size/power tradeoff is simple and direct when grammars are unambiguous (when any given pattern can be generated in only one way). The connection is less direct when, as is usually the case with natural languages, grammars are ambiguous.

Learning

In this theory of learning, it is assumed that a child starts with a small very general *grammar* like the first one above and gradually extends it. As the grammar is extended, it will become progressively more *powerful* as a means of encoding information. The term *grammar* in this context is shorthand for 'syntactic/semantic structure'.

Whether or not it becomes less general at the same time depends on whether the original general rules are retained in the grammar or discarded. They are almost certainly retained *in reserve*, so to speak, for occasions when generality is needed.

Additions to the set of rules should not be made indiscriminately. At every stage, it is likely that the child will choose the more *useful* rules in preference to less useful or powerful rules. According to the theory, the child should, at all times, try to maximize the effectiveness of each new rule as a means of encoding data economically: he or she should try to maximize the *compression capacity* (CC) or descriptive *power* of the grammar. At the same time, the child should try to minimize the *size* of the grammar which is being built; the size of the grammar is termed S_g.

The ratio between the descriptive power of the grammar and its size (i.e. CC/S_g — which is termed the *efficiency* of the grammar) should at all stages be maximized.

It is in the nature of the search process that the most powerful elements (those giving a large increase in CC for a relatively small increase in S_g) will be found early, and progressively less powerful elements will be found as learning proceeds. There is no reason to suppose that learning will cease when CC/S_g reaches a maximum. Rather, we may suppose that learning will cease when candidate elements that the child discovers or constructs do not add enough to the grammar's CC to justify the attendant increase in S_g. This point will depend on the relative value to a given child of CC and the information storage space corresponding to S_g. These values may depend on motivational factors and on the total available storage space among other things; they are likely to vary from one child to another.

The foregoing ideas are illustrated diagrammatically in Fig. 2.2. The graphs show the tradeoff between the compression capacity or power of a grammar and its size. In general, big grammars are more powerful than little ones. Independent of this tradeoff is the efficiency of a grammar, meaning the ratio of power to size. The most efficient grammars lie along the line marked '1'; the least efficient grammars lie along the line marked '4', and intermediate grammars lie in between these lines. The learning process starts near the bottom left of the diagram in the region of small grammars which are not powerful. The learning process gradually builds the grammatical system keeping as close as possible to the highest of the lines ('1') in the diagram, thus maintaining as much efficiency in the grammar as possible at all times.

Other factors
Only the two functions mentioned have so far been considered in detail but it is clear that at some stage others will need consideration. An obvious candidate is the facility with which information may be retrieved from a knowledge structure. As with information transmission, it seems that economy in storage may sometimes be bought at the cost of cumbersome retrieval. Likewise, reliability of cognitive operations may demand the preservation of some redundancy in knowledge structures. A point worth stressing here is that concepts like *efficiency* and *optimization* are *functional* notions: it is meaningless to say that something is efficient unless one can say what ends are efficiently served. The theory thus offers a bridge between the cognitive and motivational aspects of mental life.

Realization of the abstract principles of SNPR
Program SNPR appears to be a realization of the first five of the optimization principles which have been described. No doubt, other realizations are possible. A model incorporating the sixth principle has not yet been attempted.

Constructs like CC and S_g are not employed explicitly by the procedures in SNPR. The effects to be described appear to be *emergent* properties of the SNPR algorithm.

The SNPR model builds its knowledge structures from an initial small base. The effect of the building operation is apparently to increase progressively the CC of the structures while maintaining a high efficiency. The key to this building process is the use of frequency as a heuristic to discriminate *good* structures from *bad* ones. The general tendency of the building mechanisms is to maximize the sum of the products of frequency and size of the structures being built; this promotes a high efficiency.

The generalization mechanisms usually have the effect of reducing S_g without a corresponding reduction in CC; the overall effect is thus usually an increase in efficiency. The rebuilding mechanism apparently has the effect of increasing CC for a given S_g and thus promotes a high efficiency. In general, the mechanisms which have been shown to succeed in discovering a grammar from a sample of its language appear also to be mechanisms that promote high descriptive efficiency in the knowledge structures.

Other concepts
Before leaving this outline description of the theory and the computer model in which some aspects of it are embodied, we may note some general points about the

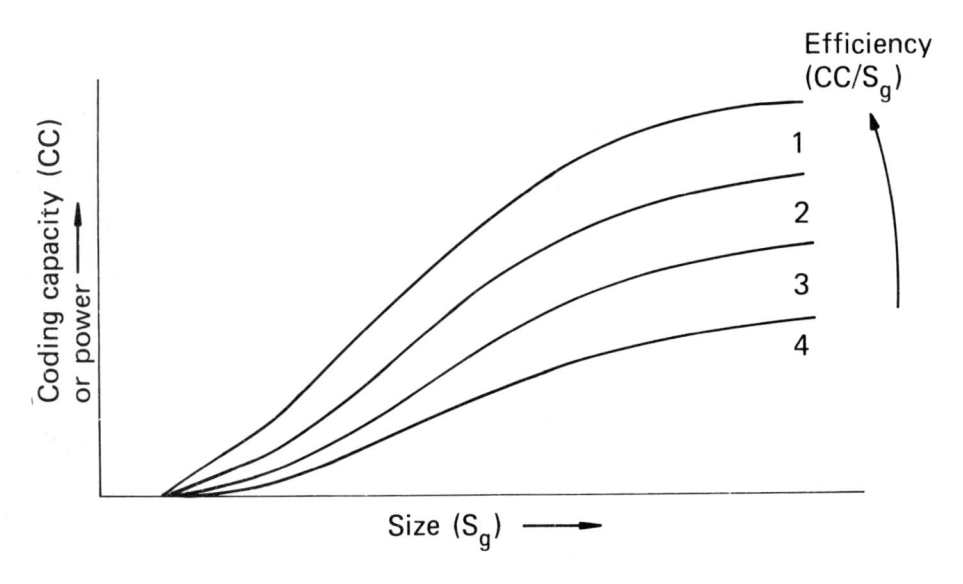

Fig. 2.2 — A search space of grammatical systems.

character of the theory. It gives expression to a number of rather potent ideas, most of which have a fairly long history in psychology and cognitive science.

One of these ideas is the notion that the acquisition of one skill may be a *stepping stone* or foundation for the acquisition of another. This principle is exemplified in SNPR in the way that the program builds a heterarchy of elements, corresponding to a heterarchy of language skills, with complex elements constructed from simpler constituents.

Another useful principle, more recent in origin but now widely recognized, is the idea that knowledge structures may with advantage be constructed from *discrete modules* together with a *restriction on the range of module types* allowed. This feature, realized in the theory by the three types of element, has the advantage that it facilitates the processes of building or modifying a knowledge structure much in the same way that modularity facilitates construction and repair of buildings or electronic systems (or Lego models).

An idea in the theory which seems not to be widely recognized is the *separation of conjunctive groupings and disjunctive groupings* into distinct modules. The significance of this idea depends on a recognition of the significance of conjunction and disjunction in data compression and optimization. The conjoining of elements represents a reduction of *choice* in the knowledge system and thus an increase in its information content (*information* being used here in the Shannon sense). Conversely, the disjunctive grouping of elements represents a preservation of choice and a corresponding reduction of information content. The quest for an optimum balance between S_g and CC is facilitated if the groupings which, so to speak, pull in one direction are kept separate from the groupings which have the opposite tendency. This design feature of a knowledge system facilitates the process of moulding the structure to fit accurately the patterns of redundancy in the database.

Mention may be made, finally, of a fourth idea, not new, which appears to have a broad significance in psychology and elsewhere. A modular knowledge structure can be optimized by processes akin to the processes of *natural selection* operating in the evolution of animals and plants. Those modules that are *useful* can be allowed to survive while the many rival modules that are less useful or, in some sense, less efficient may be progressively eliminated. This kind of *evolutionary principle* can be seen to operate in SNPR in the way that absolute and contextual frequency governs the retention or elimination of elements.

EMPIRICAL EVIDENCE

Although the theory is by no means fully developed, it is substantial enough for one to ask how well it fits with available data on people's mature knowledge of language and on the developmental processes leading to the mature system. Most of the evidence I review has been presented piecemeal in previous publications; the intention here is to summarize relevant evidence and to expand the discussion of certain points not previously considered in any detail.

Part of the empirical support for the theory lies in the presuppositions discussed above. To the extent that these presuppositions derive from observations (and in this they vary a good deal) the theory is likewise supported.

A second kind of empirical support is provided by the observed phenomena which the theory was designed to explain. To the extent that the theory does demonstrably succeed in providing explanations for these phenomena, they constitute validating data.

There is, lastly, a kind of empirical support, not always very distinct from the other two, which is phenomena not directly addressed by the theory which do nonetheless turn out to be explicable in terms of the theory; this kind of explanatory bonus can be quite persuasive. There are quite a few phenomena in this category that are considered after a review of those observations which the theory was originally designed to explain.

This section on empirical evidence ends with a discussion of certain observations that appear to be incompatible with the theory in its present form.

Phenomena addressed by the theory

The main phenomenon addressed by the theory is the observation that children can apparently discover a generative grammar from a sample of language, given only that sample as data. Insofar as SNPR does broadly the same thing, albeit with simpler grammars, it may be regarded as empirically valid. As an example, SNPR has successfully retrieved the grammar shown in Table 2.2, given only a sample of the corresponding language as input (Wolff, 1982).

In the following subsections, the components of this grammar-abstraction process are examined individually to see how well the theory fares in each domain.

1. Segmentation

The first sub-problem chosen for this project was to find a sufficient mechanism to explain how children could learn the segmental structure of language given the apparently insufficient and unreliable nature of clues like pause and stress. The problem was artificially purified by assuming, contrary to probable fact, that such clues made no contribution to the segmentation process. The main alternative is some kind of distributional or cluster analysis designed to reveal statistical discontinuities at the boundaries of words and other segments. Ideas of this kind were, of course, central to distributional linguistics and had been explored by linguists (Gammon, 1969; Harris, 1961, 1970) developing tools for linguistic analysis and also by psychologists (e.g. Olivier, 1968) interested in psychological processes.

Table 2.2 — Artificial grammar and fragment of a corresponding language sample

$$S \rightarrow (1)\ (2)\ (3)\ |\ (4)\ (5)\ (6)$$
$$1 \rightarrow DAVID\ |\ JOHN$$
$$2 \rightarrow LOVES\ |\ HATED$$
$$3 \rightarrow MARY\ |\ SUSAN$$
$$4 \rightarrow WE\ |\ YOU$$
$$5 \rightarrow WALK\ |\ RUN$$
$$6 \rightarrow FAST\ |\ SLOWLY$$

Part of the sample used as input to SNPR:

JOHNLOVESMARYDAVIDHATEDMARYYOURUNSLOWLY ...

Word structure
After a good deal of experimentation, a program was developed (a precursor of program SNPR called MK10) which produced good results in discovering word structure in artificial and natural language texts (Wolff, 1975, 1977).

A variety of search heuristics were tried, including transition probabilities between elements and measures derived from standard indices of correlation, but the best results by far were obtained with a simple measure of conjoint frequency of elements. In terms of the compression principles (which were recognized after MK10 was developed) this model may be seen as a fairly direct expression of principles (1) and (3).

Fig. 2.3 shows part of a sample of an unsegmented text taken from book 8A of the Ladybird reading scheme; the tree markers show the parsing developed by the program at a late stage of processing. There is an extremely good fit between these markers and the conventionally recognized word structure of the text, showing clearly that the program is sensitive to structures at this level. There is some evidence that the process is also sensitive to structures smaller than words. The performance of the program in identifying structures larger than words is considered in the next section.

```
   ╱╲   ╱╲╲   ╱╲╲  ╱╲  ╱╲╲  ╱╲
ANDDADDY THINK SIT DOES US
```

```
  ╱╲╲  ╱╲╲  ╱╲  ╱╲╲  ╱╲
GOOD TO GET OUT IN THE SUN
```

```
 ╱╲╲╲  ╱╲  ╱╲  ╱╲╲  ╱╲  ╱╲
WE WILL BE OUT EVERY DAY WHEN
```

```
 ╱╲╲ ╱╲╲╲ ╱╲ ╱╲ ╱╲ ╱╲
THE SUN COMES OUT DO YOU KNOW
```

```
 ╱╲╲╲  ╱╲  ╱╲  ╱╲╲
THERE IS AN OLD DONKEY
```

Fig. 2.3 — Part of a 10,000 letter sample from book 8A of the Ladybird Reading Series showing a parsing developed by program MK10 at a late stage of processing (Wolff, 1977).

Phrase structure

If program MK10 is run on a text like the one just described, it will, given time, build up structures which are larger than words and which look like phrase-structure trees. The results obtained with the Ladybird text, and others, showed a rather poor correspondence between these trees and the trees which would be assigned to the texts in conventional surface structure analyses.

One possible reason for this poor performance is that the program was not designed to discover disjunctive groupings of elements. Program SNPR does seek disjunctive groupings but it is not yet efficient enough to be run far enough on natural language for its performance with phrase structures to be judged.

A stop-gap solution to the problem of disjunctive relations was to transcribe a text as a sequence of word classes and to use this transcribed text as data for MK10. This is not a wholly satisfactory procedure because it does not provide for disjunctive groupings above and below the level of words. Despite this shortcoming and the other clear shortcomings of MK10 (not taking account of semantics, for example) surprisingly good results were obtained (Wolff, 1980).

Fig. 2.4 shows one sentence (and a bit) from 7600-word sample from Margaret Drabble's novel *Jerusalem the Golden*, which was transcribed as a sequence of word class symbols and processed in that form by MK10. The dendrogram above the sentence shows a supposedly uncontroversial surface structure analysis assigned by a linguist and the author. The dendrograms beneath show the parsing developed by the program at a late stage of processing. There is quite a good correspondence between the two analyses in this and many other cases. Statistical tests have confirmed that the correspondence is very unlikely to be an artefact of chance coincidences.

As we have seen, these results on segmentation cannot be construed as proof that children actually do distributional analyses of this kind. They merely demonstrate that such processes are plausible candidates, perhaps sufficient by themselves to explain how children learn to segment language or perhaps working in conjunction with processes which use available prosodic and semantic cues. It is perhaps worth observing that the use of such cues as a guide to structure is, in a deep sense, also distributional. If redundancy and structure are in some sense equivalent (Garner, 1974) then all modes of discovering structure may ultimately be seen in terms of redundancy abstraction.

2. Parts of speech and other disjunctive categories

In the same way that the theory has developed ideas from taxonomic linguistics about the discovery of segmental structure, it has adopted and extended what is perhaps the most distinctive idea from this tradition: how part-of-speech and other disjunctive categories are established.

The basic idea of course is to look for groups of elements where the members of the group share one or more contexts (where *context* means either or both of syntactic and semantic context). If, for example, the child finds the two patterns AX and BX in the language that he hears then X may be treated as a *context* and a structure (1)X may be created where 1 is a pointer or reference to the disjunctive grouping (A | B).

The principle is quite simple but its proper realization in a fully specified working system has proved quite difficult. What has been achieved in SNPR is the precise specification of a process in which the searches for segmental and disjunctive groupings are *integrated* in such a way that elements of one type may be incorporated in elements of the other kind and this at any level. The discovery procedure produces a generative grammar rather than some less explicit description of the data.

The observations that languages contain disjunctive categories like nouns, verbs, and adjectives is, like any other observation, partly a product of one's theoretical preconceptions. There are, no doubt, other descriptive frameworks one could employ which do not use them. But categories like these seem to be so strongly determined by the linguistic data that it seems reasonable to characterize them as observed phenomena rather than theoretical constructs. Less well supported but still reasonably clear is the observation that categories like these are a (usually unconscious) part of every adult's unschooled knowledge of language structure. The main evidence for this derives from word association tests (e.g. Deese, 1965; but see the discussion below on the 'S–P shift') and from speech errors (e.g. Fromkin, 1973).

If it is accepted that there is indeed something here requiring explanation we may ask how well the theory does in this respect. The performance of SNPR with artificial texts gives some indication of its ability to find disjunctive groups but, given that these groups have been artificially created, we cannot tell directly how it would do with natural categories.

Some attempt has been made to run SNPR on natural language but it requires impracticably long program runs to get useful results. (This in itself should not be an objection to the model given that children, with much more computational power at

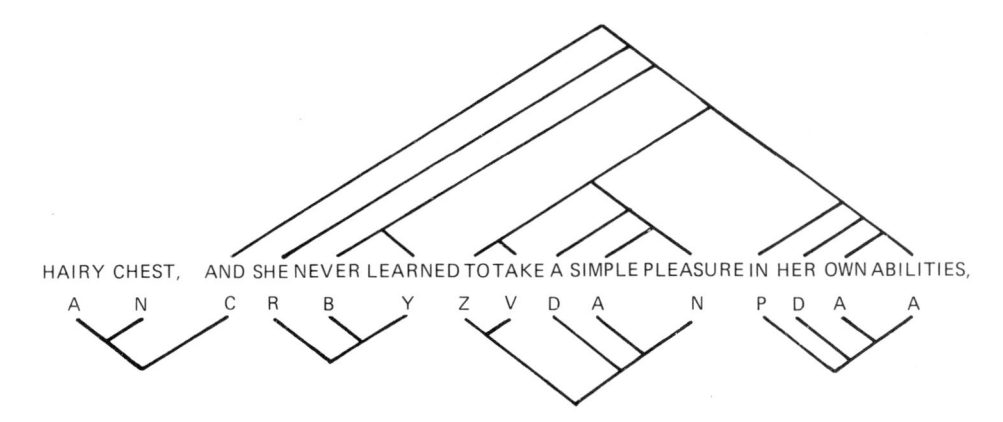

Fig. 2.4 — One sentence from a 7600-word sample from *Jerusalem the Golden* (Margaret Drabble) showing (above the text) a surface-structure analysis assigned intuitively and (below the text) the parsing developed by program MK10 at a late stage of processing (Wolff, 1980). This figure is reproduced by kind permission of Kingston Press Services Ltd.

their disposal, take several years to develop their linguistic knowledge.) Nevertheless, the program does develop some categories which correspond fairly well with recognized categories in English.

Validation of this general approach, though not the precise details of the current model, is provided in an interesting study by Kiss (1973). (Rosenfeld, Huang, & Schneider (1969) obtained similar results although their theoretical interests were rather different.)

Using a rather simple definition of the *context* of a word (the word immediately preceding the given word and the word following), Kiss measured the extent to which each of a set of selected words in a sample of natural language shared contexts with other members of the set. He then applied a standard clustering algorithm to these data to determine the *strength* of association between words. The clusters of words identified in this way corresponded quite well with the categories conventionally recognized by linguists (nouns, verbs, etc.).

Mention may be made here of observations which provide some supporting evidence for the idea that children do do a systematic comparison of linguistic structures in an attempt to find elements shared by more than one structure, much as in SNPR. In Ruth Weir's classic study (1962) of her young son's pre-sleep soliloquies one may find sequences of the child's utterances in which a word or a group of words recurs:

> ... *which one; two; one; right one; now left one; this one* ... (p. 180)

and later,

> ... *I'm taking the yellow blanket; too much; I have the yellow blanket; down; don't step in the blanket* ... (p. 181)

and many similar examples.

One gets the impression (supported by direct evidence appearing elsewhere in

Weir's protocols) that the child is repeating bits and pieces of language heard during the preceding day. The recurrence of words like 'one' and 'blanket' may simply reflect their recurrence in the original sequence of adult utterances but the overall impression one gets from Weir's records is that utterances are being brought together from disparate sources on the strength of shared constituents. We may here be witnessing part of the process of sorting and sifting required to establish disjunctive groupings of distributionally equivalent elements.

3. Generalization of grammatical rules and correction of overgeneralizations

The theory (in common with a number of other artificial intelligence theories of language acquisition) provides for the generalization of linguistic rules. Something like this is essential in any (empiricist) theory of language acquisition in order to explain how it is that both children and adults produce novel constructions which they are unlikely ever to have heard.

There is no great difficulty in creating generalizations. Almost any distortion in a grammar, including the deletion of rules, will lead it to generate constructions which it did not generate before. No strong claim is made about the particular generalization mechanisms in the present theory — it is a matter for future investigation to establish what mechanism or mechanisms children and adults actually use.

Correction of overgeneralizations

The much more difficult problem, which has received relatively little attention from psychologists or other theorists, is to establish what theoretically well-motivated process can, without the aid of a teacher or informant, eliminate the wrong generalizations and retain the good ones as permanent fixtures in the grammar.

The monitoring and rebuilding mechanisms in SNPR offer a possible explanation. Other possibilities were briefly discussed in the section outlining the workings of SNPR. Here I review some evidence that the mechanisms in SNPR are empirically valid. The evidence is provided by the results of running the program on an artificial language sample (see Table 2.2); the details are described in Wolff (1982).

An artificial text with no segmentation markers was prepared from a simple grammar but all instances of two of the (64) sentences generated by the grammar were excluded from the text. When the program was run on this text it successfully retrieved the original grammar despite the fact that the generative range of the grammar was not fully represented in the sample. In the course of building up the grammar it produced many *wrong* generalizations all of which were corrected. Every one of the *correct* generalizations, including those required to predict the missing sentences, were retained as permanent fixtures in the grammar.

In this case, the criterion of *correct* and *incorrect* was the grammar used to create the text. But this use of an artificial grammar to validate the model, although it is justified as an aid to developing the model, is potentially very misleading. The grammar used to create the text is only one of many that could have produced the same text and without some independent criterion there is no guarantee that the one employed is the *best* one. It is a mistake to allow one's knowledge of English (say) to dictate what is right and wrong when one is dealing with a text which may look superficially like a sub-set of English but whose *true* structure may be significantly different from English.

A fully satisfactory validation of the generalization and correction mechanism in SNPR is likely to prove difficult. No proper judgement can be made until a model has been developed which can give results with natural language including a satisfactory semantic input. If the mechanism allows wrong generalizations through (*wrong* now in the sense that they are not acceptable to a native speaker of the language) this would be clear evidence against the mechanism. But the model may fail more subtly if it eliminates generalizations that native speakers would in fact accept. Errors like these may be very difficult to detect.

Apart from validating the model against the judgements of native speakers of a natural language it is also necessary to demonstrate that the model does in fact realize the optimization principles on which it is based. This is chiefly a matter of demonstrating that CC increases as learning proceeds and that CC/S_g is maintained at a high level. In order to validate the optimization principles themselves it will be necessary to show that improved performance on measures of optimization correlates with success in discovering satisfactory grammars as judged by native speakers of the language. These are matters for future research.

Explanatory spin-off
The distinction between explanations considered in this section and those in previous sections is not very clear-cut because the prominent facts of language acquisition have been borne in mind at all times and they have affected the selection and rejection of hypothesized learning mechanisms. However, what follows was not a primary focus in developing the theory and may reasonably be counted as explanatory bonus, at least in part.

1. The rate of acquisition of words
Children typically produce their first word at about 12 months. In the following 6 months, new words are acquired rather slowly but then the pace quickens to produce a flood of words in the period of 18 months to 3 years. Because many of these new words are object names, this phenomenon is often called the 'naming explosion'. The rate at which new words are learned continues to be high throughout most of the rest of childhood; this is not as noticeable as the first burst of activity because it is not quite as dramatic. It is also quite difficult, without special techniques, to assess the size of the person's vocabulary when it is anything but very small. From early adulthood the rate of acquisition of new words declines progressively into old age.

The picture of vocabulary growth just sketched derives mainly from observations of spoken words but it seems to be similar for receptive vocabulary.

This pattern of vocabulary growth can be explained quite well by the theory. We have supposed that children are, from birth, busy building up bits and pieces of language structure starting with very small primitives. Eventually, one of these pieces reaches word size or near word size and, particularly if it is meaningful, it will be identified by adults as the child's first word. The reason suggested by the theory for the initial slow growth of vocabulary is that the child is still engaged in constructing the elements from which new words are built. With only a restricted range available, vocabulary growth will be slow. When the range is bigger, the rate of acquisition of new words will increase because relatively little processing is required in the construction of each new word; the rate should remain high for some time.

We may expect an eventual decline because opportunities to observe new words will eventually become rare enough to put a damper on the learning of new words (but see later discussion of this question). There is some evidence that rare words are constructed from a greater variety of constituents than common words and this might also tend to limit the rate of vocabulary growth.

This kind of informal explanation of the way vocabularies grow is not entirely satisfactory because observed patterns of growth depend in a complex way on the processing characteristics of the child and the statistical structure of the language being learned. A better way of matching the theory with empirical data is to construct a working model and see what patterns of vocabulary growth emerge when it operates with natural language. This has been done and the patterns produced correspond quite well with the picture sketched above (Wolff, 1977).

2. The order of acquisition of words and morphemes

Except for an anomaly to be discussed, there is a clear tendency for children to learn common words before rare ones (Gilhooly & Gilhooly, 1979). Given that in most languages rare words tend to be longer than common words and the variety of rare words is greater than the variety of common words (Zipf, 1935) we would expect children to learn long words later than short ones and we would expect the increases in lengths of words at successive ages to become progressively smaller.

A clear implication of the theory is that common structures should be learned earlier than rare ones. The implication that long words should be acquired later than short ones depends purely on the known relationship between frequency and word length and is nothing to do with the fact that the program builds large structures from small ones: this feature of the program would be entirely compatible with zero or even negative correlation between word length and age of acquisition.

As in the previous section, a working model is needed to see in detail how well expected patterns of acquisition correspond with observed patterns. Program MK10 produces a very good match with available data (Wolff, 1977).

Fig. 2.5 shows the relationship between the lengths of words acquired by a young child and the ages at which they were acquired (data from Grant, 1915). Fig. 2.6 shows comparable data for program MK10 applied to three different samples of natural language. In both figures, the progressive increase in the lengths of words can be seen and also the progressive decrease in the rate at which lengths increase.

Over the age range covered in Fig. 2.5, the decreasing rate at which word lengths increase is not very obvious. But it is easy to establish that the curve will be less steep at later ages because a linear extrapolation of the curve in Fig. 2.5 would lead one to predict that children would be acquiring absurdly long words in their late childhood and teens.

The anomaly mentioned above is that, in the early stages of language acquisition, function words tend to appear later than content words (McCarthy, 1954) although they are, typically, amongst the most frequent words in any language (Fries, 1952).

The best available explanation of this exception to the general pattern is that function words are largely meaningless until the larger syntactic patterns in which they function have been built up. A child may know the sound patterns of 'and',

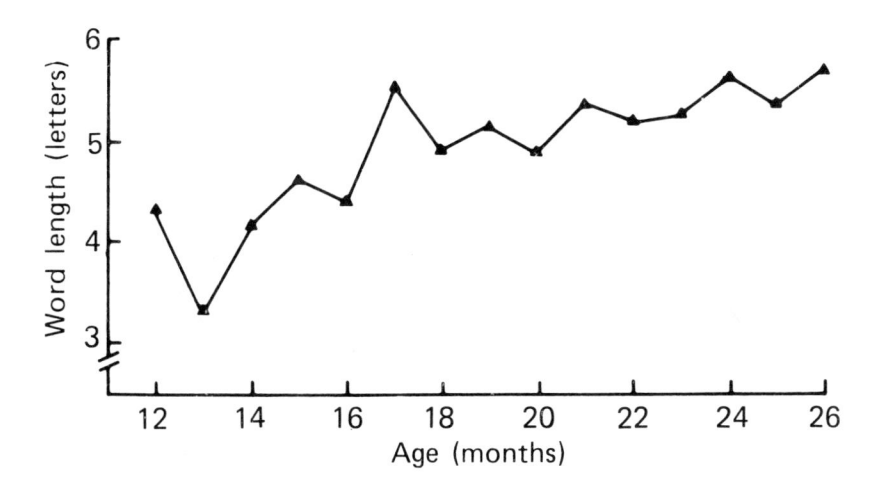

Fig. 2.5 — The average lengths of words acquired by one child at different ages (Wolff, 1977; data from Grant, 1915). This figure is reproduced by kind permission of the The British Psychological Society.

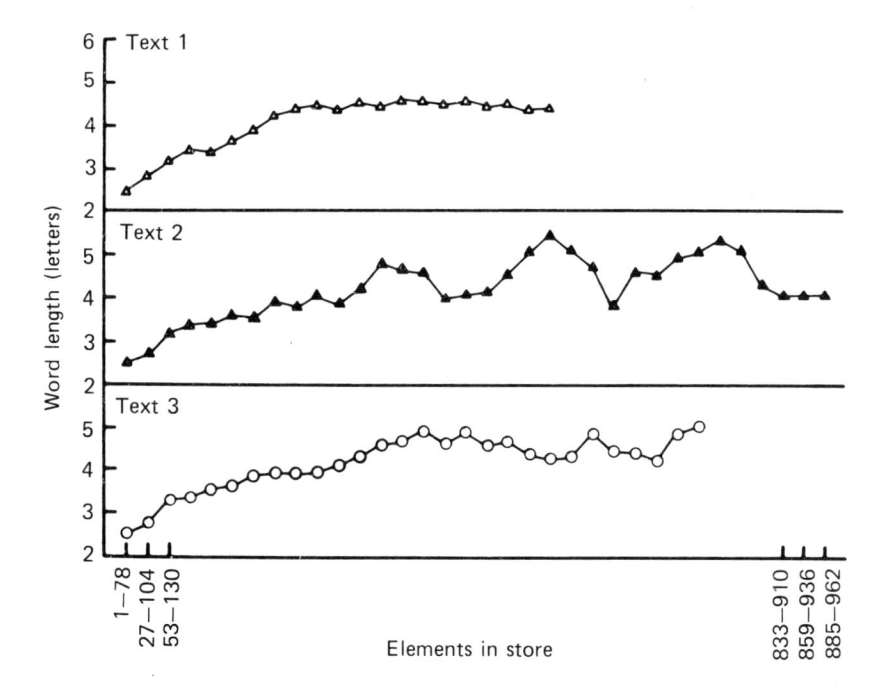

Fig. 2.6 — The average lengths of words isolated by program MK10 from three language texts at different stages of processing (Wolff, 1977). This figure is reproduced by kind permission of The British Psychological Society.

'the', 'into', etc., at an early age but have no cause to use them until they can be fitted into coordination constructions, noun phrases and prepositional phrases respectively. By contrast, words like 'table', 'Mummy', 'more', etc., are quite useful by themselves and can sensibly be used as soon as they are learned. A clear prediction of the theory, then, which would be interesting but difficult to test, is that children do have a knowledge of function words at an age before they start to use them.

Brown's (1973) observation that there is no significant correlation between frequency of use by caretaking adults and order of acquisition of fourteen functional morphemes (e.g. present progressive '-ing', preposition 'on', plural '-s', etc.) is completely at odds with the theory presented here. The argument used above (that the later acquisition of certain forms is more apparent than real) cannot be used here because all of the forms considered in this part of Brown's study are alike in that they are all functional morphemes, no one of which can sensibly be used as a meaningful utterance by itself. The criterion of acquisition was, in every case, correct use in 90% of obligatory contexts.

The conflict between the present theory and Brown's results is apparently resolved by the more recent conclusion (Forner, 1979; Moerk, 1980) that Brown's analyses of his data are in fact wrong. When defensible changes and refinements are made in the assumptions that go into the analyses then substantial and significant (negative) correlations are found between frequency of use and order of acquisition of these fourteen morphemes.

3. Brown's (1973) Law of Cumulative Complexity

Perhaps the most interesting general conclusion of Brown's (1973) classic study is that if one structure contains everything that another structure contains *and more* then it will be acquired later than that other structure. Given the variety of current linguistic theories there is some uncertainty about what the *content* of a structure might be but this 'Law of Cumulative Complexity' seems to stand up almost regardless of the theoretical framework adopted.

The law is not as trivial as it may at first sight seem although it does correspond with untutored expectations about language acquisition. It is conceivable that children might, in a certain sense, *acquire* structures whose internal organization is, initially, quite unlike the mature form eventually attained. A pattern ABC might be acquired directly or built up as (A(BC)) and then, with the subsequent recognition of AB as a discrete entity, it might be restructured as ((AB)C).

It may at first be thought that Brown's Law follows directly from the way the SNPR model has been designed; the model may be thought to be less an explanation of the law than a restatement of it. It is true that SNPR builds its structures from previously established constituents but there is nothing in the model to prevent a structure being built up initially in one form and then reconstructed in another.

The suggested reason why children (and the model) do not generally do this is that (as with the building up of words) frequency is the guiding heuristic. As a matter of observation (Brown & Hanlon, 1970) complex structures are less frequent than their constituents. According to the theory, they should, therefore, be acquired later.

4. The S–P/episodic–semantic shift

It has been recognized for some time that the way children respond in a word-association task changes as they mature. Young children tend to give as their responses words which could follow the stimulus word in a sentence (syntagmatically related words) whereas older children and adults tend to respond with (paradigmatically related) words which can be substituted for the stimulus word in a sentence (see, for example, Entwisle, 1966).

More recently, Petrey (1977) has re-examined Entwisle's data and has argued, persuasively enough, that while the syntagmatic–paradigmatic (S–P) shift remains roughly true, changes in word-association responses through childhood may be more accurately characterized as an 'episodic–semantic' shift. What this means is that young children tend to give as responses either words which could follow the stimulus word in a sentence or words which signify objects or events which could have been experienced by the child at the same time and place as the object or event signified by the stimulus word, or both of these. A seeming example of a response based on physical contiguity is a child saying 'cook' after the stimulus word 'add'. Petrey points out that this superficially bizarre response makes good sense when you see that other responses to 'add' include 'flour', 'milk', 'water', 'dinner', 'cake', etc. *Adding* things is something which young children may well typically first experience in the context of cooking.

Older children and adults tend to give responses which are related to the stimulus word in some way more abstract than mere syntactic or temporal/spatial contiguity. This abstract relationship (sometimes called 'semantic') is typically both a paradigmatic (part-of-speech) relationship and a meaning relationship as in 'long–short', 'wild–tame', 'give–take', etc.

If we assume that word-association norms at different ages reflect changing organization of stored knowledge then these phenomena make good sense in terms of our theory (see also Kiss, 1973). The theory postulates that children search for recurring clusters of spatially and/or temporally contiguous *events* both in their linguistic input and in their other experience. They also search for groups of elements in which members of the group share one or more temporal or spatial contexts. The disjunctive groups are incorporated in complex elements which represent clusters of similar patterns (see later).

The crucial point here is that the latter kind of search depends on the prior formation of clusters based on contiguity — it cannot get off the ground until there is a big enough set of simple clusters from which to derive common contexts and similarity groupings. If simple contiguity groups correspond to episodic knowledge and disjunctive/complex groupings correspond to semantic knowledge then the delay, just mentioned, in the construction of disjunctive/complex structures provides an explanation of the episodic–semantic shift; we apparently have an answer to Petrey's (1977) question: '... by what process can episodic memories of words in context lead to the abstract semantic organisation of mature lexical storage?' (p. 70).

There is other evidence supporting the present view of the S–P shift. This shift tends to occur earlier for high-frequency stimulus words than for rare ones and it correlates with the variety of syntactic contexts in which a word appears (see Kiss, 1973). The second observation is probably equivalent to the first one given that

54 LEARNING A FIRST LANGUAGE [Ch. 2

words with a wide variety of contexts will tend also to be frequent. The late appearance of an S–P shift in rare words may be attributed firstly to the fact that such words are themselves learned late and secondly to the probable fact that they tend to fall in contextual patterns which are less frequent than the most frequent contexts of common words. There are details here that need quantification.

A seeming problem for the account just given is that, as Petrey points out, children are speaking more-or-less correctly by the age of 4 whereas the S–P shift is most dramatic between the ages of 6 and 8. If, as Petrey assumes, correct speech is evidence of a knowledge of part-of-speech categories then it is hard to understand why paradigmatic responding does not appear earlier.

It is plain that children are combining words in a creative way from a very early age and it is tempting to assume, therefore, that all their speech at all stages is produced by combining elements according to rule and guided by a knowledge of permissible substitutes in particular contexts. This is not necessarily so. At least some correct utterances may be produced as essentially direct replicas of utterances previously heard. Both the theory and the observation just mentioned would lead us to expect that young children would produce a relatively high proportion of utterances of this kind. It would be interesting, although perhaps methodologically difficult, to obtain evidence on this point.

5. *Overgeneralizations*
The idea that children, in forming linguistic generalizations, might, so to speak, overshoot their target and produce wrong overgeneralizations is not merely a by-product of the theory. Clear examples of overgeneralization like 'hitted', 'mouses', etc., are very prominent in young children's speech and they are indeed one of the most salient pieces of evidence that children are abstracting general rules.

The theory not only provides a mechanism for correcting wrong generalizations but it seems to explain a quirk which has been observed in the way these generalizations arise. Children apparently produce irregular plurals and past tense verbs like 'geese', 'mice', 'fought', etc., in their *correct* form initially. *Only later* do they substitute the overgeneralized 'gooses', 'mouses', 'fighted', etc., and then revert eventually to the correct forms again (Slobin, 1971).

This pattern fits the theory well because, as explained in the section on the S–P shift, disjunctive groupings (and the generalizations that derive from them) can only be formed at a stage when there is a range of simple patterns to generalize from. The irregular nouns and verbs will be learned as they are observed and then displaced by generalizations when they are formed. The correction mechanism will restore them later.

6. *The slowing of language development in later years*
The way in which vocabulary growth eventually slows down echoes the more pronounced way in which a child's learning of grammatical patterns is accomplished largely before the age of 5 and then tails off in later years (see Chomsky, 1969).

A common-sense explanation of these effects would be that the child cannot continue to build up his knowledge of language if he or she has extracted all the available patterns in the data. In order to account for a progressive slowing in language learning rather than a sharp cessation of learning one could refine this view by taking account of the way unlearned structures would become progressively rarer as the data becomes exhausted. The opportunities to observe new structures would become more and more sparse. Notice that this explanation does not depend on the observations that common structures are learned earlier than rare ones although it is entirely compatible with it. Plausible as this *exhaustion* explanation may appear, it is very probably wrong or at least only partly true.

Although there are many uncertainties and methodological difficulties in estimating the total size of the person's vocabulary (Ellegard, 1960; Seashore & Eckerson, 1940), it is clear that most people in their lifetimes do not come anywhere near exhausting the word forms in their native language, certainly for a language like English with its exceptionally large vocabulary. While people may reach a stage in their learning where the frequency of any particular unlearned word is very low, the variety of as yet unlearned words is so great that the frequency of this class of words as a whole is relatively high.

There are considerable difficulties in determining the extent of a person's knowledge of grammatical patterns and there are uncertainties in what should or should not be regarded as a distinct pattern, but it seems reasonably clear that there are many esoteric patterns that people do not generally bother to learn.

> We found 9-year-olds and 10-year-olds who could not, even with prodding, respond with the correct answer: 'What should I feed the doll?' (in response to the instruction 'Ask L what to feed the doll'). The question that we wish to raise is whether these children are still in a process of acquisition with respect to this structure and will at some future time be able to interpret it correctly, or whether perhaps they may already have reached what for them constitutes adult competence. We have observed from informal questioning that this structure is a problematic one for many adults, and there are many adult speakers who persist in assigning the wrong subject to the complement verb. This seems to be a structure that is never properly learned by a substantial number of speakers. (Chomsky, 1969, p. 101)

Before we proceed to consider an alternative or supplementary explanation of the slowing down in the acquisition of new language patterns, one other common-sense explanation may be noted. Part of the cause of a slowing up in language learning may be a reduction in processing capacity because of physical deterioration in the brain. Barring disease, such an effect looks unimportant before old age. Even then it would seem to be only a minor factor because of the informal observation that people can pick up new words rapidly at almost any age if they are introduced to a new language.

The explanation suggested by the theory for why language learning slows up in later years has to do with the tradeoffs which are basic in the theory. The two that have been considered so far will serve the argument. Children are supposedly miserly in their use of storage space for long-term storage: new information will only be stored in a long-term form if it adds significantly to the usefulness of the knowledge structures for encoding information. In the early stages of learning, plenty of such patterns are observed and quickly incorporated in the child's long-term knowledge structures. Later on, patterns that are useful enough to warrant long-term storage will be encountered less and less often and acquisition will slow.

We might imagine that this gradual slowing in the growth of linguistic knowledge would have a sharp terminus when the child's database is finally exhausted of all structures that are useful enough to be worth storing. Given a continually expanding linguistic corpus and the resulting fluctuations in the observed frequencies of linguistic patterns, we have a second reason for expecting a gradual tailing off in language learning rather than an abrupt end to it.

The essential difference between this *tradeoff* explanation and the *exhaustion* explanation mentioned at the beginning of this section, is that it proposes optimization as a limiting factor rather than the availability of patterns in the data. Given uniform linguistic experiences and given variations in how miserly individuals need to be with storage (this in turn presumably depending in part on the total available storage), the preferred view predicts variations among individuals in how big their mature system will be while the other view does not. The two views differ also in that the preferred view does not require anyone to exhaust the data available to them whereas the other view does.

7. Nonlinguistic cognitive structures

As already stated, a working assumption in this project has been that a set of principles may be found to operate in all spheres of knowledge acquisition (which is not to say that differences may not also be found). Nonetheless, most work to date in this project has been done with input data and knowledge structures which are most clearly analogous to syntax. There has been a relatively unsuccessful attempt to develop ideas in the nonlinguistic sphere (Wolff, 1976), this at a stage before several important insights had been achieved. Wolff (1987) argues for a uniform system for encoding syntactic and semantic knowledge but relatively little is said about the latter. Only a little is said here. The topic really warrants a whole paper to itself.

The chief merit of my 1976 paper is to establish a set of target criteria of success for a theory of how classes of objects (*concepts* in this context) may be developed. Briefly, these are:

(1) Natural classifications of objects differ from the artificial classes studied by, for example, Bruner, Goodnow, and Austin (1956), in that they are in some sense *salient*: they reflect structures inherent in the world which our concept learning systems can abstract without *explicit teaching*.
(2) Our concepts are arranged in hierarchies and heterarchies.
(3) There is overlap among conceptual groupings.
(4) The boundaries of natural classes are in some sense *fuzzy*.
(5) Natural classes are often *polythetic*: no single attribute or group of attributes need be shared by all members of the class. (This together with (3) and (4) above are the chief differences between natural classification systems and those developed by the majority of clustering algorithms.)
(6) Attributes of objects carry varying *weights* in the process of recognizing new instances of a class.

The model described in Wolff (1976) was reasonably successful at meeting all the criteria, except the requirement of polythesis. Now it seems that program SNPR, although it was developed primarily as a model of syntax learning, meets all six criteria completely. This is not to say that it is a wholly satisfactory model of concept acquisition — there are other criteria that may be added to these six which it would not be able to model.

The reason that SNPR can be seen as a model of concept learning is that it develops disjunctive classes and it also develops complex elements that can be seen as intensional descriptions of classes of *similar* entities. For example, a complex element with the structure (A|B) X (C|D) Y (where | represents exclusive 'OR') describes the extensional class of entities AXCY, BXCY, AXDY and BXDY. The members of this class are similar, obviously because they share attributes X and Y and, less obviously, because there is some commonality among them in the attributes A, B, C, and D. Because X and Y are common to all members, this particular class is not polythetic. But SNPR is quite capable of developing intensional descriptions like (A|B)(C|D)(E|F) where the members of the corresponding extensional class (ACE, ACF, BCE, BCF, ADE, ADF, BDE, BDF) have no single attribute in common. This is a truly polythetic category.

The term *attribute* used here need not be confined to conventional perceptual attributes like shapes and colours. It may also cover functional attributes like the fact that a ball can roll (Nelson's (1974) example). Contextual properties of concepts — fish are typically found in water, for example — are handled quite straightforwardly by the system because of the way it develops part–whole hierarchies: the concept of fish can be incorporated in a larger element representing fish environments. Contextual or extrinsic attributes of concepts are arguably equal in importance to conventional intrinsic attributes in establishing the nature of a category.

SNPR also meets the other five criteria. The elements developed by the model are salient in the sense that they express redundancies in the input data and are discovered without explicit teaching. SNPR can develop part–whole hierarchies and it can also develop class-inclusion hierarchies in which overlap between classes can occur. Fuzziness of concepts and differential weighting of attributes can be dealt with by allowing the identification of new entities as belonging to one or other of pre-established categories to be a probabilistic matter (as in my 1976 model).

The relevance of the theory to the realm of nonlinguistic cognitions is underlined by the similarity between the complex elements developed by SNPR and the well-known notions of *schema* (Bartlett, 1932; Bobrow & Norman, 1975), *frame* (Minsky, 1975), and *script* (Schank & Abelson, 1977). Like these theoretical constructs, a complex element in the theory is a generalized pattern which reflects a commonly recurring set of entities, be it a set of cultural expectations (Bartlett) or the things found inside a typical room (Minsky) or the typical pattern of events that occur when you eat a meal in a restaurant (Schank & Abelson). All these notions share the idea that there are *slots* in the framework where alternatives may be inserted, and they share the idea that one of the alternatives may function as a default — the assumed filler for the slot when there is no contrary evidence. In the syntagmatic elements developed by SNPR the disjunctive constituents are equivalent to slots. Since members of each disjunctive set typically vary in their contextual probability, the most probable one may be regarded as a default element.

The foregoing is intended to indicate how a theory largely developed with reference to syntactic phenomena may indeed generalize to semantic phenomena with little if any adjustment, in accordance with the working hypothesis of uniform structure-abstracting principles. The major gap in these ideas is some principled account of the origin and growth of *relational* concepts. This is a matter for future work (but see Wolff, 1987).

8. Nativist arguments

Three planks of the nativist position have been that a knowledge of language structure must be largely known in advance because the available evidence contained in the language which a child hears is too much obscured by *performance* errors and distortions of various kinds; because the vagaries of individual experience of a given language and individual variations in ability do not square with the way everyone acquires essentially the same grammar; and because language acquisition apparently happens too fast to be explained by learning alone.

> A consideration of the character of the grammar that is acquired, the degenerate quality and narrowly limited extent of the available data, the striking uniformity of the resulting grammars, and their independence of intelligence, motivation, and emotional state, over wide ranges of variation, leave little hope that much of the structure of the language can be learned by an organism initially uninformed as to its general character. (Chomsky, 1965, p. 58)

And later:

> '... there is surely no reason today for taking seriously a position that attributes a complex human achievement entirely to months (or at most years) of experience, rather than to millions of years of evolution or to principles of neural organization that may be even more deeply grounded in physical law .... (Chomsky, 1965, p. 59)

That the data available to the child has a 'narrowly limited extent' seems to be simply wrong. Anyone who has had any dealings with the recording of what adults say to children or in their presence will know that the quantities of data are enormous.

That the data are very often corrupted in terms of what native speakers with mature knowledge would judge to be correct, is clearly true; attempts to show otherwise seem to be misplaced. The 'dirty data' problem is illustrated in Fig. 2.1. A strength of the theory is that it neatly explains how children can learn from such data without being thrown off by errors: any particular error is, by its nature, rare and so in the search for useful (common) structures, it is discarded along with many other candidate structures. (If an error is not rare it is likely to acquire the status of a dialect or idiolect variation and cease to be regarded as an error.)

In practice, the programs MK10 and SNPR have been found to be quite insensitive to errors (of omission, addition, or substitution) in their data. A good example with respect to omissions is the way SNPR was able to discover a grammar from data containing less than the complete range of terminal strings of that grammar.

It is probably true that the members of any given language community have grammatical systems which are quite similar, one to another. But they are not identical. There are many more-or-less subtle differences between individual systems (Broadbent, 1970). The uniformity of grammatical systems across a wide ability range seen by authors like Lenneberg (1967) may be attributed in part to unsophisticated methods of assessment. With more penetrating techniques like those pioneered by Chomsky (1969) many differences come to light which can otherwise easily be overlooked.

Even though there is wide variation in children's experience of any given language, we should not be surprised to find quite a lot of similarity between the grammatical systems that they develop. The reason is that, within one language community, children's experience of language can be varied at the level of particular sentences but quite uniform at the level of the grammatical patterns on which those sentences are modelled and uniform in terms of the words out of which they are constructed. (Without this uniformity it would not be reasonable to say that the children belonged to one single linguistic community.) Abstraction processes like those in SNPR which are guided by constancy (redundancy) are not distracted by idiosyncratic realizations of recurrent patterns.

The third argument, that language development is too fast to be explained by learning mechanisms, need not detain us. The computational power of a child's brain is clearly huge. The computational demands of current models are quite high but there is no reason to think they are unrealistically high. Given what has already been achieved with only a few hours of a conventional computer's time, there is every reason to think that with more computing power exercised over months and years this kind of process may discover the full complexity of language structure quite easily.

9. The word frequency effect

One of the most fully documented phenomena in psychology is the observation that a spoken or written word or other perceptual pattern is, in some sense, more easily perceived if it is frequent in the observer's experience than if it is rare. This effect is rather insensitive to varying modes of testing and to varying measures of perception.

There have been many attempts to explain the effect, all of which necessarily assume that people have a knowledge of the relative frequencies of these perceptual patterns. But none of them suggest any reason *why* people should have this knowledge. Now, in the theory, we have a natural explanation: a knowledge of the relative frequencies of perceptual patterns (linguistic or otherwise) is a by-product of search processes which are, so to speak, *designed* to construct an optimal cognitive system.

Neutral and disconfirming evidence

Most of the empirical evidence presented so far is apparently explicable in terms of the theory and most of it provides support for the theory. There are of course many other observations of children's language development about which nothing has been said. This large residual set of observations may be divided into two parts: observations, which are in a sense neutral with respect to the theory, which will be considered briefly, and some that seem to be incompatible with the theory, which are discussed at more length.

An example of the kind of observation which is neutral with respect to the theory would be the particular utterances recorded by Braine (1963). It happened that the child, Andrew, said 'all done', 'all buttoned', 'all clean', among other things, but he might just as well have said 'all eaten', 'all black', and 'all found', etc.; no current theory can explain why Andrew said the particular things he did say. It would require an extraordinarily precise theory of motivation and the like to pin such things down.

There seems at present to be only one class of observations which conflicts directly with the theory. In its current form the theory makes a clear statement that children progress from small structures to larger ones by concatenating contiguous elements. What this means is that an utterance like 'hit the ball' may only be built up as (($hit\ the$)$ball$) or (more likely) (hit($the\ ball$)) and children should never produce telegraphic utterances like 'hit ball' as they have been observed to do (Brown, 1973). Likewise, at the level of word structure, it should be possible for a child to learn a *schema* of salient features of a word with interstitial elements missing and then subsequently fill these details in (as claimed by Waterson, 1971). No child should ever say '[byʃ]' at an immature stage in the attainment of the adult word 'brush', as Waterson's son was heard to do. In this example there is vowel substitution (which is explicable by the theory in terms of generalization) but the missing [r] represents a supposedly unbridgeable gap between the beginning and the end of the word.

CONCLUSION

A theory may suffer many ills. It may be a loose sketchy affair which does not allow one to make reliable inferences. It may be trivial in the sense that it does not do much more than redescribe the data it is meant to explain. Or it may be trivial because it is an overgeneral catch-all theory which cannot be falsified. Many theories in psychology are weak because they are applicable to only a narrow range of phenomena, often ones observed in a laboratory setting which may lack 'ecological validity' (Neisser, 1976). 'Micro theories' like these are usually weak also because they do not suggest any connections with a broader theoretical framework.

These points are made, of course, to introduce the claim that the theory described in this chapter is reasonably free from these defects. Certainly these pitfalls have been borne in mind and considerable efforts have been made to avoid them.

As a theory of language development, the theory seems also to fare quite well against the useful criteria proposed by Pinker (1979) for evaluating such theories. It cannot yet meet the most stringent of these criteria: that it should propose mechanisms which are powerful enough to learn a natural language. But it does show promise in this direction.

The second criterion, that the theory should not propose mechanisms that are narrowly adapted to a particular language, seems to be met. It is almost axiomatic that a universal feature of languages is *structure* expressed as *redundancy*. Mechanisms designed to abstract redundancy will thus be quite general in their application. There is always the possibility, of course, that a language may be found containing a type of redundancy not yet brought within the scope of the theory.

Whether or not the kinds of mechanism proposed can learn a language within the same time span as a child cannot be decided with absolute confidence. But as previously argued, there is no reason for supposing that they cannot. Pinker's fourth criterion — that the theory should not demand information in its database which is not reliably available to children — is certainly met by the theory. Stress has been laid in this chapter on the way only weak assumptions have been made about children's sensory input.

That a theory of language development should have something to say about the phenomena observed when children progress towards a mature knowledge of language is another criterion which the theory meets fairly well. We have seen how patterns of vocabulary growth, the Law of Cumulative Complexity, and other developmental phenomena may be explained by the theory.

The last criterion is that proposed mechanisms should not be wildly inconsistent with what is known about children's cognitive abilities. Again, the theory seems quite satisfactory in this regard. The child is seen as taking repeated samples of data and abstracting linguistic structures from them. No single sample needs to be very large and all potential problems of combinatorial explosion are met by the heuristic devices embodied in the theory. Quite a lot of computation is required but there is no reason to think that it is beyond the scope of the 10^{10} neurons which are available.

Future work
Probably the most useful first step to take in future development of this theory would be to test and refine the ideas of Wolff (1987) by constructing a new computer model which embodies them. One aim would be to establish more clearly how parsing and production processes may be married to the proposed representational system. But the main goal would be to examine how well the proposed learning principles may operate with this system. At some stage a resolution must be found to the mismatch between the theory and the previously discussed observations on telegraphic speech.

An area that needs closer attention is the application of optimization principles to the acquisition of relational concepts. Also in need of fuller treatment is an examination in quantitative terms of how well different learning mechanisms can serve the optimization goal. Related to this is the need to test whether or not success in optimization correlates with success in discovering *correct* linguistic structures as judged by native speakers of a language.

Most of the empirical predictions of the theory have been tested against observations that are already recorded in the literature. There are however a few predictions from the theory that invite further empirical work. If a suitable testing method could be found, it would be interesting to see whether or not children really do have some kind of knowledge of function words at a stage before they use them. Likewise, it would be interesting to test whether babies do indeed have a developing receptive knowledge of word fragments at stages before they utter their first words as theory predicts they should.

One other empirical question that deserves attention concerns children's developing knowledge of disjunctive grouping and the extent to which their utterances are constructed from smaller constituents or are direct readouts of stored patterns. The theory predicts, and the evidence from word-association tests confirms, that children's knowledge of distributional equivalences should lag behind their knowledge of acceptable strings of words. It would be useful if a method could be found of establishing, for any given utterance, exactly how it was produced. One might then be able to test the theory's prediction that the building of utterances from smaller constituents should become increasingly important as the child's linguistic knowledge matures.

The ideas discussed in this chapter are not intended to be a new dogma. As with any theory in this area there are too many points of uncertainty to warrant rigid views. The theory does, however, seem to have sufficient merit to serve as a framework for future theoretical and empirical work on linguistic and cognitive development.

SUMMARY

The chapter has provided a broad perspective on an *optimization* theory of language learning and cognitive development, details of which have been considered elsewhere.

The basic idea in the theory is that linguistic and cognitive development is, in large measure, a process of building cognitive structures towards a form which is optimally efficient for the several functions to be served.

The theory assumes among other things that language learning does not depend on overt speaking or gesturing by the child, it does not require any kind of reinforcement or error correction or other intervention by a 'teacher' and it does not require graded sequences of language samples. But it may be helped by any of these things.

The theory provides or suggests explanations for a wide range of phenomena. These include the acquisition of segmental structures in language at word, phrase and sentence levels, the acquisition of part-of-speech and other disjunctive categories, generalization of grammatical rules (including recursive generalizations), correction of overgeneralizations (including some observed peculiarities of how overgeneralizations appear in children's speech), the varying rates at which words and other structures are acquired throughout childhood and beyond, the order of acquisition of words and more complex grammatical structures, the S–P or episodic–semantic shift, the development of semantic/conceptual structures, and some other observations. The theory fits well into a biological framework and is broadly consistent with current thinking about language comprehension and production.

There are some observations which are in conflict with the theory in its present form.

ACKNOWLEDGEMENT

I am grateful to Alan Wilkes and Philip Quinlan of the University of Dundee for useful comments on an earlier draft of this chapter.

The chapter was first drafted while I was a lecturer at Dundee. I am grateful to the university for supporting this work and to my colleagues in the Department of Psychology for friendly criticism and stimulating discussion.

Some of the research described in the chapter was supported by a Personal Research Grant to me (HRP8240/1(A)) from the British Social Science Research Council.

REFERENCES

Anderson, J. R. (1981). A theory of language acquisition based on general learning principles. *Proceedings of the Seventh International Conference on Artificial Intelligence IJCA1-81,* pp. 97–103.

Bartlett, F. C. (1932). *Remembering: An Experimental and Social Study*. London: Cambridge University Press.
Bobrow, D. G., & Norman, D. A. (1975). Some principles of memory schemata. In D. G. Bobrow & A. Collins (Eds), *Representation and Understanding*. New York: Academic Press.
Braine, M. D. S. (1971). On two types of models of the internalization of grammars. In D. I. Slobin (Ed.), *The Ontogenesis of Grammar*. New York: Academic Press.
Braine, M. D. S. (1963). The ontogeny of English phrase structure. The first phrase. *Language* **39**, 1–13.
Broadbent, D. E. (1970). In defence of empirical psychology. *Bulletin of the British Psychological Society* **23**, 87–96.
Brown, R. (1973). *A First Language: The Early Stages*. Harmondsworth, England: Penguin.
Brown, R., & Hanlon, C. (1970). Derivational complexity and order of acquisition in child speech. In J. R. Hayes (Ed.), *Cognition and the Development of Language*. New York: Wiley.
Bruner, J. S., Goodnow, J. J., & Austin, G. A. (1956). *A Study of Thinking*. New York: Wiley.
Carr, H. A. (1931). The laws of association. *Psychological Review* **38**, 212–228.
Chomsky, C. (1969). *The Acquisition of Syntax in Children from 5 to 10*. Cambridge, MA: MIT Press.
Chomsky, N. (1965). *Aspects of the Theory of Syntax*. Cambridge, MA: MIT Press.
Coulon, D., & Kayser, D. (1978). Learning criterion and inductive behaviour. *Pattern Recognition* **10**, 19–25.
Deese, J. (1965). *The Structure of Association in Language and Thought*. Baltimore, MD: Johns Hopkins University Press.
Ellegard, A. (1960). Estimating vocabulary size. *Word* **16**, 219–244.
Entwisle, D. R. (1966). *Word Associations of Young Children*. Baltimore, MD: Johns Hopkins University Press.
Forner, M. (1979). The mother as LAD: interaction between order and frequency of parental input and child production. In F. R. Eckman & A. J. Hastings (Eds), *Studies in First and Second Language Acquisition*. Rowley, MA: Newberry House.
Fries, C. C. (1952). *The Structure of English*. London: Longmans.
Fromkin, V. (Ed.) (1973). *Speech Errors as Linguistic Evidence*. The Hague: Mouton.
Gammon, E. (1969). Quantitative approximations to the word. *Tijdschrift van het Instituut voor Toegepaste Linguistiek (Leuven)* **5**, 43–61.
Garner, W. R. (1974), *The Processing of Information and Structure*. Hillsdale, NJ: Lawrence Erlbaum.
Gilhooly, K. J., & Gilhooly, M. L. (1979). The age of acquisition of words as a factor in verbal tasks. Final report to the British Social Science Research Council on Research Grant HR/5318.
Grant, J. R. (1915). A child's vocabulary and its growth. *Pedagogical Seminary* **22**, 183–203.
Harris, Z. S. (1961). *Structural Linguistics*. Chicago: University of Chicago Press.

Harris, Z. S. (1970). *Papers in Structural and Transformational Linguistics*. Dordrecht: Reidel.

Kiss, G. R. (1973). Grammatical word classes: a learning process and its simulation. *Psychology of Learning and Motivation* **7**, 1–41.

Lakatos, I. (1978). Falsification and the methodology of scientific research programmes. In J. Worral & G. Curry (Eds), *The Methodology of Scientific Research Programmes*. Philosophical Papers, Vol. I, Cambridge, England: Cambridge University Press.

Langley, P. (1982). Language acquisition through error recovery. *Cognition & Brain Theory* **5**, 211–255.

Lenneberg, E. H. (1967). *Biological Foundations of Language*. New York: Wiley.

McCarthy, D. (1954). Language development in children. In L. Carmichael (Ed.), *Manual of Child Psychology*. New York: Wiley.

Minsky, M. (1975). A framework for representing knowledge. In P. H. Winston (Ed.), *The Psychology of Computer Vision*. New York: McGraw-Hill.

Moerk, E. L. (1980). Relationships between parental frequency and input frequencies and children's language acquisition: a reanalysis of Brown's data. *Journal of Child Language* **7**, 105.

Neisser, U. (1976). *Cognition and Reality*. San Francisco: W. H. Freeman.

Nelson, K. (1974). Concept, word and sentence: inter-relations in acquisition and development. *Psychological Review* **81**, 267–285.

Olivier, D. C. (1968). Stochastic grammars and language acquisition mechanisms. Unpublished doctoral dissertation, Harvard University.

Petrey, S. (1977). Word association and the development of lexical memory. *Cognition* **5**, 57–71.

Pinker, S. (1979). Formal models of language learning. *Cognition* **7**, 217–283.

Rosenfeld, A., Huang, H. K., & Schneider, V. B. (1969). An application of cluster detection to text and picture processing, *IEEE Transactions on Information Theory*, **IT-15**(6), 672–681.

Schank, R. C., & Abelson, R. P.(1977). *Scripts, Plans, Goals and Understanding: An Inquiry into Human Knowledge Structures*. New York: Wiley.

Seashore, R. H., & Eckerson, L. D. (1940). The measurement of individual differences in general English vocabulary. *Journal of Educational Psychology* **31**, 14–38.

Slobin, D. I.(1971). Data for the Symposium. In D. I. Slobin (Ed.), *The Ontogenesis of Grammar*. New York: Academic Press.

Waterson, N. (1971). Child phonology: a prosodic view. *Journal of Linguistics* **7**, 179–211.

Weir, R. (1962). *Language in the Crib*. The Hague: Mouton.

Wolff, J. G. (1975). An algorithm for the segmentation of an artificial language analogue. *British Journal of Psychology* **66**, 79–90.

Wolff, J. G. (1976). Frequency, conceptual structure and pattern recognition. *British Journal of Psychology* **67**, 377–390.

Wolff, J. G. (1977). The discovery of segments in natural language. *British Journal of Psychology* **68**, 97–106.

Wolff, J. G. (1980). Language acquisition and the discovery of phrase structure. *Language & Speech* **23**, 255–269.

Wolff, J. G. (1982). Language acquisition, data compression and generalization. *Language & Communication* **2**, 57–89.
Wolff, J. G. (1987). Cognitive development as optimization. In L. Bolc (Ed.), *Computational Models of Learning*. Heidelberg: Springer-Verlag.
Zipf, G. K. (1935). *The Psycho-biology of Language*. Boston: Houghton Mifflin.

3
The SNPR model

The article reproduced in this chapter is mainly a description of the SNPR model with results showing how it performs. Although there is some overlap with Chapter 2, the article has been included in the book because it provides a much fuller and more detailed description of SNPR and the results it produces than in Chapter 2 and this level of detail is needed to understand fully how the model works.

As described in the introduction to Chapter 2, the main features of SNPR are:

- The discovery of un-augmented CF-PSGs in unsegmented text without the use of negative samples or a teacher.
- The integration of the discovery of segmental (conjunctive) structure with the discovery of class (disjunctive) structure.
- A mechanism for generalizing grammatical rules and correcting overgeneralizations without external error correction of any kind.

The way in which the learning of conjunctive structure is integrated with the learning of disjunctive structure seems to be the key to two problems:

- One of these has been one of the main problems for the taxonomic tradition and one of the main objections to that programme of research. A key part of taxonomic linguistics was the idea that word classes (nouns, verbs etc.) may be inferred from shared contexts. Using one of the examples given by Fries (1952), the class of 'nouns' (or 'Class I' words in Fries's terms) are words which may be substituted for 'clerk' in 'The clerk remembered the tax'. This idea cannot be used directly in a learning system because it is so rare in ordinary language to find sets of sentences which differ, one from another, by only one word.

    In SNPR, the way in which the learning of segmental structure is integrated with the learning of class structure means that:

    - Classes may be inferred from fragments of sentences and it is much less rare to find fragments of sentences which differ, one from another, by only one word or other segment.
    - 'Context' may be defined in terms of the abstract structures being built by the program. It is much easier to find abstract structures which differ in the required way than to find specific sequences of words.

- The way in which SNPR removes overgeneralizations without eliminating correct generalizations depends on the integration of the learning of conjunctive and disjunctive structures. This should be clear from the description of the mechanisms which is given in the article.

LANGUAGE ACQUISITION, DATA COMPRESSION AND GENERALIZATION†

INTRODUCTION

This article is concerned with a continuing attempt to develop an empirically adequate theory of first language acquisition building on previous work by the author which will be outlined below.‡ The theory in its current state of development is embodied in a computer model, program SNPR, which will be described together with illustrative results.

One important aim in developing this model has been to explore the nature of generalization processes which may explain how, given only the finite corpus of language heard during childhood, we can learn to produce and comprehend an infinite range of novel but grammatically acceptable utterances. In particular, an attempt has been made to understand how acceptable generalizations which need to be retained in the developing language system can be distinguished from unacceptable 'overgeneralizations' (like children's *mouses* or *buyed*) which must eventually be eliminated even if there is no error correction by a 'teacher' or informant. Syntactic overgeneralizations like these have been considered before (e.g. Braine, 1971; Ervine, 1964, Slobin, 1971) but it seems that this is the first serious attempt to answer the question posed. Semantic generalizations and overgeneralizations will not be discussed, although the principles described here may prove relevant to that domain.

Previous work on the project will be described together with a statement of methodology. This will be followed by a discussion of 'cognitive economy' and its relevance to language acquisition. The proposal to be developed is the notion that certain aspects of language acquisition are manifestations of data compression principles which have the effect of optimizing the balance between space required for storage of cognitive structures and the effectiveness of those structures for the economical encoding of cognitive data. Related ideas which have been put forward before (Horning, 1969; Feldman, 1972; Cook & Rosenfeld, 1976; Coulon & Kayser, 1978) are extended and elaborated here. This section on cognitive economy will serve as a basis for discussing generalization and for the description of SNPR which follows.

There is, of course, some overlap with other attempts to create working models of language acquisition or to construct grammar discovery procedures. (See reviews by Biermann & Feldman (1972), by Fu & Booth (1975) and by Pinker (1979), and also articles by Anderson (1977), Gammon (1969), Hamburger & Wexler (1975), L. R. Harris (1977), Z. S. Harris (1970), Kelley (1967), Kiss (1973), Knobe & Knobe (1976), Olivier (1968), Power & Longuet-Higgins (1978), Salveter (1979), Siklossy (1972), Stolz (1965), Wexler & Culicover (1980).) Reference to some of these studies will be made at appropriate points below.

---

† From the article with the same title by J. G. Wolff, 1982, *Language & Communication* **2** (1), pp. 57–89. Copyright 1982 by Pergamon Press PLC. Reprinted with permission.

‡ Papers outlining the main ideas in this article have been presented at the London Conference of the British Psychological Society in December 1979, and at the AISB-80 conference on Artificial Intelligence in Amsterdam in July 1980 (Wolff, 1980a).

Methodology and background

The method of theory development which has been employed is to identify and attempt to solve manageable sub-problems and then to integrate, modify and extend the answers, using empirical data together with pre-established theory as clues to the nature of acquisition processes and as checks to the validity of theoretical proposals. At each stage in this 'bootstrapping' process, target criteria of success or failure are established which are progressively tightened in succeeding stages.

By exploring the properties of simple mechanisms which have complex implications and by relating these properties to known features of language development we may, in the interests of theoretical parsimony, hope to find simplicity behind the apparent complexity of language acquisition. An imperative feature of this approach is that theoretical proposals be embodied in computer-based working models which can run through the implications quickly and accurately. In the course of this project a number of apparently promising ideas have been subjected to this discipline — and most have been discarded.

The main effort to date has been the development of a computer program or programs which, given only a language-like text as data, will be capable of discovering or retrieving the grammar which was used to create the text. Examples of grammars and texts are shown in Fig. 3.1. Whether or not this is accepted as a reasonable sub-goal in the search for sufficient mechanisms to explain the phenomena of language acquisition depends on an acceptance of these texts as analogues of the linguistic data available to children.

The simplest view of the texts is that they correspond to the speech which young children hear, although they differ from speech in obvious ways. Letters in a text may be seen as representing discrete perceptual elements roughly equivalent to phonemes or something smaller and simpler than phonemes: features, formant ratios or the like. The assumption implicit in the use of discrete symbols is merely that linguistic material, at some (fairly low) level, is encoded as discrete 'perceptual primitives'.

Phrase-structure grammars (PSGs) like those shown in Fig. 3.1 are, of course, insufficient to handle natural language, but they are a simple embodiment of two structural principles which seem to be prominent (perhaps universal) features of natural languages: segmental (syntagmatic) and disjunctive (paradigmatic) groupings of linguistic elements. They can also express a number of other characteristic features of natural languages, and they can thus serve as a useful test-bed for discovery procedures intended ultimately for use with natural languages.† The first grammar in Fig. 3.1 shows, in its first rule, a discontinuous dependency between PUT and ON. Notice that the relation between these two elements is independent of the complexity of rule 2 which separates them; despite assertions to the contrary (e.g. Postal, 1964), PSGs are quite capable of expressing discontinuous dependencies between constituents. Overlap amongst word classes, which is another prominent feature of natural languages, appears in the grammar of Text 2, where the classes described by rules 1 and 3 both contain the word IT. The grammar of Text 3 exhibits a

---

† Gazdar (forthcoming) argues that a version of PSG is as good as other systems like transformational grammar for handling the complexities of natural language. In another paper (in preparation, a) I have adapted these ideas and those of Woods (1970) and Winograd (1972) to show how optimization principles discussed in this article may apply to 'transformation' and 'semantic' linguistic structures.

Text 1
\# → (1)PUT(2)ON|(1)MADE(2)
1 → JOAN|LIZ|YOU|HE
2 → SOME|THEM|FOUR|IT
Sample: YOUPUTITONHEPUTTHEMONHEMADEITLIZMADESOME...

Text 2
\# → (1)(2)ES(3)|(4)(2)(3)
1 → IT|TOM|JANE|JOAN
2 → MISS|WATCH
3 → BIRDS|LIZ|THEM|IT
4 → YOU|MEN|WE|THEY
Sample: TOMMISSESTHEMYOUWATCHBIRDSTHEYMISSLIZ...

Text 3
\# → (1)(4)(5)|(6)(7)(8)
1 → (2)(3)|JOHN
2 → A|THE
3 → BOY|GIRL
4 → LIKES|ATE
5 → FISH|MEAT
6 → WE|THEY
7 → WALK|RUN
8 → FAST|SLOWLY
Sample: AGIRLATEFISHTHEYWALKFASTJOHNATEMEAT...

Text 4
\#→ (1)(2)(3)(4)|(5)(6)(7)
1 → BOB|MARY
2 → LIKES|ATE
3 → φ|SOME
4 → FISH|MEAT
5 → WE|THEY
6 → WALK|RUN
7 → FAST|SLOWLY
Sample: WEWALKSLOWLYMARYATEFISHMARYLIKESSOMEMEAT...

Text 5
\# → (1)(2)(3)|(4)(5)(6)
1 → DAVID|JOHN
2 → LOVES|HATED
3 → MARY|SUSAN
4 → WE|YOU
5 → WALK|RUN
6 → FAST|SLOWLY
Sample: JOHNLOVESMARYDAVIDHATEDMARYYOURUNSLOWLY...

Text 6
This text has the same grammar as Text 5 but all instances of JOHNLOVESMARY and WEWALKFAST are omitted.

Text 7
\# → (1)(2)(3)(4)|(5)(6)(7)
1 → A|THE
2 → VERY|VERY(2)
3 → FAST|SLOW
4 → CAR|SHIP
5 → SOME|FEW
6 → LARGE|SMALL
7 → MEN|BOOKS
Sample: SOMESMALLMENAVERYVERYSLOWSHIPTHEVERYFASTCAR...

Fig. 3.1 — Six grammars used to create seven texts for analysis by discovery procedures. Small samples of text are shown with each grammar. Brackets are used to distinguish terminal from non-terminal symbols. Vertical bars mean exclusive OR.

hierarchical organization in that rule 1 has to be unpacked in two stages before all its terminal symbols are reached. The Text 4 grammar contains a null element expressing the optional nature of the word SOME, and the last grammar shows recursion. Texts 5 and 6 will be considered later.

These texts do not contain any representations of meanings and there are not overt markers of segmental structure corresponding to pause or stress in natural languages. The omission of these structural cues may be justified on the grounds that it is heuristically valuable to see what can be achieved without them despite their probable relevance to a fully developed theory of language acquisition. Although these texts are semantics-free it has been supposed that principles and processes developed to abstract structure from them may prove relevant to the nonlinguistic domain (see Wolff, 1976) and to a unified model which would abstract an integrated structure of linguistic and nonlinguistic cognitions.† Meanings seem not to be actually necessary for experimental subjects to learn something of the structure of artificial languages, but they do seem to be helpful (Moeser & Bregman, 1972, 1973). Similarly, there is evidence that adult subjects can develop some sensitivity to the segmental structure of artificial speech without the need for overt segmental markers (Hayes & Clark, 1970). Further, it seems unlikely that children could learn segmental structure exclusively from such markers because many segment boundaries in natural speech are not marked by either pause or stress.

Another presupposition of this project is that children are capable of constructing their language system by observing language in use, without the intervention of any kind of 'teacher'. They do not need to produce overt speech in order to learn a language (Lenneberg; 1962, Brown, 1954) and thus they do not need anyone to correct mistakes or otherwise provide positive or negative reinforcement of any kind (Chomsky, 1959). This belief is of some significance because it rules out a class of mechanisms for correcting overgeneralizations. It is not shared by some other workers in this field (Klein & Kuppin, 1970; Knobe & Knobe, 1976; Power & Longuet-Higgins, 1978). Another assumption of the project is that children do not need to hear 'baby talk' or other special forms of adult language in order to learn a language (see Wexler & Culicover, 1980). One further assumption which may be mentioned is that language acquisition is an incremental or evolutionary process rather than a process of wholesale selection and rejection of pre-established grammars (see also Hamburger & Wexler, 1975). Presuppositions of the project are discussed more fully in another paper (Wolff, 1980b).

The target problem has been tackled in two stages corresponding to the two structural principles mentioned earlier. The first sub-goal or target was to develop a program which could discover the segmental structure of language-like texts without the need for any overt segment markers. A solution was found in program MK10 which is capable of isolating 'word' and 'sentence' segments from artificial language texts like those shown in Fig. 3.1 (Wolff, 1975). The program builds a set of hierarchically related segments of elements which is equivalent to a set of rewrite rules or productions — a PSG in fact. An integral part of the program is a parsing routine which assigns segmental structure to the text in accordance with the current

---

† In this article the terms *linguistic* and *nonlinguistic* will be used to distinguish phonetic, phonological and syntactic knowledge of language substance from semantic and general world knowledge. There is no presumption that the boundaries between these domains are sharply defined.

state of the grammar. The performance of the program may be judged from the structure of the grammar and also from the correspondence between the known structure of the text and parsings assigned by the program.

The second target was to modify or extend MK10 so that it would not merely discover the segmental structure of the sample text but would retrieve the grammar used to generate that text. Program GRAM15 (Wolff, 1978a, b) is an extension of MK10 which seeks disjunctive classes of elements amongst the elements created by MK10 and at the same time modifies the grammar built by MK10 to produce a new PSG. For each of the first four texts shown in Fig. 3.1 there is a satisfactory match between the grammar created by MK10/GRAM15 and the grammar used to construct the original text. These grammars are successfully retrieved, however, only if MK10 is stopped exactly at the point where all the 'sentence' types in its sample text have been built up. This is a significant weakness of these two programs which SNPR was designed to correct.

Although MK10 was developed with the limited objective of isolating segments from artificial texts, it has also been run on unsegmented natural language texts both alphabetic (Wolff, 1977) and phonetic (Collet & Wolff, 1977). There is a good correspondence between the word structures of these texts and parsings developed by the program, and there are interesting similarities between the way the program adds words to its dictionary and patterns of vocabulary growth in children (Wolff, 1977). The program is also apparently relevant to the abstraction of surface structures in natural language (Wolff, 1980b).

EFFICIENCY AND DATA COMPRESSION

The theoretical developments mentioned so far seem to have made reasonable contact with empirical data not only in meeting the target criteria but also in other ways which were not anticipated at the outset. Theory construction has not, however, been merely a data-driven bottom-up process but has, as indicated earlier, been guided in a top-down mode by pre-established theory. A biological perspective serves to remind us that the systems being investigated, and indeed brain structures and functions generally, are the products of evolutionary processes of natural selection and they are, in consequence, likely to be governed in some sense by principles of efficiency.

There are obvious affinities here with Zipf's (1949) Principle of Least Effort and with the notion of cognitive economy which has been of intermittent and sometimes controversial interest in psychology since the 1950's (Attneave, 1954, 1959; Oldfield, 1954; Conrad, 1972). A rigorous definition of some putative Law of Maximal Efficiency would, in accordance with Zipf's 'singular of the superlative', need to define a unified measure of efficiency which, in turn, would probably incorporate unified notions of benefit and cost. The latter might be defined as some multiplicative blend of information storage and transmission, while the former would cover such concepts as speed, accuracy and reliability, with allowance for the variable importance of these elements in various task domains. Whether or not such a law could be defined with sufficient precision to permit validation is probably not important for our theoretical purposes. We need only recognize that selection pressures are likely to have favoured modes of information processing which increase the effectiveness of cognitive operations or reduce their computational costs, or both.

Prime candidates here are techniques for reducing or eliminating redundancies in data. They have an obvious relevance to information storage, but their impact can be at least as great on information transmission — from one person to another or from one part of the nervous system to another. So great are the potential advantages of data compression principles in increasing the volume of data that may be handled by a given system, or in reducing costs for a given body of data, that it is hard to imagine how any biological information processing system could evolve without incorporating some at least of these principles in one form or another. The general tendency of vertebrate and invertebrate nervous systems to respond to changing rather than homogeneous conditions, exemplified by the phenomena of habitation, lateral inhibition and compensation (Von Bekesy, 1967), by 'on', 'off' and 'on–off' responses of nerve cells, is familiar evidence in support of this position (see also Barlow, 1969). A basic supposition of the work described in this article is that data compression principles provide a useful perspective on the form and functioning of linguistic and nonlinguistic cognitive structures and, in particular, on the processes which acquire, discover or create those structures.

The view to be described, that linguistic and cognitive development can be usefully seen as a process of optimizing a cognitive system using data compression principles, contrasts with the view typically adopted in other studies, that language acquisition is a process of discovering a 'target' grammar or cognitive system. There is at least one logical problem arising from the latter view which has been spelt out by Gold (1967) and which will be considered briefly at the end of the article.

We shall proceed to consider the role of data compression in language acquisition, but first it is as well to emphasize that the form of cognitive structures is probably conditioned in a complex way by the several functions that they perform — they are not merely minimum redundancy versions of sensory data. There is, for example, no conflict between the view expressed here and multiple-copy theories of memory with all the redundancy they imply. Indeed, to the extent that memory traces are replicated there is an advantage in minimizing the storage required for each trace. This issue aside, we may expect to find redundancies in cognitive structures because they can increase the reliability of cognitive processes and they can increase processing speeds: information which is stored in a compressed form can be slow to retrieve. We should also remember that data compression is itself a processing cost which may not always be justified by the benefits obtained.

Redundancy clearly has a role in cognition, but this does not invalidate our view that compression can give useful insights into acquisition processes and can illuminate our target problems. In the rest of this section five candidate compression principles will be described, with some discussion of their possible roles in language acquisition. This discussion will be extended in the following sections on generalization and program SNPR.

Compression principles

(1) Where a pattern occurs more than once in perceptual input then it may be advantageous to record the structure of the pattern only once, and then replace each of its occurrences by a label, pointer or reference number which identifies the record (Schuegraf & Heaps, 1974). For example, a sequence ABCDPQ

RABCDABCDPQRABCDPQRPQR may be reduced to $(x)(y)(x)(x)(y)(x)(y)(y)$, where x is a pointer to the pattern ABCD and y is a pointer to PQR. The use of subroutines and calls in computer programs is a familiar example of this device, which is essentially the same as Miller's (1956) notion of chunking.

(2) Where two or more patterns share one or more contexts then they may be grouped into a disjunctive set which may be accessed via its pointer in the same way. For example, the sequences ABCIJKDEF and ABCLMNDEF may be collapsed into ABC(x)DEF, where x is a pointer to the disjunctive group LMN|IJK (Kang et al., 1977).

(3) Where conflicting syntagmatic groupings are possible then it is advantageous to choose the grouping which will include the greatest amount of the input corpus. In general, frequently occurring groupings are preferred to less frequent ones and big ones are preferable to little ones, so that the product of frequency and size is maximized. For example, in the sequence ABCDPQRABCDABCDPQ RABCDPQRPQR, given above, there are repeating sequences like CDPQ and RAB which could be formed into chunks. It should be clear, however, that greater compression is achieved by using the chunks ABCD and PQR, which occur more frequently. Likewise, ABCD and PQR are more useful than smaller chunks like ABC or PQ.

Similar arguments apply in the case of disjunctive groups: frequent groups are more potent for compression than rare ones, and the frequency of a disjunctive group usually increases with the addition of new elements to the group.

(4) If a pattern is repeated as a sequence of contiguous instances then the sequence may be reduced to one instance of the pattern coded for repetition, perhaps also with a record of the number of instances. This method of reducing redundancy is a compression technique with communication engineering applications (e.g. Ruth & Kreutzer, 1972) and corresponds approximately with the previously mentioned tendency of nervous tissue to respond more to changing than to steady or homogeneous stimulation. Recursion is a similar device which will be discussed in connection with the fifth principle and with generalization.

(5) The last compression technique to be mentioned, which is superficially the crudest, is simply to ignore parts of the data to be coded or to delete parts of the record, or both. Crude as it seemingly is, this technique is related directly to generalization, as will be seen.

The notion of 'schema plus correction' (Attneave, 1954), which has not been mentioned so far, is implicit in each of the first two of our compression principles. When a symbol sequence is coded by joining two chunks of data together, then one of these chunks may be regarded as a 'schema', while the other can be seen as a 'correction' to that schema. In this case the roles of schema and of correction may be interchanged. In the case of disjunctive relations, a pattern like ABC(x)DEF, described above, may be regarded as a schema which can be used to encode a symbol sequence if it is 'corrected' by the specification of one out of the set of alternatives referenced by the pointer x. If that set contains a null element (or if every symbol in the schema is regarded as being in paradigmatic relation with a null element) then it is possible, by specification of one or more null elements, to give expression to the logical operator NOT. As pointed out elsewhere (Wolff, 1976), it is often useful in the quest for cognitive economy to be able to delete or negate one or more parts of a pattern.

These compression principles probably do not exhaust the possibilities, but they will serve for the present discussion. That some of them at least are relevant to language acquisition is evidenced by familiar features of language itself. It is hardly possible to describe language structure without using segmental and disjunctive groupings (principles (1) and (2)) and recursion (principle (4)). At the level of semantics, the use of words as pointers to complex conceptual structures is a clear example of the first principle. The role of frequency in language acquisition is considered briefly below and more fully in the final discussion.

There is, of course, abundant evidence for the psychological significance of language segments like phrases and clauses (e.g. Johnson, 1965; Wilkes & Kennedy, 1969) and the word structure of language has clear psychological relevance even for young children. They show themselves sensitive to word boundaries in their single word utterances and in those inventive combinations like *more high* (Braine, 1963) which are not likely to have been taken directly from adult speech.

Groupings of words by shared context was an important feature of taxonomic linguistics (e.g. Fries, 1952). Kiss (1973) and Rosenfeld *et al.*, (1969) have shown how cluster analysis based on commonality of contexts may produce word groups which resemble the part of speech groupings traditionally recognized by linguists. There is some evidence for the psychological significance of word classes from studies of speech errors (Fromkin, 1973). Weir's (1962) study provides some evidence that children actually do search for groupings with shared contexts. Her young son, in his pre-sleep soliloques, produced several sequences of utterances where the utterances in each sequence had a word or a group of words in common (e.g. *Go for glasses*; *go for them*; *go to the top*; *go throw*; *go for blouse* and *On the leg*; *Anthony's leg*; *put some Mommy's legs*; *Mommy's legs*).

Some but not all of our compression principles are exemplified in program MK10 which, as we have seen, operates by building a set of elements which is equivalent to a PSG. The first principle is exemplified in the way these elements or chunks can be used for the economical coding of the data from which the grammar was abstracted or other data having similar structure. Since many of the elements are constituents of other elements, the same principle is used to reduce the storage demands of the set, which thus acquires an hierarchical organization. In accordance with the third principle, frequent elements are selected in preference to rare ones and then, for a given frequency of occurrence, elements are built to be as large as possible. Owing to the fact that in natural and artificial language texts the frequency of a symbol string is approximately an inverse power function of its length, this search strategy, which gives priority to frequency, is more likely to maximize the product of frequency and size than the alternative strategy giving priority to size. The relevance to language acquisition of this kind of frequency-guided search has been demonstrated at the level of words (Olivier, 1968; Wolff, 1977) and of phrases (Stolz, 1965; Wolff, 1980b).

The parsing problem in MK10 is to choose from amongst the manifold possibilities a segmentation which maximizes the average size of the elements assigned to the text. The routine used in MK10 simply seeks the biggest element available to match the text at successive points in the text, so that much less processing is required than other segmentation routines like the shortest-path algorithm employed by Olivier (1968). This device, like the use of frequency information to minimize search times, allows speedy processing, but the benefit is obtained at the expense of the occasional occurrence of 'run-on' errors (Wolff, 1975, 1977) and failure to maximize the average size of elements. This tradeoff provides an interpretation for the similar 'garden-path' errors which we occasionally make in language comprehension. It is one example of the several tradeoffs which seem to operate in cognition under the rubric of efficiency. In program GRAM15, the second of our compression principles is exemplified by the creation of disjunctive groups of elements. This operation, which is governed by the third principle much as in MK10, allows a dramatic reduction in the size of the grammar created by MK10, although there is some offsetting cost which will be considered later.

We can see, then, how the first three of our data compression principles are embodied in programs MK10 and GRAM15, and how data compression is promoted in two distinct ways. The programs serve to create grammars which can encode data economically for storage or transmission. They also serve to minimize the sizes of the grammars themselves. The effectiveness of a grammar for compressing data (its 'compression capacity' or CC) may be defined as $(V-v)/V$, where v is the volume, in bits, of a body of data after encoding by the grammar and V is the volume of the data in unprocessed form. Compression values of a similar kind for MK10 have been presented previously (Wolff, 1977). The size (S_g) of a grammar is simply the number of bits of information required to specify it.

CC and S_g are not usually independent. A tradeoff exists such that an improvement in CC may be achieved at the expense of a larger grammar and vice versa. In these circumstances it would seem necessary to assign weights to CC and to S_g, representing their relative importance biologically, so that an optimum balance may be found between the two. *A priori*, however, we do not know what these weights should be. In fact, such a decision on priorities can be largely shelved when grammar construction is begun. By building a grammar in such a way that CC increases monotonically with S_g then the decision about the balance between S_g and CC becomes largely a decision about when to stop the building process.

Whatever this decision, it will always be advantageous to maximize CC for a given S_g. Therefore it is appropriate, at every step, to choose that structure which gives the greatest improvement in CC for unit increase in S_g. Generally speaking this means choosing frequent structures before infrequent, and maximizing size for a given frequency much as in MK10. In a system like this the gains in CC for unit increase in S_g will decrease progressively, and the compression value of a grammar (CV_g), defined as (CC/S_g), will therefore change as the analysis proceeds. In discussion below, the value of CV for any given S will be referred to as ($CV_g[S_g]$). When CV_g is referred to in this way, the intention is to emphasize that comparisons between values of CV_g should only be made when their corresponding S values are equal.

The chief shortcoming of MK10 is that it cannot recognize disjunctive relations and cannot therefore take advantage of corresponding reductions in storage costs which disjunctive structures make possible. One aim in developing SNPR was to get rid of the unnatural division between processes for establishing syntagmatic and paradigmatic relations which exists in MK10/GRAM15; these two processes have been integrated in SNPR so that both may operate from the beginning of grammar construction. One advantage of this integration is that successful retrieval of a grammar does not depend on the first process being stopped at any particular point.

Despite its shortcoming, program MK10 serves to illustrate a general point concerning the relative importance of size and frequency of grammatical structures. Each addition of a new element to the grammar built by MK10 allows a reduction in the size of a coded text equal to $f(S-s)$, where f is the frequency of the element in unit text, S is the size of the element and s is the size of the pointer used to replace the element. The storage cost of this element is equal to its size (S) or perhaps a little less, depending on the extent to which compression principles can be applied to the grammar itself. We shall suppose that the storage cost of an element is a fixed proportion (q) of S. If the compression value of an element (CV_e) is defined as the reduction which it allows in unit text for unit storage cost then:

$$CV_e = \frac{f(S-s)}{Sq} = \frac{f(1-S/s)}{q}.$$

From this formula it is clear that (CV_e) increases in direct proportion to f but it is a negatively accelerated function of S. Here then is a second reason, additional to that mentioned above, for giving priority to frequency in the search for new elements.

So far in this section we have considered the first three of our compression principles in relation to programs MK10 and GRAM15. The third and fourth principles are intimately connected with generalization and will be discussed in the next section under this head. The notions considered in these two sections will provide a foundation for the subsequent description of program SNPR.

GENERALIZATION

Generalization is related to data compression through our fifth principle: that we may make economies by simply discarding some of our data. Consider the simple text given earlier to illustrate the first compression principle: ABCDPQRABC DABCDPQRABCDPQRPQR may be coded as $(x)(y)(x)(x)(y)(x)(y)(y)$ if $x \rightarrow$ ABCD and $y \rightarrow$ PQR. The two rewrite rules are a simple grammar which, in conjunction with the coded sequence $(x)(y)(x)(x)(y)(x)(y)(y)$, constitutes an exact, faithful record of the original text. If we discard the coded sequence we have lost some of the original data but, in the grammar, we have retained some useful information about the structure of the text.

Implicit in this grammar are other sequences of non-terminal symbols like $(y)(x)(x)(x)(y)(y)(x)$... and $(x)(y)(y)(y)(x)(y)(x)$... and many others, each of which may be decoded into a corresponding text. These, then, are inductive generalizations or predictions derived from the original text. In this rather trivial sense of generalization, the grammar produced by MK10, with or without further processing by GRAM15, can be said to generalize from its data. Indeed, the elementary grammar with which MK10 is equipped at the start of processing ($1 \rightarrow A1|B1|C1 \ldots |Z1|\phi$) can also be said to generalize from the text.

The limitation of the two programs in respect of generalization is that the generative potential of every rewrite rule is restricted to sequences of terminal symbols corresponding to symbol sequences in the original corpus. There is no possibility with either program of creating productions which will generate sequences of symbols not found in the sample from which the grammar was abstracted.

A solution to this problem is provided by the technique employed by Cook & Rosenfeld (1976) and Harris (1977)† for reducing the size or complexity of a grammar. If a production or all its terminal strings can be generated by another production, then the first production, which may be said to be 'covered' by the second, may be replaced by that second production.

Consider, for example, a grammar like this:

$1 \rightarrow$ NP V NP|NP is A
$2 \rightarrow$ NP V NP
$3 \rightarrow$ NP said that (2).

Rule 2 is covered by rule 1, so that it may be deleted and pointers to the production may be replaced by 1. The grammar may thus be reduced to the following form:

$1 \rightarrow$ NP V NP|NP is A
$3 \rightarrow$ NP said that (1).

As a result of this simplification the grammar can generate the new string *NP said that NP is A*.

If this technique is employed so that part of a rule is replaced by the rule itself then the result is recursion, the fourth of our data compression principles (see Harris, 1977). Consider, for example, the following grammar:

$1 \rightarrow$ NP V NP|NP said that (2)
$2 \rightarrow$ NP V NP

If 2 is deleted and its pointer replaced by 1 then we arrive at a structure like this:

$1 \rightarrow$ NP V NP|NP said that (1)

This is a recursive structure which will predict:

NP said that NP V NP and *NP said that NP said that NP V NP*
and *NP said that NP said that NP said that NP V NP* etc.

We can see from these examples how a reduction in the size of a grammar can lead to an increase in its 'range', the variety of terminal strings which the grammar can generate. As Cook & Rosenfeld (1976) have pointed out, there is a tradeoff between the complexity or size of a grammar and what they call its discrepancy, roughly the same concept as range.

Basic information theory indicates that the specification of one out of many alternatives requires more information than identifying one from amongst a few possibilities. Thus generally speaking, an increase in discrepancy or range means an increase in the information required to encode a text and thus a reduction in CC. In

---

† Harris's use of the term 'folding' in this connection is different from how the term is used later in this article.

short, the tradeoff between complexity and discrepancy is essentially the same as the trade-off between S_g and CC which we encountered in the previous section.

It is instructive in this connection to compare two primitive grammars. The one mentioned earlier $(1 \rightarrow A1|B1|C1| \ldots |Z1|\phi)$ is essentially a list of the basic symbols used in a text. Such a grammar can be regarded as a very compact (if crude) statement of the structure of the input corpus. This paucity of information about the structure of the text leads the grammar to generalize to an infinite variety of other alphabetic texts. The compactness of the grammar contrasts with its inability to introduce any compression into its encoding of the sample text — its CC is zero. The second primitive grammar is one with a single rewrite rule of the form: $1 \rightarrow$ *the complete sample of text*. Unlike the first example, this grammar is not at all compact and does not generalize, but it can encode the sample text using just one bit of information. A 'realistic' grammar for a text sample is some kind of compromise between these two extremes.

At first sight, reductions in the size of a grammar and corresponding increases in its range are merely a reversal of the building process described in the last section, which offers nothing but a reduction in S_g with a corresponding reduction in CC. This view is too simple, however, because it overlooks the facts that we are at all times trying to maximize $CV_g[S_g]$ and that simple building processes alone may not achieve this. If processes for increasing the size of a grammar are interwoven with other processes for reducing its size and if, at every stage, we try to maximize $CV_g[S_g]$ we may hope to avoid 'local peaks' in the hill-climbing search. When the size of a grammar is reduced by the formation of disjunctive classes there may be some decrease in CC, but it seems that the reduction in S_g is not, for the most part, completely offset by the fall in CC. The reduced grammar may have a better CV_g than a grammar of the same size without disjunctive classes — an improvement in $CV_g[S_g]$. Likewise, when reductions in S_g are achieved by deleting some rules and modifying others (and thus producing generalizations) there is not necessarily a completely offsetting reduction in CC. If some of the new strings predicted by the modified rules turn out to have some compression value, if their occurrence in the corpus is 'confirmed', then there may be an improvement in $CV_g[S_g]$.

The distinction between predicted strings which are confirmed in the corpus and those which are not suggests at first sight an answer to one of the central questions of this article: how does a child come to distinguish between legitimate generalizations which are retained in his linguistic system and overgeneralizations which are weeded out? We can quickly see that this idea is false because, in a narrow sense of generalization, an utterance which has occurred in the sample from which linguistic knowledge is abstracted is not a generalization at all. As Chomsky (1957, 1965) and many others have stressed, most utterances of everyday use, including many that are grammatically acceptable, are novel and have never been encountered before. Why these are regarded as acceptable, while childish forms like *hitted* and *mouses* are not, is the problem confronting us.

The tentative answer offered in the next section seems to be a further example of the principle described above. By increasing the size of a grammar in a way to be explained, we can increase its CC more than enough to offset the increase in S_g so that there is an overall gain in $CV_g[S_g]$.

PROGRAM SNPR

The general principles which we have considered so far may now be reconsidered in a more concrete form: the program SNPR, which is an attempt to embody these ideas in a working model which can be tested against target criteria. The gap between general principles and a model which actually works is considerable. SNPR in its present state is the product of a fairly lengthy period of development in which several attempts at realizing the principles were constructed and tested and generally found to fail in one way or another. Some reference will be made below to blind alleys of this sort which have been entered, but they will not be described exhaustively. To some extent, general theoretical principles evolved through experience with the several versions of SNPR but, in the interest of clarity, principles and realization have been presented one after the other.

The objectives or target criteria set for this program were these:

(1) That the program should be able to retrieve simple PSGs like those in Fig. 3.1 from unsegmented, semantics-free texts, much as MK10/GRAM15 can do.
(2) The program should generalize effectively. What this means in concrete terms for the artificial languages used is that it should be possible to construct a text containing less than the complete range of terminal strings of its grammar, and that SNPR should be able to retrieve the complete grammar from this incomplete text and thus predict the legitimacy of the missing terminal strings.
(3) That the program should have a means of distinguishing legitimate generalizations like these from erroneous generalizations, and should be able to eliminate the latter while retaining the former.
(4) The program should seek syntagmatic and paradigmatic groupings at all stages of processing, and should not separate the two kinds of search as in MK10/GRAM15. As we have seen, a justification for this objective is the desirability of growing the grammar in such a way that $CV_g[S_g]$ is maximized at every stage, much as in MK10. Another justification, possibly more cogent, is that children clearly develop an early sense of both segments and classes and no sharp break is apparent, comparable with the division between MK10 and GRAM15.
(5) The process or processes which seek generalizations should also seek recursive structures successfully without *ad hoc* provision.

The current version of SNPR has been dubbed SNPR14. The number reflects the extent of the development process and the range of alternatives tried, although some of these were merely programming variants with no theoretical significance. SNPR14 meets all five criteria more or less successfully, except that no attempt has been made to seek null elements as in GRAM15, and the program fails in other ways which will be described.

Program SNPR14 (and procedure MK10/GRAM15) operates with elements of more than one type, which may be described here as a preliminary to what follows. Minimal or M elements are basic symbols used in the text, typically the letters of the alphabet. A syntagmatic or SYN element is any element which expresses sytagmatic relations in the text and a paradigmatic or PAR element is one whose constituents are in paradigmatic or disjunctive relation to each other. SYN elements may be simple (S) elements, which are strings of two or more M elements like those formed by MK10, or they may be complex (C) elements. Each of the latter must contain at least one PAR element, or at least one C element, or both, amongst its constituents and it may also contain one or more M elements. Since PAR elements may themselves contain M, S or C elements as constituents, it is clear that C elements can be arbitrarily complex. An element of any type functions as the right-hand side of a rewrite rule in a PSG and its reference number is equivalent to a non-terminal symbol on the left-hand side. There are points of similarity between the notion of an element, particularly a C element, and the concepts of *schema* (already mentioned), *frame* (Minsky, 1975) and *script* (Schank & Abelson, 1977). One of the features shared by these concepts is modularity, a desirable attribute of any cognitive system which is to be built or modified.

Outline description of SNPR

The basic concept of SNPR, which has remained more or less unchanged throughout the program's development, is that it would 'build' elements by concatenation in the same way as MK10, but that a process like GRAM15 would operate at the end of every scan to find disjunctive groups and compress or 'fold' the grammar by using these groups. PAR elements and C elements would thus be introduced at an early stage, the parsing routine would be designed to recognize elements of all types, and the high frequency pair of elements selected at the end of each scan would comprise elements of any type.

This modification of the MK10 format means that the search for syntagmatic groupings is interwoven with the search for paradigmatic groupings, as our fourth criterion dictates, and it also means that concatenation of elements can lead to generalizations. A C element like $(m)X(n)Y$ (where $m \rightarrow A|B$ and $n \rightarrow P|Q$) may be created by concatenation of $(m)X$ and $(n)Y$ when the text contains only AXPY, BXPY and AXQY amongst the four possible terminal strings of this element. The string BXQY is a generalization predicted by the element $(m)X(n)Y$. Program SNPR14 forms generalizations in this way, but it can also form them in one other way to be described later.

One possible solution to the problem of overgeneralization which has been considered and rejected is that the program should keep a record of the symbol strings corresponding to elements identified during each parsing and should, at the end of each scan, completely rebuild the grammar from these strings using the folding mechanism. In the example above, the strings AXPY, BXPY and AXQY can be folded to produce (m)XPY and AXQY (or BXPY and AX(n)Y) with the elimination of the generalized string BXQY. Apart from the heavy computational cost of a complete rebuilding of the grammar after every scan, this idea is completely implausible because it would eliminate generalizations of all kinds, and would not therefore distinguish correct generalizations from incorrect ones.

An answer to this problem, which is the basis of the mechanism employed in SNPR14, is that the program should monitor the PAR elements contained at all levels within every C element, and should rebuild any PAR element and the C element which contains it if some of the constituents of the PAR element fail to occur within the context of the containing C element. Consider, for example, the strings AXPY, BXPY, AXQY and BXQY, which would each identify an element $(m)X(t)Y$

(where $m \rightarrow A|B$ and $t \rightarrow P|Q|R$). If these were the only instances of the element in a text sample, then the PAR element t would be rebuilt as an element with the structure $P|Q$ which would replace t in the C element. If the PAR element $P|Q$ already exists in the grammar as, say, n then the C element would become $(m)X(n)Y$. If $P|Q$ does not already exist then it would be given its own number, say p, and the C element would become $(m)X(p)Y$. Notice that t is replaced *only* in the C element which led to its rebuilding. The presence of R in t may seem arbitrary, but comparable examples will be seen in the results presented later.

The same ideas may be illustrated with a more real-life example using phonetic symbols (in which certain complexities of phonological and semantic conditioning have been glossed). A syntactic/semantic structure like PLURAL((1)əz) (where 1→ boks | matʃ| kis | maus | ...) would correctly generate words like /boksəz/, /matʃəz/ and /kisəz/, but would also produce the childish form /mausez/. If 1 is reduced to 2 (where 2→ boks | matʃ| kis | ...) then the new structure, PLURAL((2) əz), will not over generalise in this way. The adult form /mais/ may be built up independently and then at some stage, presumably, it would be incorporated in a PAR element like PLURAL(2) əz | mais ...). If the incorporation of /mais/ in the new structure coincides with or overlaps with the reduction of 1 to 2, then one might speak of /mausəz/ being 'driven out' by /mais/. Whether the formation of new structures precedes, follows or coincides with the destruction of their erroneous counterparts are matters for future investigation.

The attraction of this kind of mechanism for eliminating over generalizations is that it offers an answer to our problems of removing some generalizations but leaving others permanently in the grammar. If the C element $(m)X(t)Y$ (where $m \rightarrow A|B$ and $t \rightarrow P|Q|R$) is identified by the three strings AXPY, BXPY and AXQY, and if the string BXQY fails to occur in the text, then t will be reduced to $P|Q$ as before and BXQY will remain as a permanent generalization, because the three strings contain all of A, B, P, and Q in the context of the C element. Whether or not permanent generalisations like this are correct, or in what sense they can be said to be correct, are questions without clear answers at present and will be discussed later.

The foregoing account of SNPR is intended as a bird's-eye view of the program and some of its rationale. We are now in a position to give a more detailed description of the program, sufficiently precise for it to be recreated, and to expand on certain points given only a mention so far.

Detailed description of SNPR14

As we have seen, the format of SNPR14 is similar to MK10. Starting with the basic set of minimal or M elements in its grammar, the program scans its sample of text repeatedly (or uses new text on successive scans) and, on each scan, it parses the text in accordance with its current grammar, keeping a count of all contiguous pairs of elements. A list structure is used to record these frequencies rather than a simple array, which would be wasteful of storage space. The program also records the frequencies of occurrence of individual elements, both those identified at the top level and those accessed at lower levels. At the end of each scan the program selects the most frequently occurring pair (or chooses arbitrarily between ties) and adds that pair to its grammar as a new element.

The constituents of the new element are not merely a conjunction of the reference numbers of the two elements being joined, but are a concatenation of the constituents of those elements. Joining of ABC and PQR (reference numbers x and y) would give ABCPQR and not $(x)(y)$. Prior to this building operation at the end of each scan are two other operations, 'rebuilding' and 'folding', in that order. They will be described in reverse order together with the parsing routine which analyses the text on each scan.

Folding

The folding process is essentially the same as the set of operations in GRAM15, although the detailed programming is rather different. The folding process uses a list of 'contexts' and a list of 'connections' which are updated every time a SYN element is formed or modified by rebuilding, folding or building. Maintenance of these lists will be described first.

Whenever a SYN or M element matches part of another SYN element, a context can be created by replacing the matched part by a * or other symbol to show the position of the missing part. For example, if a grammar contains, amongst others, the elements A, B, C, AB, BC and ABC, then five contexts may be derived from ABC: *BC, A*C, AB*, *C and A*. Every newly created or modified SYN element is matched with every other SYN or M in this way. Each of the derived contexts is then added to the master list of contexts and assigned a reference number, unless it is already present on the list, in which case the reference number of the pre-existing entry is used for identification. The connections list has three-item entries for the reference numbers of the containing element (B-EL), the contained element (L-EL) and the context (CXTREF). Entries with the same CXTREF are grouped together to facilitate later comparison processes.

The folding routine itself first examines the connections list systematically to find those two elements which occur most frequently in one or more shared contexts. The frequency of occurrence of a pair of elements in any one context is the sum of the current frequencies of occurrence of the corresponding B-ELs. The pair of elements with the highest contextual frequency is formed into a PAR element and added to the grammar with an assigned reference number. Then all the SYN elements in the grammar from which the shared contexts were derived are modified so that the contained element is replaced by the pointer or reference number for the new PAR element. For example, if the new PAR element (with reference number, x were AB|XY then SYN elements ABC and XYC would each become (x)C. In addition, all other SYN elements which contain one or other of the two PAR element constituents are modified in the same way, so that the contained element is replaced by a pointer to the new PAR element. This extension of the range of application of the PAR element is the second of the two ways in which the program generalizes, to be discussed later.

Since there are now duplicated C elements in the grammar, one of each identical pair is deleted, and its storage location is put back on the stack which supplies storage locations for newly created elements. All pointers to the deleted element are replaced by pointers to its matching partner and the current frequency value of the deleted element is added to the frequency of the partner. Appropriate adjustments are made in the connections list, so that outdated entries are removed and new entries derived from the new C element or elements are added, including one or more entries showing the PAR element as L-EL. On the subject of duplicates, it is actually necessary to check for duplication whenever any SYN or PAR element is created or modified at any stage of analysis. Whenever a newly created or modified element is found to duplicate a pre-existing element then the recent element is retained and the older one is deleted. Adjustments to pointers are made in the way indicated.

When these operations have been completed, the whole folding cycle is iterated on the modified and reduced grammar exactly as described, until all PAR elements with a frequency greater than zero have been found. It is quite possible for one or both elements which form a new PAR element to be PAR elements themselves. When this happens their constituents are written out in the new PAR element, as was the case with the conjoining of SYN elements.

Parsing

The parsing process in SNPR14 is a fairly straightforward 'top-down' analysis which works in the following way. At every point in the text where an element is to be identified, the program checks elements in the grammar against symbols in the text to the right of the given point until a match is found between an element and symbols in the text. Elements are listed in the grammar and checked against the text in descending order of recency. Whenever a new element is created by building, folding or rebuilding it is put at the top of the list. Whenever the composition of an existing element is changed by folding but not by rebuilding, it is moved to the top of the list. Generally speaking, this means that larger elements are checked before the smaller elements which are contained within them, so that the program will usually find the largest possible element in the grammar which will match symbols to the right of the given point in the text, in accordance with the maximum-size principle discussed in the previous section.

Checking of any given SYN or PAR element against the text means that those constituents of the element which are M elements are matched with the appropriate symbol in the text directly. Other constituents are 'unpacked' down to the level of M elements which can then be checked against symbols in the text. If a constituent PAR element at any level fails to match the text then the system 'backs-up' to try the other constituents in turn. The PAR element is considered not to match the text if none of its constituents match the text. A 'parsing list' (P-DN) is maintained to keep track of constituents at all levels within the element which is being checked and to record which of the constituents are successfully identified in the text. When an element has been successfully matched with a segment of text, P-DN contains a record of the internal structure of that segment as determined by the parsing process. The program can output this information for every segment, so that the complete structure assigned to the text by the parsing routine on any scan can be seen. The structural information in P-DN is also used by the rebuilding routine described below.

The parsing routines in MK10 and in earlier versions on SNPR are mixed bottom-up/top-down processes which capitalize on frequency information to speed up processing. The mixed process was eventually abandoned in SNPR in favour of the current top-down system based on recency, because it proved too difficult and cumbersome to implement. But a process of this type is probably more plausible psychologically than a simple top-down process, and the use of frequency information suggests explanations for the well-known effects of frequency in perceptions. There are interesting questions concerning the relation of frequency and recency and their psychological relevance, but these are beyond the scope of this article.

Rebuilding

In earlier versions of SNPR the PAR elements contained within any given C element were monitored only when that C element had first been formed. (At that stage in the program's development PAR elements could not be identified except as constituents of C elements.) The assumption was that a C, once rebuilt, would need no further attention, but this assumption proved false. Experience of running these early versions showed that the creation of new elements could change the parsing behaviour of other elements, which might then require rebuilding. It was therefore necessary to monitor elements at all stages of grammar development. In every scan, SNPR14 monitors all PAR elements identified as constituents of C elements, but not those identified at the top level as discrete elements. Less frequent monitoring of elements may be adequate, but this possibility has not been explored. A data structure is used for monitoring, which allows a record to be kept of the position of those PAR elements within their containing C elements.

At the end of the scan a rebuilding routine examines each of these records and, where necessary, rebuilds elements in the way which was previously described. The one or more incomplete PAR elements contained within a C element may occur at any level within that element. It may, in consequence, be necessary to rebuild C elements below the top level in addition to the given C and its incomplete constituent PAR element or elements. A C element rebuilt at the top level retains its reference number, but any other rebuilt element is given a new reference number.

If, in the course of rebuilding, a PAR element is reduced to one constituent, then it loses its status as a PAR element and converts to the SYN element to which it has been reduced. The constituents of this SYN element are 'written out' in the containing C elements. For example, a PAR element, x, with the structure PQ|RS contained in the C element A(x)B, may be reduced to PQ. In this case, A(x)B becomes APQB.

It should be stressed again that the replacement of an element by its rebuilt counterpart occurs *only* in the context which led to the rebuilding. However, an element identified and rebuilt at the top level may also be a constituent of one or more other elements in the grammar. The effect of rebuilding may therefore be to alter the structure of those other elements so that the variety of terminal strings which they can generate would be reduced. This is a theoretical possibility which has not yet been encountered in practice. It is anticipated that any errors created in this way would be corrected automatically by later processing.

Realization of general principles

The detailed description of SNPR14 is complete and we may relate the program to the general principles set out in the previous two sections. As in MK10 and GRAM15, SNPR14 constructs SYN and PAR elements on the maximum frequency principle and, for a given frequency, each element is built as large as possible. The parsing system is designed to seek large elements in preference to smaller ones so that the average size of segments assigned to the text approaches a maximum. SNPR14 and MK10 share this feature but differ in how they achieve it.

Generalizations arise from two sources. (1) When new elements are created by building, one or both of the two concatenated elements may be C or PAR elements. (2) PAR elements created during folding may be incorporated in contexts other than those from which they are derived.

This second mechanism has the potential for forming recursive structures without *ad hoc* provision, because any element in which a PAR element is incorporated may itself be a constituent of that PAR element, either immediately or at depth. Consider, for example, a grammar containing the elements A, B, C, BB, ABC, ABBC amongst others. A PAR element (x) with the structure B|BB may be formed and then ABC and ABBC will each become A(x)C (and one of them will be deleted). BB will become (x)(x), so that the structure of x will therefore be B|(x)(x), which is recursive. Such strings as ABBBC, etc. would then fall within the generative range of the grammar. The example of recursion given earlier would be handled in a similar way.

The recursive generalization in the example above looks plausible if we take B to represent the word *very* and consider how a child's hearing *very* and *very very* in the same context may lead him or her to the adult intuition that the word may be repeated any number of times. Adults retain this intuition, although they never hear all its possible realizations. Likewise, the generalization in the earlier example is consistent with native speakers' intuitions about the structure of English. The system does from time to time produce erroneous recursive generalizations which are then corrected by rebuilding.

The rebuilding mechanism relates to our general principles in the following way. Its function is to reduce the range of terminal strings which can be generated by C and PAR elements and thus to reduce the generative range of the grammar of which they are a part. This reduction is made in such a way that the range of strings in the sample text which can be encoded by the grammar remains unchanged. Generative range is, as we saw before, inversely related to CC, so the effect of the rebuilding mechanism should be to increase the CC of a grammar.

The creation of new PAR elements means that this increase in CC may be offset by an increase in S_g. However, some of the new elements may be identical with existing elements and in that case there will be no increase in S_g. Even when a new element is not identical with an existing element, the increase in S_g may be minimized by the encoding techniques discussed previously. It seems, in short, that the rebuilding mechanism may increase CC without a completely offsetting increase in S_g, so that $CV_g S_g$ is increased. Taken as a whole, program SNPR14 can be viewed as an embodiment of three interwoven processes designed to maximize $CV_g[S_g]$. The building process increases CC and S_g in such a way that the increase in CC for the unit increase in S_g is maximized, while the folding decreases S_g without, apparently, producing a completely offsetting decrease in CC. Rebuilding increases CC with some cost in increased S_g but, seemingly, there is an overall gain in $CV_g[S_g]$. Quantified tests of these suppositions have not yet been attempted.

As noted earlier in connection with MK10, it appears that gains in CC for unit increase in S_g are likely to be greatest in the early stages and decrease progressively thereafter. Additions to a grammar should become progressively less 'profitable' in terms of increases in CC and this may explain why the pace of language development is apparently greatest in the early years and decreases throughout childhood and beyond.

ILLUSTRATIVE RESULTS

When program SNPR14 is run on a sample of Text 5 it produces a grammar which is nearly equivalent to the original grammar, but with anomalies which will be explained.

The program has also been run on another text (Text 6) which has the same grammar as Text 5, but without any instances of JOHNLOVESMARY or WEWALKFAST. The sequence of elements derived from this text by the program is shown in Table 3.1. These results exhibit the same kinds of features as those from Text 5, including the anomalies, and they will also serve to illustrate how the program can correctly induce missing sentences. Because of the weaknesses in this version of SNPR no attempt has yet been made to run it on natural language texts.

Each built element (B in column 4) marks the end of a program cycle and it may be preceded by zero or more rebuilt elements R, or elements created or modified by folding F. For the first 14 scans, elements are formed only by building and then, on the fifteenth scan, a PAR element (42) is formed with the structure U|SUSA, derived from UN and SUSAN. The S elements 32 and 41 are converted to identical C elements (with the structure of (42)N), 41 is deleted and its frequency (58) is added to the frequency of 32 to give a total frequency of 124. On the same scan, a new element (shown in line 18) is formed by building. This element, with the structure R(42)N, is the first example of generalization by building. It can generate the string RUN and the erroneous string RSUSAN. This and other examples of overgeneralization appearing in these results do not much resemble *mouses*, *buyed* etc., probably because the structure of the artificial text is not sufficiently close to that of natural language. When the program has been developed enough for it to be run on natural language we may look for more realistic results.

Somewhat confusingly, the new element is given the reference number (41) of the previously deleted element. The new element is derived from element R and element 41 (old version) and pointers to these two elements are stored pending the building operation. When the old element 41 is modified and deleted, its stored pointer is replaced by a pointer to 32, so that the new element is in fact built from element R, joined to the modified element 32.

During the following scan the new element 41 serves to identify instances of RUN but not SUSAN; the latter is identified by element 32. The rebuilding process converts 41 to the structure RUN, while element 32 is restored to its original structure, SUSAN. In the cycles that follow there are several similar examples where erroneous PAR elements and C elements are created and then corrected by rebuilding. The first examples of (erroneous) generalization by folding appear on lines 47 to 50. They are corrected by rebuilding on the following cycle. Another point of interest is the way PAR elements may be identified as discrete elements at the top level and may be incorporated in built elements. An example appears on line 60.

The first correct PAR element to be formed is element 69 (with the structure JOHN|DAVID shown on line 100) which is derived from DAVIDHATED (line 89)

Table 3.1 — Elements derived from a 2500-letter sample of Text 6 in order of their creation or modification by program SNPR14

	1	2	3	4	Columns[a] 5
1.	28	98	S	B	LO
2.	29	67	S	B	SU
3.	30	66	S	B	SUS
4.	31	66	S	B	SUSA
5.	32	66	S	B	SUSAN
6.	33	62	S	B	AT
7.	34	62	S	B	ATE
8.	35	62	S	B	ATED
9.	36	62	S	B	HATED
10.	37	60	S	B	AV
11.	38	60	S	B	AVI
12.	39	60	S	B	AVID
13.	40	60	S	B	DAVID
14.	41	58	S	B	UN
15.	42	124	P	F	U|(31) [U|SUSA]
16.	41	58	C	F	(42)N
17.	32	124	C	F	(42)N
18.	41	58	C	B	R(42)N [R,41]
19.	41	58	S	R	RUN
20.	32	66	S	R	SUSAN
21.	43	51	S	B	LOW [28,W]
22.	44	51	S	B	LOWL
23.	45	51	S	B	LOWLY
24.	46	51	S	B	SLOWLY
25.	47	49	S	B	OH
26.	48	49	S	B	OHN
27.	49	115	P	F	(31)|(47) [SUSA|OH]
28.	32	66	C	F	(49)N
29.	48	115	C	F	(49)N
30.	32	49	C	B	J(49)N [J,48]
31.	32	49	S	R	JOHN
32.	48	66	S	R	SUSAN
33.	50	47	S	B	LOV [28,V]
34.	51	47	S	B	LOVE
35.	52	47	S	B	LOVES
36.	53	44	C	B	0(42)
37.	53	44	S	R	OU
38.	54	44	S	B	YOU
39.	55	43	S	B	WE
40.	56	42	S	B	AR
41.	57	42	S	B	ARY
42.	58	42	S	B	MARY
43.	59	36	S	B	AS
44.	60	83	P	F	A|(51) [A|LOVE]
45.	59	36	C	F	(60)S
46.	52	83	C	F	(60)S
47.	36	62	C	F	H(60)TED
48.	40	60	C	F	D(60)VID
49.	48	66	C	F	SUS(60)N
50.	58	42	C	F	M(60)RY

88 THE SNPR MODEL [Ch. 3

Table 3.1 — Elements derived from a 2500-letter sample of Text 6 in order of their creation or modification by program SNPR14

51.	59	36	C	B	(60)ST [59,T]
52.	59	36	S	R	AST
53.	58	42	S	R	MARY
54.	48	66	S	R	SUSAN
55.	40	60	S	R	DAVID
56.	36	62	S	R	HATED
57.	52	47	S	R	LOVES
58.	61	90	P	F	W|(50) [W|LOV]
59.	55	43	C	F	(61)E
60.	51	90	C	F	(61)E
61.	46	51	C	F	SLO(61)LY
62.	52	47	C	F	(61)ES
63.	55	36	S	B	FAST [F,59]
64.	52	47	S	R	LOVES
65.	46	51	S	R	SLOWLY
66.	51	43	S	R	WE
67.	62	35	S	B	LOVESSUSAN [52,48]
68.	63	35	S	B	RUNSLOWLY [41,46]
69.	64	33	S	B	DAVIDHATED [40,36]
70.	65	29	C	B	(61)(60)
71.	65	29	S	R	WA
72.	66	72	P	F	A|E
73.	58	42	C	F	M(66)RY
74.	48	31	C	F	SUS(66)N
75.	40	27	C	F	D(66)VID
76.	36	29	C	F	H(66)TED
77.	55	36	C	F	F(66)ST
78.	52	12	C	F	LOV(66)S
79.	65	29	C	F	W(66)
80.	51	72	C	F	W(66)
81.	62	35	C	F	LOVESSUS(66)N
82.	64	33	C	F	D(66)VIDHATED
83.	36	29	C	F	H(66)T(66)D
84.	62	35	C	F	LOV(66)SSUS(66)N
85.	64	33	C	F	D(66)VIDH(66)TED
86.	64	33	C	F	D(66)VIDH(66)T(66)D
87.	65	29	C	B	W(66)L [65,L]
88.	65	29	S	R	WAL
89.	64	33	S	R	DAVIDHATED
90.	62	35	S	R	LOVESSUSAN
91.	36	29	S	R	HATED
92.	51	43	S	R	WE
93.	52	12	S	R	LOVES
94.	55	36	S	R	FAST
95.	40	27	S	R	DAVID
96.	48	31	S	R	SUSAN
97.	58	42	S	R	MARY
98.	67	29	S	B	WALK [65,K]
99.	68	29	S	B	JOHNHATED [32,36]

Ch. 3] THE SNPR MODEL 89

Table 3.1 — Elements derived from a 2500-letter sample of Text 6 in order of their creation or modification by program SNPR14

100.	69	62	P	F	(32)|(40) [JOHN|DAVID]
101.	68	29	C	F	(69)HATED
102.	64	62	C	F	(69)HATED
103.	68	23	S	B	RUNFAST [41, 55]
104.	70	58	P	F	(46)|(55) [SLOWLY|FAST]
105.	63	35	C	F	RUN(70)
106.	68	58	C	F	RUN(70)
107.	63	35	C	B	(69)LOVESSUSAN [69,62]
108.	71	97	P	F	(36)|(62) [HATED|LOVESSUSAN]
109.	64	62	C	F	(69)(71)
110.	63	97	C	F	(69)(71)
111.	64	33	C	B	WERUN(70) [51,68]
112.	72	31	C	B	(69)(71)SUSAN [63,48]
113.	72	31	C	R	(69)HATEDSUSAN
114.	73	30	C	B	(69)(71)MARY [63,58]
115.	73	30	C	R	(69)HATEDMARY
116.	63	35	C	R	(69)LOVESSUSAN
117.	74	66	P	F	(36)|(52) [HATED|LOVES]
118.	62	35	C	F	(74)SUSAN
119.	72	31	C	F	(69)(74)SUSAN
120.	63	66	C	F	(69)(74)SUSAN
121.	73	30	C	F	(69)(74)MARY
122.	72	96	P	F	(48)|(58) [SUSAN|MARY]
123.	62	35	C	F	(74)(72)
124.	63	66	C	F	(69)(74)(72)
125.	73	96	C	F	(69)(74)(72)
126.	63	29	C	B	WALK(70) [67,70]
127.	75	54	P	F	(41)|(67) [RUN|WALK]
128.	68	25	C	F	(75)(70)
129.	63	54	C	F	(75)(70)
130.	64	33	C	F	WE(75)(70)
131.	68	68	C	B	(69)(74)(72)(69)(74)(72) [73,73]
132.	76	44	C	B	YOU(75)(70) [54,63]
133.	77	87	P	F	(51)|(54) [WE|YOU]
134.	64	43	C	F	(77)(75)(70)
135.	76	87	C	F	(77)(75)(70)
136.	64	16	C	B	(77)(75)(70)(69)(74)(72)(69)(74)(72) [64,68]
137.	78	31	C	B	(77)(75)(70)(77)(75)(70)[76,76]
138.	79	50	P	F	(68)|(76) [(69)(74)(72)(69) (74)(72)|(77)(75)(70)]
139.	64	21	C	F	(79)(69)(74)(72)(69)(74)(72)
140.	78	29	C	F	(77)(75)(70)(79)
141.	64	21	C	F	(79)(79)
142.	78	50	C	F	(79)(79)
143.	64	12	C	B	(69)(74)(72)(79)(79) [73,78]

The program was stopped here.

"Columns:
1. Reference numbers of elements. Elements 2 to 27 are the letters of the alphabet. Element 1 is a dummy element.
2. Frequency of occurrence in text sample. The exact nature of this frequency value is explained in the text.
3. Type of element (P = PAR; S = S; C = C).
4. Mode of formation (R = rebuilding; B = building; F = folding).
5. Immediate constituents of elements. The structures of the constituents of PAR elements are given in square brackets. The two elements which are concatenated to form built elements are shown in square brackets in cases where they are not entirely obvious.

and JOHNHATED (line 99). C element 64 is formed as (69)HATED and then (line 107) an element is built with the structure (69)LOVESSUSAN. This leads to the formation of PAR element 71 (line 108) and C element 63 (line 110), with the erroneous structures HATED|LOVESSUSAN and (69)(71) respectively. Element 63 is incorporated inelements 72 (line 112) and 73 (line 114), which are rebuilt (lines 113 and 115) together with element 63 itself (line 116). The rebuilt elements on lines 113 and 116 lead to the formation of PAR element 74 (line 117) with the correct structure HATED|LOVES. The formation of the elements on lines 120 and 121 leads directly to element 73 (line 125) with the structure (69)(73)(72) (where 69 → JOHN|DAVID; 74 → HATED|LOVES; 72 → SUSAN|MARY). This structure is identical with one of the two sentence types in the original grammar. Another structure is formed soon afterwards (element 76, line 135) which is equivalent to the second sentence type. It has the form (77)(75)(70) (where 77 → WE|YOU; 75 → RUN|WALK; 70 → SLOWLY|FAST).

Two structures have been formed which have a generative capacity identical with the generative capacity of the original grammar. They are formed despite the fact that the text did not contain the full range of terminal strings of the original grammar. It is clear that the rebuilding mechanism cannot remove the two predicted strings, JOHNLOVESMARY and WEWALKFAST, from the set of terminal strings of these two structures.

In Fig. 3.2 is shown part of the parsing assigned to the text on the scan

$$68(69[40(DAVID)]74[52(LOVES)]72[48(SUSAN)])$$
$$69[40(DAVID)]74[36(HATED)]72[58(MARY)])$$
$$68(69[40(DAVID)]74[36(HATED)]72[48(SUSAN)])$$
$$69[40(DAVID)]74[36(HATED)]72[58(MARY)])64(77[54(YOU)]$$
$$75[67(WALK)]70[55(FAST)]69[40(DAVID)]74[36(HATED)]$$
$$72[48(SUSAN)]69[32(JOHN)]74[36(HATED)]72[48(SUSAN)])$$
$$76(77[54(YOU)]75[41(RUN)]70[46(SLOWLY)])$$
$$76(77[54(YOU)]75[67(WALK)]70[55(FAST)])$$
$$64(77[51(WE)]75[41(RUN)]70[46(SLOWLY)]69[40(DAVID)]$$
$$74[36(HATED)]72[58(MARY)]69[32(JOHN)]74)[36(HATED)]$$
$$72[58(MARY)])...$$

Fig. 3.2 — Part of the parsing assigned by SNPR14 to Text 6 on the scan following the formation of element 64 (line 136 in Table 3.1). Square brackets are used to mark PAR elements and round brackets show the boundaries of SYN elements.

immediately following the formation of element 76 (line 135). This parsing is nearly but not quite the same as the parsing which would be assigned by the original grammar. The differences are due to the presence in the grammar of two Celements: 68 (line 131) and 64 (line 136). The first is simply a concatenation of 73 with itself, and the second, which is formed in the same cycle as 76, is a similar conjunction of 64 (old version), with 68. At this stage the only elements identified in the text are elements 64 (new version), 76, 68 and 73, together with their constituents. These elements are nearly the same as the original grammar. All other elements, like elements 34 (line 7), 39 (line 12), 62 (line 123) and 63 (line 126), are 'garbage' which may be discarded. In later cycles the program continues to incorporate elements 73 and 76 in larger C and PAR elements. If it were allowed to run on, it would eventually create an element equivalent to the complete text sample.

Rather than the progressive amalgamation of elements into one 'super' element, it would perhaps be more appropriate for the program to recognize the recursion implicit in the original grammar. The form of the latter should perhaps be $1 \rightarrow A1|B1|\phi$ (with A and B representing the two sentence patterns), so that it expresses the repeated unpacking of the 1 symbol needed to create a text containing more than one sentence. If elements 64, 76, 68 and 73 belonged to the same PAR element (reference number x) then, in the way explained in the last section, SNPR14 would reduce that element to the form $(73)|(76)|(x)(x)$, which is suitably recursive. Such an element would have generative capacity equivalent to the original grammar. These considerations suggest that elements identified at the top level should perhaps be treated as if they belonged to one PAR element. A rationalization of this position would be that such elements can be regarded as having a shared context if they are regarded as having a null context.

While program SNPR14 operates more or less successfully on Texts 5 and 6, it has been less successful in retrieving the grammar used to produce the input text in other cases, like Text 3 which has a hierarchical grammar, and Text 7 which is recursive. Failure in these cases seems to be due to a general weakness in the program and not to be the hierarchy and recursion features *per se*. (The program can and frequently does create 'wrong' grammars (see below) with hierarchical and recursive structures.) For reasons that are not yet fully understood, SNPR14 sometimes fails to form key constituents as independent entities. With Text 3 it builds elements containing the letter sequence JOHN without at any stage forming a discrete element with the structure JOHN. It is therefore impossible to form the target PAR element which contains this word. With Text 7 it forms elements with the structures (64)VERY(55) and (64)VERYVERYVERY(55) (where $64 \rightarrow A|THE$ and $55 \rightarrow FAST|SLOW$, which should lead to the identification of a recursive PAR element (x) with the structure $VERY|(x)(x)(x)$. This does not happen because VERYVERYVERY does not exist as an element in its own right.

DISCUSSION

Program SNPR14 is a partial model of first language acquisition which seems to offer some insight into how children may discover segmental and disjunctive groupings in language, how they may identify recursive structures, and how they may generalize beyond the language which they hear, correcting any overgeneralizations which occur. The program comes close to meeting the criteria of success which were set.

The first of these criteria, the requirement that the program should be able to retrieve the grammar used in the creation of an input text, deserves some comment because it begs a question concerning the 'correctness' of that grammar with respect to the sample text and the 'correctness' of the generalizations required to achieve the target grammar. Since there is an infinite range of grammars which are consistent with any text, we may ask why one or some of them should be judged more appropriate than the rest. The answer suggested here is that our intuitions are based on principles of cognitive economy like those which have been presented. These principles echo linguists' concern with simplicity and may, indeed, from the standpoint of linguistic theory, represent a refinement of that traditional but somewhat vague notion. (They may also prove helpful in understanding the nature of parsimony in scientific theorizing.) These considerations suggest a reformulation of the language acquisition problem: notwithstanding the first criterion of success which was established for SNPR, we should, perhaps, cease to look on language acquisition as a process of discovering a target grammar and should, instead, view it as a process of constructing an optimally efficient cognitive system. This revised view fits more naturally into a biological perspective and allows us to side step certain logical problems which arise from the first view (Gold, 1967; Pinker, 1979). Gold proved that for certain classes of language (which probably include natural languages) it is impossible to identify the grammar of a language from a 'positive' sample of the language alone without 'negative' samples which are marked as wrong, or error correction by an informant, or constraints on the order in which linguistic material is presented. If there is no target grammar but merely an evolutionary process of improving the efficiency of a cognitive system then this proof no longer presents a problem.† The taxonomy of grammars used in discussions such as Gold's should perhaps be replaced by a new taxonomy based on what devices have been used in the optimization process and how effective they are. Those used in SNPR have been described in this article, but their full evaluation will require further work.

An important feature of the theory is the mechanism for eliminating overgeneralizations. There seem to be only two other proposed mechanisms which are intended to work without error correction by an informant, but both of them have weaknesses which seem to be more serious than anything so far discovered in the current proposal. Braine (1971) describes a mechanism which would, apparently, eliminate generalizations of all kinds, both those which are correct and those which are not. Coulon & Kayser (1978) suggest that a measure of discrepancy for distance between the generative potential of a grammar and the language sample from which it is derived could serve to keep generalizations within bounds. The evidence which they present suggests that this principle cannot reliably distinguish between correct and incorrect generalizations.

To the extent that it meets its target criteria, program SNPR14 can be regarded as empirically valid. But it is still pertinent to ask whether there are any predictions or implications of the model which may be compared with known features of language acquisition. Some points of validation have been noted at intervals throughout this article and some others will be considered here. It should be borne in mind, however, that the model is not intended as a fully developed account of language acquisition and that future extensions and modifications, as for example, the incorporation of processes for abstracting nonlinguistic structures, are likely to change the detailed patterning of its behaviour.

An examination of Table 3.1 shows that there are no errors in segmentation. The formation of whole segments is preceded by the formation of their parts, but there is no case in which part of one segment is joined to part or all of another one. A prediction of the model, therefore, is that segmentation errors in children should be rare. Casual observation of young children's speech shows that their words are frequently incomplete, but it does seem that segmentation errors of the type

---

† The assumption that there is a target grammar seems to be what led Pinker to write that '... equipping a child with Occam's Razor will not help him learn languages' (p. 231).

described are indeed rare. 'The evidence we found in the fine structure of our data suggests that segmentation is a real problem in the sense that it is something a child learns but that it is also a problem for which he has highly effective solution procedures' (Brown, Cazden & Bellugi-Klima, 1969, p. 48).

One of the strongest implications of the model and of the general principles on which it is based is that syntagmatic patterns should be acquired in descending order of frequency. The same is true of program MK10 (Wolff, 1977). The proposition requires qualification in three ways. (1) The patterns referred to are those which are functional in the mature grammar and they exclude others formed by by-products of the acquisition process. (2) Slight perturbations or anomalies sometimes occur for reasons which need not be detailed here. (3) Last, but most important, the proposition applies only to patterns of a given type. Syntagmatic patterns without disjunctive components (S elements in the model) should be distinguished from those which contain disjunctive relations (C elements). The first appearances of the words in Table 3.1 are in strict order of frequency and the more frequent of the two sentence patterns is identified before the less frequent ones. But sentence patterns are isolated later than words, despite their being relatively more frequent.

A second general prediction of the theory, then, seems to be that the appearances of disjunctive structures will tend to be delayed compared with non-disjunctive patterns. Complex structures, being syntagmatic patterns which contain disjunctive relations, will also tend to be delayed compared with simple patterns. The reason for this is that a certain range of simple patterns needs to exist before disjunctive relations can be detected. In Table 3.1 the target PAR element JOHN|DAVID and the corresponding C element cannot be created until DAVIDHATED and JOHN HATED have been built up (see lines 69, 99 and 100). The prediction apparently provides an explanation for certain phenomena which will be considered shortly.

If, as seems to be the case (see below), the complexity of complex structures is inversely related to their frequencies, then the model predicts that such structures should be acquired in approximate order of increasing complexity. It would account for Brown's (1973) Law of Cumulative Complexity which states that the components of a structure are created before the structure itself. Notice that the prediction does not arise from the way the building routine forms new elements by joining simpler constituents. In spite of this feature, the model could in principle create the sub-structure of a C element after the main framework of the element has been established.

Brown & Hanlon (1970) have shown that the order of acquisition of sentence patterns correlates with frequency and also, to essentially the same extent, with grammatical complexity. Their tentative opinion favours grammatical complexity as a determiner of acquisition order, but they acknowledge that their data provide much the same support for frequency as a controlling variable. Word length is inversely related to frequency and there is a greater variety of rare words than common ones (Zipf, 1935). So a prediction from SNPR (and from MK10) is that word length should be an increasing, negatively accelerated function of age of acquisition. Confirming evidence has been presented previously (Wolff, 1977). Significant inverse correlations have been found between word frequencies and age of acquisition (Gilhooly & Gilhooly, 1979).

However, Brown (1973) has presented evidence to show that the three children of this study gained control over fourteen morphemes in an order which bears little relation to the frequency with which these morphemes are used by the children's parents. This is the chief support for his conclusion that frequency is not relevant to language acquisition. Other evidence in the same vein is the longstanding observation that English function words tend to appear late in children's spoken vocabularies despite their relatively high frequencies of occurrence (McCarthy, 1954).

These observations are seemingly in conflict with the predictions which have been put forward, but need not be fatal for the model. Most available evidence on the order of acquisition of language patterns is based on what children actually say. This may not be the same as what, in some sense, they know (Smith, 1973). Since many function words and most of Brown's fourteen morphemes have little communicative value when they are divorced from the grammatical structures in which they normally occur, it is reasonable to suppose that, while children may have some kind of knowledge of these small function elements (their sound patterns perhaps), they will not use them until they have acquired the larger structures which contain them. If acquisition is actually defined in terms of correct use in obligatory contexts, as is the case with Brown's fourteen morphemes, then it is clear that no morpheme can be 'acquired' in this sense until its containing structures have matured. The relatively late appearance of function words may thus be explained by the relatively late appearance of complex structures predicted by SNPR14. We should expect the order of acquisition of Brown's fourteen morphemes to be related to the frequencies of the structures in which the morphemes occur, rather than the frequencies of the morphemes themselves. The prediction finds support in Brown's conclusion that the order of acquisition of these morphemes is related to the semantic/syntactic complexity of their containing structures, coupled with the observation by Brown and Hanlon that syntactic complexity correlates with frequency.

It is possible, of course, that the frequencies of the containing structures are themselves correlated with the frequencies of the functional elements contained within them. Should this be so then Brown's observation would still present a problem. However, this observation may, after all, turn out to be wrong. Recent re-analyses of Brown's data show significant correlations between the frequency and the order of acquisition of certain morphemes (Forner, 1979; Moerk, 1980).

Be that as it may, the late appearance of function words in children's spoken vocabularies still requires an explanation like that outlined above. At a stage when a child's mental 'grammar' contains only function words and content words, without any larger syntactic structures to tie them together and make the function words meaningful, one would expect a child to communicate using content words alone, because they are meaningful even when there is no syntactic structure. Strings of content words without function words are observed in children's speech and are known, of course, as 'telegraphic speech'.

The fact that children do apparently observe correct word order in their telegraphic speech (Brown, 1973) runs counter to the view of telegraphic speech being suggested here. The contradiction may perhaps be resolved by the previously noted observation that the model can in principle form sub-structures after the larger structures which contain them.†

---

† These matters are more fully discussed in another paper (in preparation, b).

Another feature of children's language development which may be explained by the model is the observation that children often produce irregular forms correctly before they regularize them by erroneous overgeneralization: '...children actually say *it came off*, *it broke*, and *he did it* before they say *it camed off*, *it breaked* and *he doed it*. Even though the correct forms may have been practised for several months, they are driven out of the child's speech by overregularization, and may not return for years. This is just one example of a widespread phenomenon, noted by investigators of child speech in many languages ...' (Slobin, 1971, p. 9). This observation seems to be in keeping with a process like SNPR14 because regularization requires the formation of a complex structure like (V)ed (where the category V contains *came*, *broke* and *do* as well as *help*, *walk*, etc.) and, as we have seen, the formation of complex (and disjunctive) structures by the program tends to be delayed relative to simple forms.

This delay in the appearance of disjunctive relations also suggests an explanation of the 'syntagmatic–paradigmatic (S–P) shift': the observation that young children tend to give responses in a word-association task which are syntagmatically related to the stimulus words, while older children and adults tend to give paradigmatically related responses. It is not hard to imagine how the progressive introduction of paradigmatic groupings into a child's linguistic system could influence word association responses in this way. Kiss (1973) has discussed ideas of this kind.

Since structure-abstraction processes like those we have been considering probably apply in both semantic and syntactic domains, we might expect the S–P shift to have a semantic as well as a syntactic dimension. Petrey's (1977) thesis that the S–P shift is better characterized as an episodic–semantic shift gives useful emphasis to semantics, although the case may have been overstated.

A seeming problem in using the S–P shift as supporting evidence for SNPR is that 'Whereas normal children are speaking correctly, and thus displaying great sensitivity to form–class distinction, by the age of four, the S–P shift is most dramatic between the ages of six and eight' (Petrey, 1977, p. 61). In answer to this it may be said that correct speech is not good evidence that young children are sensitive to form–class distinctions — they may merely have a good stock of correct phrases and sentences. It is also possible that semantic constraints may help them choose words correctly (Braine, 1976). Performance is not a simple guide to competence, especially in children.

CONCLUDING REMARKS

In this discussion and at other points in the article an attempt has been made to show how SNPR14 and its underlying principles relate to observed features of language development and other phenomena. There seem to be sufficient points of contact for the model to serve as a basis for further development into a more adequate theory of language acquisition.

An immediate goal is to remedy the faults which have prevented this model from fully meeting its target criteria. Sometimes the program fails to form one or more constituents of a grammar, as it did with Texts 3 and 7. The program needs to be able to detect null elements, and it should perhaps also be modified so that it treats elements identified at the top level as if they shared a null context. If these problems can be solved then it may be possible to get meaningful results with natural language texts, so that comparisons between the program and children can be made in more detail.

In the longer term it is possible that the ideas developed here may be applied to the abstraction of nonlinguistic cognitive structures. There seem to be parallel problems of segmentation, classification etc. which may be solved in similar ways (see Wolff (1976) and Wolff (in preparation, a). At some stage an attempt may be made to create a unified system which would abstract an integrated structure of linguistic and nonlinguistic (syntactic and semantic) cognitions.

Acknowledgements
I am grateful to Alan Wilkes, Alan Kennedy and Philip Quinlan of the University of Dundee and to anonymous reviewers for constructive comments on earlier drafts of this paper.

REFERENCES

Anderson, J. R. (1977). Induction of augmented transition networks. *Cognitive Science* 1, 125–157.

Attneave, F. (1954). Some informational aspects of visual perception. *Psychological Review* 61, 183–193.

Attneave, F. (1959). *Application of Information Theory to Psychology*. New York: Holt.

Barlow, H. B. (1969). Trigger features, adaptation and economy of impulses. In K. N. Leibovic (Ed.), *Information Processing in the Nervous System*, New York: Springer, pp. 209–230.

Biermann, A. W., & Feldman, J. A. (1972). A survey of results in grammatical inference. In M.S. Watanabe (Ed.), *Frontiers of Pattern Recognition*. New York: Academic Press, pp. 31–54.

Braine, M. D. S. (1963). The ontogeny of English phrase structure: the first phrase. *Language* 39, 1–13.

Braine, M. D. S. (1971). On two types of models of the internalization of grammars. In D.I. Slobin (Ed.), *The Ontogenesis of Grammar*. New York: Academic Press.

Braine, M. D. S. (1976). *Children's First Word Combinations*. Chicago: University of Chicago Press.

Brown, C. (1954) *My Left Foot*. London: Secker & Warburg.

Brown, R. (1973) *A First Language: The Early Stages*. Harmondsworth, England: Penguin.

Brown, R., & Hanlon, C. (1970). Derivational complexity and order of acquisition in child speech. In J.R. Hayes (Ed.), *Cognition and the Development of Language*, New York: Wiley, pp. 155–207.

Brown R., Cazden, C., & Bellugi-Klima, U. (1969). The child's grammar from I to III. In J.P. Hill (Ed.), *Minnesota Symposia on Child Psychology*, Vol. 2. Minneapolis: University of Minnesota Press.

Chomsky, N. (1957). *Syntactic Structures*. The Hague: Mouton.

Chomsky, N. (1959). Review of Skinner's 'Verbal Behaviour'. *Language* 35, 26–58.

Chomsky, N. (1965). *Aspects of the Theory of Syntax*. Cambridge, MA: M.I.T. Press.
Collet, R. J., & Wolff, J. G. (1977). From phoneme to morpheme–revisited. *Bulletin of the Association for Literary and Linguistic Computing* **5**, 23–25.
Conrad, C. (1972). Cognitive economy in semantic memory. *Journal of Experimental Psychology* **92**, 149–154.
Cook, C. M., & Rosenfeld, A. (1976). Some experiments in grammatical inference. In J. C. Simon (Ed.), *Computer Oriented Learning Processes*, Leyden: Noordhoff, pp. 157–174.
Coulon, D., & Kayser, D. (1978). Learning criterion and inductive behaviour. *Pattern Recognition* **10**, 19–25.
Ervin, S. M. (1964). Imitation and structural change in children's language. In E.H. Lenneberg (Ed.), *New Directions in the Study of Language*. Cambridge, MA: M.I.T. Press.
Feldman, J. (1972). Some decidability results on grammatical inference and complexity. *Information and Control* **20**, 244–262.
Forner, M. (1979). The mother as LAD: interaction between order and frequency of parental input and child production. In F. R. Eckman & A. J. Hastings (Eds), *Studies in First and Second Language Acquisition*. Rowley, MA: Newberry House.
Fries, C. C. (1952). *The Structure of English*. London: Longmans.
Fromkin, V. (Ed.), *Speech Errors as Linguistic Evidence*. The Hague: Mouton.
Fu, K. S., & Booth, T. L. (1975). Grammatical inference: introduction and survey 1 and 2. *IEEE Transactions on Systems, Man and Cybernetics*. **SMC 5**, 95–111; **SMC 5**(4), 409–423.
Gammon, E. (1969). Quantitative approximations to the word.*Tijdschrift van het Instituut voor Toegepaste Linguistiek, Leuven* **5**, 43–61.
Gazdar, G. (forthcoming). Phrase structure grammar. To appear in G. K.Pullum & P. Jacobson (Eds), *The Nature of Syntactic Representation*.
Gilhooly, K. J. & Gilhooly, M. L. (1979). The age of acquisition of words as a factor in verbal tasks. Final report to the Social Science Research Council on Research Grant HR/5318.
Gold, M. (1967). Language identification in the limit. *Information and Control* **10**, 447–474.
Hamburger, H., & Wexler, K. (1975). A mathematical theory of learning transformational grammar. *Journal of MathematicalPsychology* **12**, 137–177.
Harris, L. R. (1977). A system for primitive natural language acquisition. *International Journal of Man–Machine Studies* **9**, 153–206.
Harris, Z. S. (1970). *Papers in Structural and Transformational Linguistics*. Dordrecht: Reidel.
Hayes, J. R., & Clark, H. H. (1970). Experiments on the segmentation of anartificial speech analogue. In J. Hayes (Ed.), *Cognition and the Development of Language*, New York: Wiley, pp. 221–234.
Horning, J. J. (1969). A study of grammatical inference. Technical Report No. CS 139. Computer Science Dept., Stanford University, Stanford, CA.
Johnson, N. F. (1965). The psychological reality of phrase-structure rules. *Journal of Verbal Learning and Verbal Behaviour* **4**, 469–475.

Kang, A. N. C., Lee, R. C. T., Chang, C.-L., & Chang, S.-K. (1977). Storage reduction through minimal spanning trees and spanning forests. *IEEE Transactions on Computers* **C-26**(5), 425–434.

Kelley, K. L. (1967) Early syntactic acquisition. Rand Corporation Report P-3719.

Kiss, G. R. (1973). Grammatical word classes: a learning process and its simulation. *Psychology of Learning and Motivation* **7**, 1–41.

Klein, S., & Kuppin, M. (1970). An interactive, heuristic program for learning transformational grammar. Technical Report No. 97. Computer Sciences Dept., University of Wisconsin, Madison, WI.

Knobe, B., & Knobe, K. (1976). A method for inferring context-free grammars. *Information and Control* **31**, 129–146.

Lenneberg, E. H. (1962). Understanding language without the ability to speak. *Journal of Abnormal and Social Psychology* **65**, 419–425.

McCarthy, D. (1954). Language development in children. In L. Carmichael (Ed.), *Manual of Child Psychology*, New York: Wiley, pp. 492–630.

Miller, G. A. (1956). The magical number seven, plus or minus two: some limits on our capacity for processing information. *Psychological Review* **63**, 81–97.

Minsky, M. (1975). A framework for representing knowledge. In P. H. Winston (Ed.), *The Psychology of Computer Vision*. New York: McGraw-Hill.

Moerk, E. L. (1980). Relationships between parental input frequencies and children's language acquisition: a reanalysis of Brown's data. *Journal of Child Language* **7**, 105–118.

Moeser, S. D., & Bregman, A. S. (1972). The role of reference in the acquisition of a miniature artificial language. *Journal of Verbal Learning and Verbal Behaviour* **11**, 759–769.

Moeser, S. D., & Bregman, A. S. (1973). Imagery and language acquisition. *Journal of Verbal Learning and Verbal Behaviour* **12**, 91–98.

Oldfield, D. C. (1954). Memory mechanisms and the theory of schemata. *British Journal of Psychology* **45**, 14–23.

Olivier, D. C. (1968). Stochastic grammars and language acquisition mechanisms. Unpublished doctoral thesis, Harvard University.

Petrey, S. (1977). Word associations and the development of lexical memory. *Cognition* **5**, 57–71.

Pinker, S. (1979). Formal models of language learning. *Cognition* **7**, 217–283.

Postal, P. (1964). Limitations of phrase structure grammars. In J. A. Fodor & J. J. Katz (Eds), *The Structure of Language*, Englewood Cliffs, NJ: Prentice-Hall, pp. 137–151.

Power, R. J. D., & Longuet-Higgins, H. C. (1978). Learning to count: a computational model of language acquisition. *Proceedings of the Royal Society (London)* **B200**, 391–417.

Rosenfeld, A., Huang, H. K. & Schneider, V. B. (1969). An application of cluster detection to text and picture processing. *IEEE Transactions on Information Theory* **IT-15**(6), 672–681.

Ruth, S. S., & Kreutzer, P. J. (1972). Data compression for large business files. *Datamation* (Sept.), pp. 62–66.

Salveter, S. C. (1979). Inferring conceptual graphs. *Cognitive Science* **3**, 141–166.

Schank, R. C., & Abelson, R. P. (1977).*Scripts, Plans, Goals and Understanding: An Enquiry into Human Knowledge Structures*. New York: Wiley.

Schuegraf, E. J., & Heaps, H. S. (1974). A comparison of algorithms for data base compression by use of fragments as language elements. *Information Storage and retrieval* **10**, 309–319.

Siklossy, L. (1972). Natural language learning by computer. In H. Simon & L. Siklossy (Eds), *Representation and Meaning: Experiments with Information-Processing Systems*. Englewood Cliffs, NJ: Prentice-Hall.

Slobin, D. I. (1971). Data for the symposium. In D. I. Slobin (Ed.), *The Ontogenesis of Grammar*, New York: Academic Press, pp. 3–16.

Smith, N. V. (1973). *The Acquisition of Phonology: A Case Study*. Cambridge: Cambridge University Press.

Stolz, W. (1965). A probabilistic procedure for grouping words into phrases. *Language and Speech* **8**, 219–245.

Von Bekesy, G. (1967). *Sensory Inhibition*. Princeton, NJ: Princeton University Press.

Weir, R. (1962). *Language in the Crib*. The Hague: Mouton.

Wexler, K., & Culicover, P. W. (1980). *Formal Principles of Language Acquisition*. Cambridge MA: MIT Press.

Wilkes, A. W. & Kennedy, R. A. (1969). Relationship between pausing and retrieval latency in sentences of varying grammatical form. *Journal of Experimental Psychology* **79**, 241–245.

Winograd, T. (1972). *Understanding Natural Language*. Edinburgh: Edinburgh University Press.

Wolff, J. G. (1975). An algorithm for the segmentation of an artificial language analogue. *British Journal of Psychology* **66**, 79–90.

Wolff, J. G. (1976). Frequency, conceptual structure and pattern recognition. *British Journal of Psychology* **67**, 377–390.

Wolff, J. G. (1977). The discovery of segments in natural language. *British Journal of Psychology* **68**, 97–106.

Wolff, J. G. (1978a). The discovery of syntagmatic and paradigmatic classes. *Bulletin of the Association for Literary and Linguistic Computing* **6**(2), 141–158.

Wolff, J. G. (1978b). Grammar discovery as data compression. Proceedings of the AISB/GI Conference on Artificial Intelligence, Hamburg, pp. 375–379.

Wolff, J. G. (1980a). Data compression, generalisation and overgeneralisation in an evolving theory of language development. Proceedings of the AISB-80 Conference on Artificial Intelligence, Amsterdam, pp. Wolff–1–10.

Wolff, J. G. (1980b). Language acquisition and the discovery of phrase structure. *Language and Speech* **23**, 255–269.

Wolff, J. G. (in preparation, a). An optimisation account of the acquisition of 'transformational' and semantic cognitive structures.

Wolff, J. G. (in preparation, b). Overview of a theory of language development.

Woods, W. A. (1970). Transition network grammars for natural language analysis. *Communications of the ACM* **13**, 591–606.

Zipf, G. K. (1935). *The Psycho-biology of Language*. Boston: Houghton Mifflin.

Zipf, G. K. (1949). *Human Behaviour and the Principle of Least Effort*. New York: Hafner.

4

The SP Theory

The article reproduced in this chapter is the first substantial presentation of the SP theory as a theory of computing. As I explained in Chapter 1, the realization that concepts developed to explain language learning and cognitive development might generalize to mainstream computing emerged first through seeing the similarity between the pattern matching and unification processes in the learning models (MK10 and SNPR) and the pattern matching and unification processes in Prolog. Subsequent work at Praxis in developing an integrated project support environment (IPSE) highlighted similarities between the problem of representing and integrating knowledge in that kind of system and the problem of integrating syntax and semantics in a language learning model. It was from these insights that the proposals in this article grew.

Since this article was written, there have been some refinements of the SP theory — they are described in Chapter 5. This article provides the rationale for the proposals and describes how they may be applied in several different areas of computing.

In this article, the term *simplicity* has been used as a synonym for the *size* or *complexity* of a body of information. Because this is confusing, and not very logical, *simplicity* is now defined as the reciprocal of complexity. This adjustment has been made in Chapter 5.

SIMPLICITY AND POWER — SOME UNIFYING IDEAS IN COMPUTING[†]

ABSTRACT

The article develops the conjecture that the organization and use of all kinds of formal system, knowledge structure or computing system may usefully be seen in terms of the management of *redundancy* in information.

Every formal system, knowledge structure or computing system has two key dimensions — *simplicity* (complexity or size) and expressive or descriptive *power* — and there is a *tradeoff* between them. The balance between simplicity and power corresponds to a balance between *OR relations* and *AND relations* in the system.

The *efficiency* of the system (the ratio of power to size) depends on the extraction of redundancy from the system. Key mechanisms for the extraction of redundancy

---

[†] This article is reproduced from the *Computer Journal* **33**(6), 518–534, 1990. It is printed here with the permission of the publishers, the British Computer Society.

are *pattern matching* and *search* (by *hill climbing* or equivalent mechanism) for the greatest possible *unification* of patterns.

These principles are the basis of a proposed new language and associated computing machine, called SP, which combines simplicity with high expressive power. SP is a Prolog-like pattern-matching system well suited to high levels of parallelism in processing.

In SP, the boundary between 'knowledge engineering' and other kinds of information engineering breaks down. In SP there is the potential for full integration of artificial intelligence, software engineering and other aspects of computing — with Shannon's information theory as a unifying framework. SP also offers a bridge between 'connectionist' and 'symbolic' views of computing.

1. INTRODUCTION

There is a Babel of languages, formalisms and representational systems in computing and a diversity of concepts. Some of this variety is useful but much of it is not. There is a need to rationalize and integrate computing ideas and to achieve a corresponding simplification of the subject.

Simplicity in itself is not enough. We could, for example, propose the very simple theory that all (digital) computing is about storing and manipulating bits. This theory is too simple to be illuminating. We need a view of computing which is simple but which also has explanatory and expressive power.

This article proposes some principles which can lay some claim to providing that desirable marriage of simplicity and power. The principles are embodied in a proposed new computing language and associated computing machine called 'SP'. The name SP is mnemonic for 'Simplicity' and 'Power'; it is also mnemonic for 'Syntagmatic' and 'Paradigmatic', two concepts from taxonomic linguistics which figure prominently in the system.

SP is a Prolog-like pattern-matching system well suited to high levels of parallelism in processing. The justification for creating yet another language is the expectation that it will lead to an overall simplification of the field.

In SP, the boundary between 'knowledge engineering' and other kinds of information engineering breaks down. In SP there is potential for the full integration of artificial intelligence, software engineering and other aspects of computing — with Shannon's information theory as a unifying framework. SP also offers a bridge between 'connectionist' and 'symbolic' views of computing.

The principles and the system have potential applications in several areas of computing including:

- Logic and logical inference.
- Formal specification of computing systems.
- Inductive learning.
- Pattern recognition.
- Principles of object-oriented design and conceptual modelling: class-inclusion relations, part–whole relations, inheritance of attributes — and the integration of these constructs. SP supports intensional and extensional descriptions of classes and the creation of entity-relationship models.

- The representation of knowledge in expert systems and databases; information retrieval and content addressable memory.
- Probabilistic inference and reasoning with uncertain and incomplete knowledge.
- The representation of plans and the automatic generation of plans.
- Specification of the organization of natural languages including 'context-sensitive' features.
- Software re-use and configuration management.
- The integration of diverse kinds of knowledge which is required in many applications including integrated project support environments; facilitation of translations between computer languages and between one form of knowledge and another.

2. SIMPLICITY AND POWER IN GRAMMARS AND COMPUTING SYSTEMS

The ideas to be described derive most immediately from work on the inductive learning of grammars and from an analysis of cognitive development (see, for example, Wolff (1982, 1987); an overview is presented in Wolff, 1988). I don't intend to discuss these fields in detail — merely to sketch the ideas which are relevant here.

From this work on inductive learning has emerged the conjecture that knowledge representation and inductive learning may both usefully be seen in terms of the management of *redundancy* in information. The idea has now been generalized to the conjecture that: *the organization and use of all kinds of formal system, knowledge structure or computing system may usefully be seen in terms of the management of redundancy in information.*

Key ideas in the management of redundancy in a knowledge structure are:

- The detection of redundancy by *pattern matching*.
- The reduction of redundancy in the structure by *searching* for the greatest possible *unification* of patterns (using *hill climbing* or a related process).

As I shall try to show, the extraction of redundancy by pattern matching and unification of patterns can provide a unified view of several concepts in computing. Since the concept of redundancy is part of Shannon's information theory, information theory is a foundation for the theory to be described.

The idea of searching for economical structures has figured in research on 'neural computing' (see, for example, Rumelhart & McClelland (1986)) and, indeed, in research on cluster analysis and numerical taxonomy. This article presents a view of computing which is not tied to any particular architecture (such as neural networks) and which is in several other respects different from work on neural computing or cluster analysis. In many ways it is complementary to these fields. In particular, it may be seen as a bridge between the purely connectionist and 'sub-symbolic' views of computing associated with research on simulated neural nets and the more traditional 'symbolic' views of computing.

2.1 Redundancy, structure and inductive reasoning

Before we proceed to examine these ideas, there are some general points to be made about redundancy:

- *Redundancy means repetition of information.* Although this is not always obvious, redundancy in information (and thus all kinds of structure — see below) always means repetition of information. Repetition of information means redundancy when the repeating patterns are more frequent than other patterns of the same size.
- *Redundancy and structure.* The concept of redundancy (in the Shannon sense) is closely related to the concept of *structure*. A body of information which has no redundancy is entirely random; it is 'white noise' with a maximum of entropy; it has no structure. The structure of a body of information may be equated with the patterns of redundancy in it. Thus any discussion of the structure or organization of a body of information may be mirrored by a corresponding discussion about the redundancy in the information.
- *Redundancy and inductive reasoning.* Whatever the particular reasons for storing and manipulating information (in computing systems, on paper, or in our heads) the underlying reason is always to make *predictions*. The principle of inductive reasoning — that the past is a guide to the future — is the basis of all kinds of natural or artificial cognition.

Inductive reasoning depends on repetition of information: patterns of information which have repeated in the past are assumed to repeat in the future. Given that repetition of information also means redundancy, we can see that inductive reasoning (and thus all kinds of natural and artificial cognition) depends on the existence of redundancy in the world.

The idea that the storage and manipulation of information is always about prediction may seem obscure if we think of some humdrum computing task like the storage and processing of accounts. But the accounts of a company (or any other organization) are only interesting in relation to the future: Should there be changes in how the company is managed? Should the receiver be called in? Should we buy more shares in the company or sell the ones we have got?

A world without redundancy would not permit prediction. It would lack any structure; there would be no point in storing or manipulating information because that information would provide no means of anticipating the future.

These ideas have a bearing on the philosophical problem of finding a rational basis for inductive reasoning but it would take us too far afield to discuss this interesting question here.

In the following sub-sections I discuss the significance of redundancy in more detail using grammatical inference (inductive learning) as a way of introducing the main concepts.

2.2 Grammatical inference

Grammatical inference is a process of discovering, inducing or constructing a grammar from a body of 'raw' data — typically a string of characters or a set of strings of characters. The grammar which is inferred from the string or strings may be seen as a means of succinctly describing those strings.

There are always many grammars which are compatible with a given body of raw data, in the sense that they can 'generate' that body of data; some of these alternative grammars are, in some sense, 'better' than others. The inference problem is to find the 'best' grammar or, more realistically, to find one which is 'good enough'.

Two key measures of 'goodness' are: the compactness, size or *simplicity* of a grammar; and its usefulness, expressiveness or *power* for describing data. The words with emphasis have been chosen deliberately to show the parallel with the need for both simplicity and power in how we think about computing.

Consider Fig. 4.1. The 'raw' data at the top of the figure may be represented by a number of alternative grammars. In the first, labelled 'Primitive Grammar 1', we simply give a label '1' to the whole string of data. This primitive grammar is not at all compact: apart from the label, it is exactly the same size as the original data. But it is very 'powerful' in the sense that it may be used to represent the original data succinctly in other contexts by means of the symbol '1'.

The same raw data may also be represented by 'Primitive Grammar 2' in which each type of letter is represented by a digit. If rules are selected repeatedly from this primitive grammar it can 'generate' the original data. This grammar is very simple and compact — but it is not at all powerful: a description of the original data using the grammar is as big as the original data (see Fig. 4.1).

These two primitive grammars represent extremes of a *tradeoff* between simplicity and power. Between the two extremes lies a whole range of grammars covering a whole range of combinations of simplicity and power. The problem of grammatical inference is to find grammars, like the two 'well-structured' grammars in Fig. 4.1, in which that combination is at or near a maximum.

The first well-structured grammar in Fig. 4.1 is just as expressive (powerful) as the first primitive grammar (because the original data may be represented with the single symbol '1') but it is more compact (simple) and thus represents an improvement over the first primitive grammar.

The second well-structured grammar in Fig. 4.1 is as simple as the second primitive grammar but it is more powerful because the grammar may be used to encode the original data in a more economical form than with the second primitive grammar (as shown in Fig. 4.1).

As a contrast to the two well-structured grammars, consider the two badly structured grammars in Fig. 4.1. The first badly structured grammar is as powerful as the first well-structured grammar but it is less compact. We can say that it is relatively 'inefficient' compared with the first well-structured grammar because it has a relatively poor ratio of power to size.

The second badly structured grammar is as simple as the second well-structured grammar but it is less powerful. Again, its efficiency is low compared with the corresponding well-structured grammar. There are many possible inefficient grammars like this which should be rejected by the grammar induction process.

2.3 Grammars and other systems

There is a more than superficial analogy between these example grammars and other kinds of formal system. The analogy extends to cognitive and computing systems in general — hardware, software or both:

- Every system has a *size* measurable in terms of the amount of information (bits) needed to specify the system.

RAW DATA
A,B,C,D,P,Q,R,A,B,C,D,A,B,C,D,P,Q,R,A,B,C,D,P,Q,R,P,Q,R,A,B,C,D

PRIMITIVE GRAMMAR 1

1→ A,B,C,D,P,Q,R,A,B,C,D,A,B,C,D,P,Q,R,A,B,C,D,P,Q,R,P,Q,R,A,B,C,D

Encoding of raw data: 1

PRIMITIVE GRAMMAR 2

1→ A
2→ B
3→ C
4→ D
5→ P
6→ Q
7→ R

Encoding of raw data:
  1,2,3,4,5,6,7,1,2,3,4,1,2,3,4,5,6,7,1,2,3,4,5,6,7,5,6,7,1,2,3,4

WELL STRUCTURED GRAMMAR 1

1→ 2,3,2,2,3,2,3,3,2
2→ A,B,C,D
3→ P,Q,R

Encoding of raw data:1

WELL STRUCTURED GRAMMAR 2

1→ A,B,C,D
2→ P,Q,R

Encoding of raw data: 1,2,1,1,2,1,2,2,1

BADLY STRUCTURED GRAMMAR 1

1→ A,B,3,2,C,D,A,B,3,2,3,Q,R,P,2,C,D
2→ Q,R,A,B
3→ C,D,P

Encoding of raw data: 1

BADLY STRUCTURED GRAMMAR 2

1→ Q,R,A,B
2→ C,D,P

Encoding of raw data: A,B,2,1,C,D,A,B,2,1,2,Q,R,P,1,C,D

Fig. 4.1 — Data and grammars to illustrate concepts of simplicity and power.

- Every system has more or less *power*, comparable with the expressive power of the example grammars. For example, a 'bare' computing machine, without software, is a relatively poor tool for doing any particular kind of task, e.g. processing accounting data and producing accounting reports. The addition of an operating system makes it more powerful in this sense and the further addition of an accounting package makes it even better. 'Power' in this context means much the same as 'usefulness' or 'functionality' and seems to be equivalent at some level of abstraction to the notion of expressive power introduced in last section.

In addition to the dimensions of simplicity and power seen in grammars and in computing systems, there is the concept of *efficiency* (the ratio of power to size) which we saw in connection with grammars and which seems also to apply to other systems. Efficiency in this discussion means 'doing a lot with relatively little'. It corresponds with the intuitive notion of 'elegance' or 'prettiness' of design.

A method of calculating *simplicity* (*size*), *power* and *efficiency* of grammars is described in the Appendix.

2.3.1 An abstract space for grammars and computing systems

Fig. 4.2 summarizes the ideas introduced so far. It is a set of graphs representing an

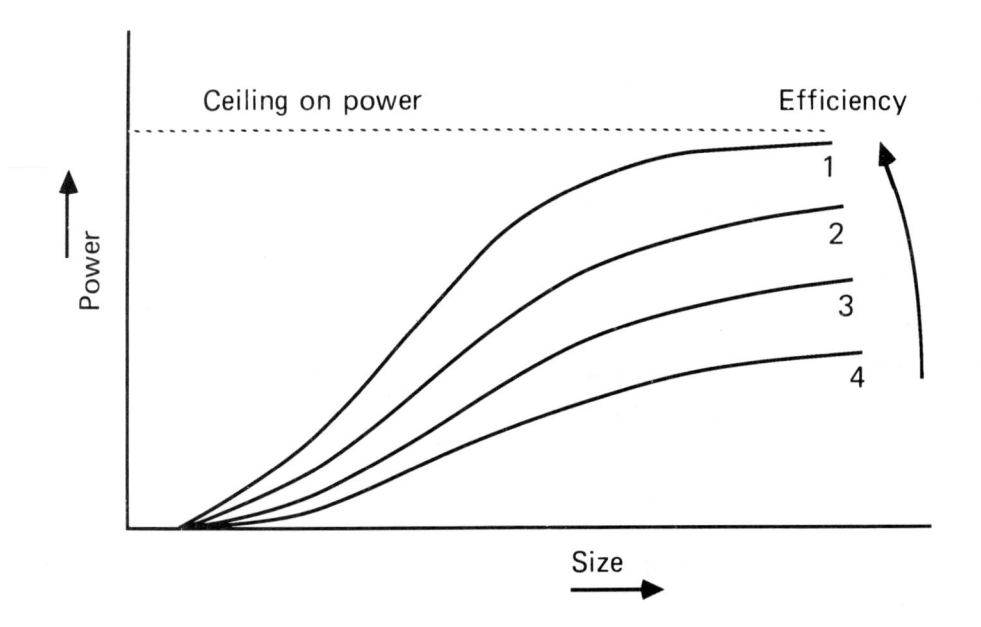

Fig. 4.2 — An abstract space for grammars and computing systems.

abstract 'space' within which any grammar, formal system, knowledge structure or computing system may be placed. Each structure is a point in the space. The 'x' axis records the size of a structure; the 'y' axis records its descriptive power. These graphs represent imaginary data but are similar to unpublished graphs obtained from program SNPR — the program for grammatical inference which is described in Wolff (1982).

Each of the curves in the figure represents the tradeoff between size and power. Each of the higher curves represents a set of well-structured, efficient systems with good ratios of power to size. The lower curves are for poorly structured, inefficient systems with low ratios of power to size.

Where a structure should be positioned up or down a curve depends on the relative importance of size and power and this will vary with the application. However, in all circumstances, the aim should be to maximize efficiency — the ratio of power to size. In grammatical inference, we need to find or create grammars which fall on or near the line marked '1' in the figure. In the design of computing systems we need to create systems which fall on or near that line.

No system can have more descriptive power than the raw data to which it relates. Hence the 'ceiling on power' in Fig. 4.2.

2.4 An analogy

It may be helpful at this point to describe an everyday analogy for the relationships shown in Fig. 4.2. The analogy is fairly accurate but not completely so.

The relationship between size and power (in the senses intended here) is similar to the relationship between cost and value in the purchase of goods or services. The tradeoff between size (simplicity) and power is like the dimension from 'down market' to 'up market' which is so familiar when we are buying things. For a given type of commodity we may choose to go for lower cost and less value or we may choose to pay more for something which is higher quality or in some other way more valuable.

Of course, we all know that you do not always 'get what you pay for'. Independent of the up-market/down-market dimension is the notion of 'value for money'. Whether we are buying at the low or high ends of the market, a given sum of money can yield either poor value or good value. The notion of value for money is analogous to the notion of efficiency introduced earlier.

The cost and value analogy should not be stretched too far. Value, in particular, can be subjective and relative to a particular buyer. By contrast, the notions of size, power and efficiency can in principle be measured precisely in terms of information theory and without reference to subjective judgements.

2.5 Constraint and freedom, power and simplicity, AND relations and OR relations

The tradeoff between simplicity and expressive power in a grammar corresponds with a balance between freedom and constraint in the grammar. The second primitive grammar in Fig. 4.1 provides the freedom to generate an infinite range of strings using the basic symbols. The first primitive grammar in Fig. 4.1 is constrained to one string of symbols.

'Freedom' in this context corresponds to OR relations and 'constraint' corresponds to AND relations in the grammar. The tradeoff between compactness and expressiveness is mirrored by the balance between OR relations and AND relations in a grammar.

These ideas also map onto basic information theory: 'freedom' means choice which means low information content; 'constraint' means reduced choice and raised information content.

Fig. 4.3 illustrates the way the dimensions of 'freedom–constraint', 'simplicity–

```
raw machine              freedom/simplicity/low functionality
microcode
assembler
high level language
application program      constraint/complexity/high functionality
```

Fig. 4.3

complexity' and degrees of 'functionality' are related. At the top of the diagram is a 'raw' computing machine representing relative simplicity, a high degree of freedom but low functionality. Below this are layers of organization representing decreasing freedom but increasing complexity and increasing functionality.

2.6 Efficiency and redundancy extraction

The efficiency of our two well-structured grammars was achieved by the *extraction of redundancy* in the original data and a corresponding compression of those data. Extraction of redundancy appears to be the key to achieving a favourable ratio of simplicity to power.

2.6.1 Avoid repetition of information

The basic idea in extracting redundancy from information is to avoid storing information more than once when once will do. Here are three ways in which this can be achieved:

- *Method 1*. In the two well-structured grammars in Fig. 4.1, the patterns A,B,C,D and P,Q,R, which repeat themselves irregularly in the raw data, are stored once and accessed via pointers or references from inside the grammar in the case of the first well-structured grammar and from outside the grammar in the case of the second.
- *Method 2*. These two patterns:

    A,B,C,D,P,E,F,G,H
    A,B,C,D,Q,E,F,G,H

    may be reduced to A,B,C,D,x,E,F,G,H, where $x \to P|Q$. Alternatively, the two patterns may be represented as A,B,C,D(P|Q)E,F,G,H.
- *Method 3*. Where a pattern or type of pattern repeats in a sequence of contiguous instances, this may be reduced to a single instance with some indication that it repeats. A sequence like A,A,A,A,A,A,A,A,A,A may be reduced to a recursive rule or it may be treated as 'iteration'.

The first of these examples illustrates the principle of *structure sharing* as a means of reducing or eliminating redundancy in data: a repeating pattern of information is stored once and accessed via *references* from the several contexts in which it occurs. *A major motivation for using references in computing is to achieve the extraction of redundancy from data by means of structure sharing.* A commonplace example is the use of named procedures and functions in computer programs, and calls to those procedures or functions from diverse contexts.

2.7 Pattern matching and the hill-climbing search for efficient structures

The three methods of extracting redundancy from information, described above, all depend on *pattern matching* and *unification* of patterns. Where a pattern of information repeats itself, the repetition can be avoided by creating one copy to replace all instances of the pattern: the replicated patterns are *unified*.

In most realistically large bodies of data there is a very large number of alternative ways in which patterns may be matched and unified. In these circumstances, the set of unifications to choose is the one which maximizes C where:

$$C = \sum_{i=1}^{i=n} f_i s_i ,$$

f is the frequency of pattern i in a body of raw data, s is its size (in bits or some equivalent measure) and n is the number of different kinds of pattern.

The patterns A,B,C,D and P,Q,R used in the two well-structured grammars in Fig. 4.1 are better according to this measure than the patterns Q,R,A,B and C,D,P used in the two badly structured grammars.

There is no algorithmic way of ensuring that C is always maximized. Except for trivially simple cases, it is always necessary to use the kinds of *search* techniques familiar in artificial intelligence (most notably, *hill climbing*). These techniques cannot guarantee a perfect solution but they provide a practical means of finding at least an approximation to the desired goal.

An example of the application of hill climbing to redundancy reduction by pattern matching and unification is described in detail in Wolff (1982). Winston (1984, Ch. 4) provides a useful introduction to the concept including the the idea of 'local peaks' and methods of avoiding them. In the context of computing with simulated neural networks, the technique of 'simulated annealing' has proved to be an effective means of reducing the chances of the system getting stuck on local peaks (see, for example, Hinton & Sejnowski (1986)).

2.8 De-referencing as pattern matching and unification

As described above, when two or more patterns have been unified, references are often used to mark the contexts in which the original patterns occurred. A pattern may be brought back into its original context by *de-referencing* its identifier. *But de-referencing is itself an example of pattern matching and unification of patterns*. To achieve de-referencing, a match must be found for the reference elsewhere in the structure — and the two matching patterns must be unified.

A good example to illustrate this point is the way a named procedure in a computer program may be 'called' from several different contexts. The procedure name is associated with the body of the procedure in one part of the program. A reference to the procedure appears wherever the procedure is needed in other parts of the program. A 'call' to the procedure means searching for the name which matches the reference and unifying them.

Memory 'pointers' and memory 'addresses' may also be seen in these terms. Accessing an area of memory means searching for the address which matches a pointer and unifying them. The search process in this case is rather simple but it is search, nevertheless.

2.9 Modelling the world

As we have seen, there is a close connection between the concept of structure and the concept of efficiency. Efficient grammars are well-structured grammars and they are also the grammars which capture the redundancy (or structure) in the raw data.

When these ideas are generalized to other kinds of computing system, we find ourselves in familiar territory: a computing system is well structured to the extent that it reflects ('captures', 'models') the structure of its inputs and of its outputs. This principle has been propounded most persuasively by Michael Jackson (1975). It figures in the use of 'entity-relationship models' as a basis for the design of commercial software systems (LBMS, 1986). The principle is also an important part of the philosophy of object-oriented design (see, for example, Birtwistle *et al*. (1979); Cook, 1986).

The principle of modelling a computer system on the structure of the material it has to deal with is well-recognized but the significance of this principle is, perhaps, not fully appreciated. Normally it is justified on the grounds that it facilitates thinking about design and it makes it easier to modify designs. Both these justifications are sound but there is the additional, and related, reason that it is a means of maximizing the functionality of the system for a given cost in the complexity of the system (or minimizing complexity for a given functionality). Systems designed to conform to this principle are more efficient (in the sense defined above) than otherwise.

In general, systems which are 'efficient' are ones whose structure reflects or models the 'natural' structures in the external data. 'Natural structures' are patterns in the data which are 'coherent'. Patterns are 'coherent' when they repeat frequently in the data. Natural structures in this sense include such things as 'objects', 'entities', 'relationships' and, as we shall see later, 'classes' of these things.

2.10 Useful and useless redundancies

The idea that 'elegance' or 'prettiness' in design are closely bound up with the extraction of redundancy in information is not in conflict with the well-known uses of redundancy in computing systems to increase speed of processing or the reliability of systems or both.

For example, it is normal practice in computing to create 'backup' or security copies of information as a protection against losing the information altogether. A backup copy is redundant in the sense that it replicates the original data. Here, the redundancy between the original and its copy is useful. By contrast, redundancy within each copy arising from poor structuring of the information is not useful and should be minimized. 'Management of redundancy' means, to a large extent, the removal of *unnecessary* redundancy or complication in a structure.

The use of references or identifiers to achieve structure sharing is an interesting example of useful redundancy. To achieve this effect, the identifier must appear in association with what it identifies and it must also appear in each of the contexts where the material is referenced. In this case a small amount of redundancy is introduced into a knowledge structure as a means of achieving a relatively large reduction in redundancy: structure sharing only makes sense if the material to be shared is bigger than the identifier used to achieve the sharing.

2.11 Summary
Here is a summary of the ideas introduced so far:

(1) Fundamental principles for the organization of formal systems and computing systems may be seen in a relatively transparent form in the organization of simple grammars.
(2) Any grammar, other formal system, knowledge structure or computing system may be seen as a means of succinctly describing information which is external to the system — inputs, outputs or both.
(3) Any system has a place in a space defined by two dimensions: *simplicity* (or size or complexity — meaning the information content of the system) and expressive or descriptive *power* (meaning the effectiveness with which the system can represent or manipulate its external information).
(4) There is a *tradeoff* between simplicity and power.
(5) The balance between simplicity and power in a system corresponds to the balance between *OR relations* and *AND relations* in the system.
(6) The *efficiency* of a system is the ratio of power to size.
(7) Efficiency is obtained by capturing or extracting the *redundancy* in the external information.
(8) Efficiency in this sense seems to correspond to the intuitive notions of 'good structure' in a system, 'elegance' or 'prettiness' in design. A well-structured system reflects or models the structure of its external data: objects or entities, relationships and classes.
(9) The basic principle of *redundancy extraction* is to avoid recording a pattern more than once when once will do. Often this means the use of the principle of *structure sharing* and this means the introduction of *references* between one structure and another.
(10) Redundancy extraction may be achieved more generally by *pattern matching* and the *search* (by *hill climbing* or equivalent process) for as much *unification* as possible. Notions of 'reference' and 'de-referencing' may be subsumed by these notions.

3. ORGANIZING PRINCIPLES

A main proposition from the last section is that any system may be placed anywhere in the space of possible systems by the application of two basic organizing principles, AND relations and OR relations. Another main proposition from the last section is that *efficiency* (in the sense previously defined) may be achieved by the extraction of *redundancy* from information. Important mechanisms in this connection are *structure sharing*, *referencing* and *de-referencing*. More generally, redundancy extraction may be achieved by *pattern matching* and the search (by hill climbing or equivalent process) for the greatest possible *unification* of patterns. These principles appear to have a fundamental significance in the organization and use of formal systems, knowledge structures and computing systems of all kinds.

Some of the importance of AND relations and OR relations is recognized in Michael Jackson's principle (1975) that any sequential file of data may be described in terms of sequence, selection and iteration; and likewise for any program using that file as data (see also Bohm & Jacopini, 1966). In general, however, the fundamental significance of the principles which have been described in previous sections seem not to be widely recognized.

To get a feel for the generality of the organizing principles we can briefly survey some of the ways in which they currently appear in computing.

3.1 AND relations

Here are some examples of AND relations in computing:

- Sequences of statements in a program.
- The relationship between a and b in **If** a **then** b **else** c statements.
- The relationship between the fields in a table in a relational database.
- The sequence of structures in the body of a Prolog Horn clause.
- The relationship between the head and the body of a Prolog Horn clause.
- The relationship between an identifier and what it identifies in a wide variety of computing systems.
- The relationship between a structure in the syntax of any computing language and the semantics of that structure.
- The relationship between the (formal or actual) items in a parameter list for a function or procedure.
- The relationship between the fields of a Pascal record or COBOL record or C struct.

AND relations are often treated as being ordered; probable exceptions in the examples just given are fields in a relational table, fields in records or structs and the relationship between a syntactic structure and its semantics.

3.2 OR relations

Examples of OR relations in computing:

- The relationship between b and c in **If** a **then** b **else** c statements.
- Case statements.
- The relationship between items in a Pascal enumerated type.
- The relationship between Horn clauses in a Prolog procedure.
- The relationship between the rows in a table in a relational database.
- The relationship between items in a C union and the relationship between the variants in a Pascal 'record with variants'.

3.3 Identifiers and references

The types of identifier for an object (and thus the means by which it may be referenced) include:

(1) The position of the object in (actual or virtual) memory.
(2) The position of the object in a 'naming space'. 'Scoping rules' may be used so that a given name may be used in more than one context.
(3) A 'path' through a tree or network (e.g. Unix files or the 'dot' notation in Pascal). Path names may be abbreviated if the 'scoping' assumption is made that the current context is the default context.
(4) The contents of the structure as in 'content addressable memory'.

The use of identifiers in conjunction with AND relations and OR relations results in the trees and networks which are so widespread in computing: hierarchical directories of files, the structure of function or procedure calls in a typical computer program, plex structures in a network database, the structure of 'include' files in a typical C program or system, the structure of a non-overwriting filestore like ADAM (Peeling, Morison and Whiting, 1984).

The first three methods of identification may be seen as being 'content addressable' if the information used to identify an object is seen as being a *part* of that object.

The extreme case of identifying an object by its constituents is where the whole object stands for itself. This may seem an idiosyncratic, perhaps meaningless, view of the notion of identification but, if we do not allow this notion, we are forced into arbitrary distinctions which lead to unwelcome complications in our view of the subject.

As an illustration of the idea of an object standing for itself, each word in this text may be seen as an AND group of references to its constituent letters. Each letter is an object which stands for (is a reference to) itself. Creating special identifiers for each letter is less economical than using the letters directly.

3.4 Pattern matching, hill climbing and unification

Pattern matching is a recognized technique in computing (see, for example, Winston (1977, Ch. 14)) but the possibility that all kinds of computing may be seen as the extraction of redundancy by pattern matching and hill-climbing search for the best possible unification seems not to be generally recognized: the section on pattern matching is omitted from the second edition of Winston's book (1984) and the topic does not even get an entry in the index.

From the following examples we can see some of the range of applications of pattern matching in existing systems and, to a lesser extent, search for good unifications:

- Resolution theorem proving: pattern matching and unification are basic mechanisms.

- De-referencing of identifiers may be seen as a form of pattern matching and unification.
- Parsing is clearly an application of pattern matching and unification. Many parsers are designed to deliver only one 'correct' parsing of any given input string. More sophisticated parsers will deliver alternative parses and distinguish 'good' ones from 'bad' ones.
- Information may be retrieved from databases by pattern matching (query-by-example).
- The creation of human-like capabilities in pattern recognition clearly requires pattern matching.
- Inductive learning is largely a matter of pattern matching allied to search mechanisms designed to seek the greatest possible unification of patterns (Wolff, 1982).

4. THE SP LANGUAGE

The syntax of the SP language, shown in Fig. 4.4, is extremely simple. Since it represents a distillation of existing ideas in computing, there should be no surprise that the language is similar in certain respects to existing languages. SP owes its greatest debt to Prolog but differs from Prolog in interesting ways:

- There is nothing in SP equivalent to the distinction in Prolog between the head and the body of a Horn clause. SP deals only in 'patterns'.
- The rules for matching and unification are significantly different from Prolog.
- Indeterminacy in the results of a computation is expressed in SP by creating a disjunctive structure rather than creating a set of alternative results not incorporated in any structure. This is significant in relation to inductive learning.
- In SP, variables do not have explicit names. A variable may be given a name by associating the variable with the name inside a structure, e.g. (Clementine,_). In this way, the connection between variables and their names is recognized as being an AND relation and is brought within the small range of basic constructs in the language without any ad hoc plain principle.
- The fact that variables are not explicitly named means that there is nothing in the language like the principle in Prolog that repeated instances of a named instantiated variable within one Horn clause refer to the same structure. This has a bearing on how 'context-sensitive' structures are represented as will be described in section 5.4.

Although this will be less obvious, the language also owes a debt to object-oriented languages like Simula, Smalltalk and LOOPS. As I shall show in section 5.3, it supports the notions of classes and sub-classes, inheritance of attributes and part–whole relations. SP differs from all current OO languages in being significantly simpler and, in a theoretical sense, more 'clean'. The Lisp-like qualities of the language will be obvious.

4.1 The syntax

```
Object →   Ordered-AND-object |
           Unordered-AND-object |
           Or-object |
           Simple-object ;
Ordered-AND-object → '(' , body , ')' ;
Unordered-AND-object → '[' , body , ']' ;
OR-object → '{' , body , '}' ;
body → b | NULL ;
b → object , body ;
Simple-object → symbol | '_' ;
symbol → character , s ;
s → symbol | NULL ;
character → 'a' | ... | 'z' | '0' | ... | '9' ;
```

Fig. 4.4 — The syntax for SP.

Between any two simple objects which are immediately contiguous there must be at least one space, comma or new line. Otherwise, as an aid to readability, zero or more spaces, commas or new lines may be used in any desired combination between objects.

A 'symbol' may be a single character or a string of characters. In terms of the definition of SP, a string is an Ordered-AND-object of characters. The reason for having 'symbol' as a distinct construct (and not using the term 'string') is that symbols, unlike Ordered-AND-objects, will be treated as atomic.

To be practical, the SP language would need such constructs as 'integer' and 'real'. The assumption here is that such concepts and the operations which relate to them (addition, multiplication etc.) may be defined in SP and need not be supplied as primitives. Justification of this claim is beyond the scope of this paper.

4.2 The semantics of SP: how it is intended to work

This section describes the possible ways in which the language may be made to work — i.e. to do some computing. A formal definition of the semantics has not yet been attempted. The meanings of the types of object should be reasonably clear from their names:

- An Ordered-AND-object (OAO) represents a sequence: a collection of structures where the order of the structures is significant. An OAO represents what, in taxonomic linguistics, used to be called 'syntagmatic' relations.
- An Unordered-AND-object (UAO) represents a 'bag' of structures: the order of structures in the bag is not significant. Any given item may be repeated in a UAO but, for reasons which will become clear, any such repetition is likely to be removed as computing proceeds.
- An OR-object (ORO) represents a collection of items from which one or more may be selected. It represents an 'inclusive' OR relation amongst its constituents.

An ORO represents what, in taxonomic linguistics, used to be called 'paradigmatic' relations.
- Simple-objects are the 'atoms' of the language.
- The '_' character represents a 'variable', i.e. a place holder to which an object may be 'assigned'. As in Prolog, values are assigned to variables by unification of patterns. As in Prolog but not in most conventional programming languages, the value of a variable may not be changed once it has been assigned. In general, the language works in a 'non-overwriting' mode: non-redundant information is never destroyed in the course of computing.

The symbols '→' and '...' which appear later in the article are not part of the SP language. '→' is used to show when one SP object gives rise to another in the course of computing. '...' is used in SP examples to show where other information would go in a more fully developed description.

4.2.1 Computing

To create 'results' using SP, the 'data' and the 'program' must be associated. This is done by joining them together within an AND object. Quote marks have been used for 'results', 'data' and 'program' because these distinctions are not recognized in the system and a uniform notation is used for them all.

All computing is done by *searching* within the composite program-data object to find patterns which *match* each other; when patterns do match they may be *unified*. The search space is usually very large; where there is recursion, the search space is infinite.

Pattern matching may be 'free' or 'constrained':

- SP in 'free' mode lives in an impracticable world where all possible matches are sought and all possible unifications are delivered. This version of SP will not be discussed.
- SP in 'constrained' mode has restrictions on the kinds of match which may be sought or the kinds of unification which may be delivered.

There is a variety of ways in which constraint may be applied in the SP system and varying degrees of constraint — and there can be corresponding varieties of the SP language:

(1) *'Broad' SP*. The most general kind of constraint relies on the notion of 'goodness' or 'economy' in matching and unification. The aim is always to achieve as much unification as possible or, equivalently, to reduce the size of an SP structure as much as possible.

There is no algorithmic way to ensure that the maximum possible amount of unification is always achieved. Any practical version of 'broad' SP will have to use *hill climbing* search techniques of the kind described in Wolff (1982). These may reliably find more or less 'good' unifications but cannot guarantee that the best will always be found. To cope with big search spaces in a practical way, Broad SP also demands high levels of parallel processing in pattern matching and unification.

Like chess programs, versions of Broad SP may vary in how deeply the search tree is explored before decisions are made. Alternatively, the depth of exploration in Broad SP may be controlled by a parameter.

Broad versions of SP may be regarded as the canonical forms of SP. All other versions may be regarded as approximations to the ideal.

(2) *'Narrow' SP*. Superficially, the reliance of the most general constrained version of SP on search techniques seems to mean that computing with SP is different from the clockwork nature of conventional computing. However, on a 'simplicity and power' view, all computing systems rely on search techniques of some kind even when this is not explicitly recognized. For example, any practical parser on a conventional computer embodies a 'biggest is best' principle to help it find the 'correct' parsing from amongst the many 'incorrect' parses which the grammar may otherwise allow. The clockwork nature of Prolog derives from constraints applied to how pattern matching may be done and what will count as 'true'.

SP may be constrained to work more like Prolog or a conventional programming language (e.g. Pascal, C or functional languages like Lisp) by being more restrictive about how the search for matching patterns is done. Here are three of the more obvious kinds of restriction:

(1) The search for matches for the constituents of an object may be done always in *left-to-right sequence*. This reduces the range of possible matches which can be found and gives the language a 'procedural' flavour. If this restriction is applied only to OAOs then these objects become 'processes' and UAOs represent 'concurrency' amongst their constituents.
(2) *Nearest is dearest*. When the system seeks a match for any given object it will try other objects in order of their 'distance' from the given object in the total structure of objects rather in the manner of scoping rules in languages like Pascal.
(3) *All-or-nothing matching*. In most computer languages, the search for matching patterns is greatly reduced by insistence on all-or-nothing matching, particularly for identifiers. This kind of restriction is implied by the atomic nature of the 'symbol' construct of SP. This feature should, perhaps, be removed in any 'broad' version of SP.

These and other kinds of restriction on pattern matching may be regarded as ways of reducing the size of the space of possible unifications which the system has to search and thus making the search tractable within the limits on processing power imposed by currently available hardware. The penalty of these restrictions is that they limit the range of problems which the computing system may solve.

4.2.2 Rules for matching and unification
Here are the rules required for pattern matching and unification in SP:

(1) *Matching simple objects*. Simple objects which are not variables and which match (e.g. A and A) give a copy of either object as the unification.
(2) *Matching with variables*. An SP variable matches any object. In all cases, including when a variable is matched with another variable, the result of unifying a variable with another object (or objects) is a copy of the other object(s). For example, $[A,\_]$ matches $[A,B]$ giving $[A,B]$; $[A,\_]$ matches with $[A,B,C]$ giving $[A,B,C]$.
(3) *Matching two OAOs*. Two OAOs may match completely or partly. In both cases, unification is possible:

   (i) When one or more constituents of a OAO match one or more constituents of another OAO, in the same order, then each constituent of the one OAO may be unified with the corresponding constituent of the other. Obviously order is irrelevant when only one constituent from each OAO is involved. Notice that ordinal position is not significant. For example, A and B in (X,A,B) may be unified with A and B in (A,Y,B).
   (ii) When two OAOs match only partly, the resulting unification contains all the unmatched constituents from both OAOs — in the appropriate position relative to the constituents which have been unified. These unmatched constituents are formed into one or more OROs, each in an appropriate position in the unified pattern. For example, the unification of (X,Y,A,B) and (P,Q,R,A,B) will give $(\{(X,Y)(P,Q,R)\}A,B)$.
   (iii) Where alternative partial unifications are possible then the one giving the greatest amount of unification is preferred (unless there is a tie in which case an arbitrary choice is made). For example, if unification were sought between (A,B,C,P,D,E,F) and (A,B,C,Q,D,E,F) then $(A,B,C\{P,Q\}D,E,F)$ would be better than $(\{(A,B,C,P)(A,B,C,Q)\}D,E,F)$.

   It is normal for there to be many alternative possible unifications. A more realistic example appears in section 5.1. The 'best' set of unifications is the one which reduces the size of the structure by the greatest amount. As we have seen, there is no algorithmic method which is guaranteed to find the best set of unifications in all cases. An SP 'engine' will depend on hill climbing search techniques or something equivalent.
(4) *Matching with UAOs*. The rules for matching a UAO against another UAO or an OAO are the same as for matching two OAOs except that ordering constraints do not apply.
(5) *Matching with OROs*. Two rules apply, as follows:

   (i) An ORO matches any other object if one of its constituents matches that object. The resulting unification is a copy of the given object. For example, $\{A,B,C\}$ matched with A gives A.
   (ii) An ORO matches another ORO if one or more of its constituents can be matched with one or more constituents of the other ORO. The unification is an ORO whose constituents are the result of unifying the constituents which match, unless there is only one such unified pair of constituents in which case the result of unifying the two OROs is that unification. For example, the unification of $\{A,B,C\}$ and $\{B,C,D\}$ is $\{B,C\}$. The unification of $\{A,B,C\}$ and $\{C,D,E\}$ is C.

In general, the effect of unifying two OROs is to form the intersection of the two sets of constituents.

The rules described in this section are not fully developed — more work is needed in this area. There is a case, in future work, for introducing 'weights' on SP objects to reflect (absolute and contextual) frequencies of objects in the raw data. The metric which evaluates alternative unifications will need to accommodate these weights. The introduction of weights is likely to lead to some modification in the rules just described, particularly the rules for matching and unification with OROs. Two OROs may be unified by taking the union of their constituents (rather than the intersection) but assigning higher weights to items which are in the intersection.

5. APPLICATIONS

In this section I shall illustrate the workings of SP and the principles on which it is based using examples from several areas of computing.

5.1 Parsing with a simple grammar

This first example, showing how SP may be used to represent a simple grammar and parse a simple 'sentence', may at first sight seem remote from the mainstream of computing. The justification for first illustrating the workings of SP in this way is the belief that many aspects of computing may be seen in these terms.

In many ways SP has the organization of simple phrase structure grammars. In section 5.4 I will show how SP overcomes the limitations of such grammars and has the power to handle 'context-sensitive' features in representations of knowledge.

Fig. 4.5 shows a little grammar written in SP. In this and later examples of

```
[
(S(NP,_)(VP,_))
(NP{john,mary})
(VP(V,_)(NP,_))
(V{loves,hates})
]
```

Fig. 4.5 — A grammar written in SP.

grammars, the distinction between upper and lower case letters has no formal significance; it merely helps one to see which objects are serving as 'non-terminal symbols' and which represent 'text'. To forestall misunderstanding, it should be stressed that SP is not a rewrite system. The matching and unification mechanisms in SP may imitate the effect of a rewrite system but they are more general.

The example grammar may be used to parse a sentence by associating the sentence with the grammar inside a UAO, as shown in Fig. 4.6.

Consider, first of all, a 'top down' parsing, where the processes of matching and unification are driven by the 'top level' rule in the grammar: $(S(NP,\_)(VP,\_))$. Taking the components of this object in turn, left to right, the system tries to unify as much as possible of this object with other objects in the 'universe' of objects in the

120 THE SP THEORY [Ch. 4

[(*john,loves,mary*)
[
(*S(NP,_)(VP,_)*)
(*NP{john,mary}*)
(*VP(V,_)(NP,_)*)
(*V{loves,hates}*)
]]

Fig. 4.6 — Association of a sentence with a grammar.

combined sentence and grammar. The same applies to any new objects created by unification. The sequence of matchings and unifications is shown in Fig. 4.7.

1 (*S(NP,_)(VP,_)*)

2 (*S(NP{john,mary})(VP,_)*)
   /* By unification of (*NP,_*) with
   (*NP{john,mary}*) */

3 (*S(NP,john){VP,_)(loves,mary)}*)
   /* By unification of {*john,mary*} with
   '*john*' in (*john,loves,mary*) */

4 (*S(NP,john){(VP(V,_)(NP,_))(loves,mary)}*)
   /* By unification of (*VP,_*) with
   (*VP(V,_)(NP,_)*) */

5 (*S(NP,john){(VP(V{loves,hates})(NP,_)* with
   (*V{loves,hates}*) */

6 (*S(NP,john)(VP(V,loves){(NP,_)(mary)})*)
   /* By unification of {*loves,hates*} with
   '*loves*' in (*loves,mary*) */

7 (*S(NP,john)(VP(V,loves){(NP{john,mary})(mary)})*)
   /* By unification of (*NP,_*) with
   (*NP{john,mary}*) */

8 (*S(NP,john)(VP(V,loves)(NP,mary))*)
   /* By unification of {*john,mary* with
   '*mary*' */

Fig. 4.7 — Unifications in a 'top down' parsing of the sentence in Fig. 4.3 using the grammar in Fig. 4.3.

Ch. 4] THE SP THEORY 121

Some comments on Fig. 4.7:

- In stage 2 we see the use of the variable '_'.
- In stage 3 we see how an ORO, {*john,mary*}, is reduced to a singleton: '*john,*'; when one of its constituents matches that singleton.
- Also in stage 3 we see how SP forms a disjunction when two matched patterns both contain unmatched components. After '*john*' within (*john,loves,mary*) has been unified with {*john,mary*} within (*S*(*NP*{john,mary})(*VP*,_)), the residues of the two larger objects are formed into an ORO:

Fig. 4.8 shows how the system may work in a 'bottom up' mode, where unification starts with the sentence rather than the top rule of the grammar.

1 (*john,loves,mary*)

2 ((*NP,john*),*loves,mary*)
/* By unification of '*john*' in
(*john,loves,mary*) with
(*NP*{*john,mary*}) */

3 (*S*(*NP,john*){(*VP,_*)(*loves,mary*)})
/* By unification of (*NP,john*) with
(*S*(*NP,_*)(*VP,_*)).
There is a conflict here because (*NP,john*) may also be unified with (*VP*(*V,_*)(*NP,_*)) giving
((*VP*(*V,_*)(*NP,john*))(*loves,mary*)).
In this example, this second, 'bad', alternative will not be followed through. This kind of conflict is discussed in the text. */

4 (*S*(*NP,john*){(*VP,_*)((*V,loves*),*mary*)})
/* By unification of (*V*{*loves,hates*}) with
'*loves*' in (*loves,mary*) */

5 (*S*(*NP,john*){(*VP,_*)(*VP*(*V,loves*){(*NP,_*),*mary*})})
/* By unification of ((*V,loves*),*mary*) with
(*VP*(*V,_*)(*NP,_*)) */

6 (*S*(*NP,john*)(*VP*(*V,loves*){(*NP,_*),*mary*}))
/* By unification of (*VP,_*) with
(*VP*(*V,loves*){(*NP,_*),*mary*}) */

7 (*S*(*NP,john*)(*VP*(*V,loves*){(*NP,_*),(*NP,mary*)}))
/* By unification of '*mary*' with
(*NP*{*john,mary*}) */

8 (*S*(*NP,john*)(*VP*(*V,loves*)(*NP,mary*)))
/* By unification of (*NP,_*) with
(*NP,mary*) */

Fig. 4.8 — Unifications in a 'bottom up' parsing of the sentence in Fig. 4.6 using the grammar in Fig. 4.6.

In Fig. 4.8 we see an example, at stage 3, of how rival unifications can arise. They represent alternative solutions to the problem in hand. In principle, the system may be allowed to compute all possible alternative solutions. For most purposes, it will be necessary to nip off any branch of the search tree if it seems to be leading in an unhelpful direction. In terms of the theory on which SP is based, 'unhelpful' means uneconomical. If the 'bad' path is followed at stage 3 of Fig. 4.8 it will lead to this parsing:

$$((VP(V\{loves,hates\})(NP,john)),loves,(VP(V\{loves,hates\})(NP,mary)))$$

No further unification is possible without violating the order constraints on the sentence. This solution is clearly much less economical than the 'correct' parsing and may be rejected on those grounds.

5.2 Logic and logical inference

SP has potential as a medium for expressing logical propositions and making logical inferences. This is perhaps not surprising, given the significance in the language of the simple logical relations, AND and inclusive OR.

Here is a familiar and elementary example:

> All men are mortal.
> Socrates is a man.
> Therefore Socrates is mortal.

In first-order predicate calculus this may be expressed as:

$$\forall x \in \text{man} . \text{mortal}(x) \wedge \text{Socrates} \in \text{man} \Rightarrow \text{mortal}(\text{Socrates})$$

In SP, the same premises and the inference may be expressed like this:

> [[mortal[man,_]]]
> [man,Socrates]]
> →[mortal[man,Socrates]]

Remember that '→' is not part of SP. It simply shows what is produced in the course of computing. In the first line, the pattern [man,_] matches any UAO which has 'man' as a constituent object. Thus it may be read as 'all men' or 'any man'. The underscore symbol removes the need for a universal quantifier rather in the way that Skolemization may be used to remove universal quantifiers in predicate calculus. (Existential quantifiers are not needed either because any given object may be named.)

The conjunction of 'mortal' with [man,_] gives the pattern [mortal [man,_]]. This represents 'All men are mortal'. Likewise, [man,Socrates] represents 'Socrates is a man'. When these two patterns are matched and unified, the result is [mortal[man, Socrates]] which may be read as 'Socrates is a man and he is mortal'.

Thus SP does not derive [mortal,Socrates] directly from the two original propositions but creates a pattern with which [mortal,Socrates] will unify. In this way, the proposition 'Socrates is mortal' is validated.

The problems mentioned earlier in finding matches between patterns and in differentiating between 'good' and 'bad' matches, suggest that SP is too uncertain a medium on which to base logical inference. But it is already known that every formal system which is expressive enough to be useful is also 'incomplete' in the sense that there are truths which are expressible in the system but which cannot be proved within the system. The uncertainty of matching and unification in infinite search spaces may provide a reason for the existence of incompleteness in formal systems.

5.2.1 'True' and 'false'
SP has no explicit concepts of 'true' or 'false'. These concepts, which are primitives in other views of computing may be seen as emergent properties of the SP system. If every SP object is regarded as some kind of statement (it is, without doubt, a body of information), then it may be regarded as true if it matches some other object, much in the way that a Prolog Horn clause is regarded as true if a match can be found for it within a set of clauses.

SP differs from Prolog, of course, in that it allows partial matching. Correspondingly, it supports the notion of degrees of truth. In general, truth in an SP system will be modelled by the metrics which guide the search for 'good' structure within the system. There is no space here to discuss fully the ramifications of these ideas.

5.3 Object-oriented design and entity-relationship models
This section discusses a set of inter-related ideas associated with object-oriented (OO) design and with the creation of conceptual models.

The distinctive features of OO systems (e.g. Simula, Smalltalk and LOOPS) are as follows:

- That all data structures and procedural code are organized as *objects*. An object is an association of data structures with the procedural code ('functions' or 'methods') with which those data structures may be manipulated. In most systems, data structures are accessed *only* by means of 'messages' sent to object methods and may thus be protected from modification in illegal ways.
- Objects in an OO system may be grouped into *classes* (including super-classes and sub-classes) in the same way that biologists group animals and plants. This has the psychological advantage that groupings may be set up corresponding to the way we naturally think of these things.
- A (related) advantage is that any structure ('property' or 'attribute') in an object may be recorded just once at the appropriate level of generality and it may then be *inherited* by the lower levels. This saves space; by allowing redundancy to be minimized, it helps avoid problems of inconsistency in design and facilitates the modification of designs.

In the more sophisticated OO systems (e.g. LOOPS), cross classification is possible with the possibility of a class having multiple inheritance of attributes from two or more higher level classes. A structure of interlocking hierarchies like this is sometimes called a 'heterarchy'. In OO languages, classes serve as models for the creation of object 'instances'. This is similar to the way in which types serve as models for the assignment of values to variables in other languages.

In most OO systems, classes are themselves objects which are instances of 'metaclasses'. An idea which is complementary to the notion of class inclusion relations is the notion of *part–whole relations*. This idea tends not to be explicitly recognized in OO systems but is there nonetheless in the kinds of groupings and sub-groupings of objects which can be formed. Part–whole relations form hierarchies and heterarchies as AND trees and AND networks.

Related to OO systems are the kinds of 'entity-relationship' (ER) models which are the stock-in-trade of systems analysis (LBMS, 1986). Such models typically identify significant 'entities' in the domain being modelled, 'attributes' of those entities and named 'relationships' between entities.

Although they do not usually figure in discussions of OO systems and ER models, three other concepts will be mentioned here which relate to classes and categories. A class may be defined *extensionally* by listing all the members of the class. It may also be defined *intensionally* by describing the properties of the class. The third notion is that many of the classes we regularly use in everyday life are *polythetic*. What this means is that there need be no single attribute which is found in every example of the class. This property of natural categories has proved puzzling to theorists who try to characterize classes in terms of *defining* characteristics. Polythetic classes need not have any defining characteristics.

All the concepts described in the foregoing may be accommodated by the concept of an 'object' in SP: 'class', 'super-class' and 'sub-class', 'meta-class', 'instance', 'function', 'method', 'message', 'class-hierarchy' and 'heterarchy', 'part–whole hierarchy' and 'heterarchy', 'entity', 'attribute', 'relationship', 'extensional definition', 'intensional definition' and 'polythetic class'.

5.3.1 Class-inclusion relations, part–whole relations and inheritance of attributes

Fig. 4.9 shows how class-inclusion relations, part–whole relations and inheritance of

```
[person [name,_]
        ((head ((eyes ...)(nose ...) ...))
        (body ...)(legs ...))
        [eats ...][sleeps ...][breathes ...] ...
        [profession
             {[tinker ...]
              [tailor ...]
              ...
             }]
        [gender
             {[male ...]
              [female ...]
             }]]
```

Fig. 4.9 — The integration of class-inclusion relations, part–whole relations and inheritance of attributes.

attributes may be integrated. The sets of three dots ('...') show where other information would go in a more fully developed description. This structure shows the class '*person*' as having the attributes '*head*', '*body*', '*legs*', '*eats*', '*sleeps*' etc. These are the *parts* of which the concept of a person is composed; parts may have sub-parts down to any level.

'*Persons*' have sub-classes '*tinker*', '*tailor*' etc. and they are also cross-classified as '*male*' or '*female*'. Any number of levels is possible in this kind of classification scheme. Notice how part–whole relations equate with AND relations, while class-inclusion relations equate with OR relations.

An 'instance' of a person may be represented as:

[person [name,Tom],_,[profession[tinker,_]][gender[male,_]]]

or even more succinctly as:

[_,[_,Tom],_,[_,[tinker,_]][_,[male,_]]]

Either pattern will unify with the class schema giving a full description of 'Tom' something like this:

[person [name,Tom]
 (head ((eyes ...)(nose ...) ...))
 (body ...)(legs ...)
 (eats ...)(sleeps ...) (breathes ...) ...
 [profession [tinker ...]]
 [gender [male ...]]]

Pattern matching and unification provides a mechanism by which attributes may be *inherited* by an instance (or sub-class) in the sense understood in object-oriented design. In SP, unlike most other OO systems, the concepts of class-inclusion relation, and inheritance of attributes are *integrated* with the concept of part-whole structure.

5.3.2 Methods and messages

Narrow SP has potential as a 'procedural' language although the details will not be pursued here. An SP object may contain constituent objects corresponding to 'methods' in other OO languages. For example, a class '*person*' containing the method '*eat*' may be represented something like this:

[person,[name,_],[eat[food,_],...],...]

The first set of three dots corresponds to the details of how eating is done. The second set represents the many other attributes of the class 'person'. A particular person may be represented as, for example:

[person,[name,Mary],_]

or, more succinctly,

[person,Mary,_].

If Mary is to eat something then one can send a 'message' to the object which represents her something like this:

[person,Mary,[eat,ham-sandwich],_]

Thus, in SP, both 'methods' and 'messages' may be treated as objects, not essentially different from other kinds of knowledge. One advantage of treating 'methods' and 'messages' uniformly with other kinds of knowledge is that 'inheritance' may be exploited within them. A 'method' may be inherited by other objects and it may itself inherit objects from elsewhere. Likewise for 'messages'. Knowledge engineering systems like KEE go some way down this path.

5.3.3 Class, meta-class, instance and the evolution of classes

Most OO systems make a sharp distinction between 'classes' and 'instances'. Classes serve as templates for the creation of instances but instances may not be templates for anything. The structure of classes is established by a designer before the system runs and remains fixed while the system runs. As it runs it may create new instances of classes dynamically but not new classes. Since classes, in most systems, are regarded as objects, this means that they must be instances of something. To avoid classes being instances of classes (which would violate the sharp distinction between instances and classes) it is necessary to introduce the concept of 'meta-class'. Classes may then be instances of meta-classes. There is an infinite regress because meta-classes must be instances of meta-meta-classes — and so on (see Ungar & Smith, 1987).

In SP, the concepts of 'instance', 'class' and 'meta-class' are merged. There is no attempt to create 'strict' hierarchies or avoid Russell's paradox. The advantage of this breaking down of the distinction between classes and instances is the removal of unnecessary rigidities in the system: any object may serve as a template for the creation of other objects (i.e. any object may serve as a class) and any object may be created dynamically as the system runs. In other words, the structure of classes of the system may evolve as the system runs.

Many people find it difficult to abandon the distinction between classes and instances. The reason seems to be that the things which, in everyday life, are conventionally regarded as instances of classes (e.g. individual people) are highly salient, coherent concepts. The fact that an individual person (dog, cat, table, chair) is a very highly coherent concept should not disguise the fact that such things are in fact collections of more primitive percepts. In short, they are classes of visual, auditory and tactile images. Something which would conventionally be regarded as an instance, e.g. 'Mary', may be specialized into such concepts as 'Mary-as-wife-and-mother', 'Mary-as-magistrate' etc. These are sub-classes of the class 'Mary'.

5.3.4 Entity-relationship models

Representing the relationship between two or more entities in SP is no different from representing the structure of a given entity. The relationship may be expressed as an AND relation between the relationship identifier and identifiers of the entities to be related. For example, [*employs*,*John*,[*Harry*,*Mary*],_]

in the context of this schema:

[*employs*
    [*employer*,_]
    [*employees*,_]
    ...]

expresses the idea that '*John*' employs '*Harry*' and '*Mary*'. The ellipsis represents other information (e.g. company law) that may be associated with the relationship between employers and employees.

5.3.5 Polythetic classes
As already mentioned, most 'natural' categories are polythetic, meaning that there need not be any single attribute which is found in all examples of the class. We can recognize something as, say, a cat when any one (or perhaps more) of its distinctive features is missing or replaced by something else. This property of natural categories is puzzling if one assumes that there must be defining characteristics for classes, but it can be accommodated quite easily by SP.

As a simple example, the SP object ({A,B}{C,D}{E,F}) represents the class of three letter strings comprising *ACE*, *ACF*, *ADE*, *ADF*, *BCE*, *BCF*, *BDE* and *BDF*. No single attribute (letter) is found in every example of the class. In general, polythesis is a reflection of disjunction (OR relations) in the organization of knowledge.

5.4 'Context-sensitive' power in SP
The expressive power of systems for constructing context-free grammars is limited. Systems of this type (e.g. BNF) cannot, for example, adequately represent the syntax and semantics of most natural languages.

Although SP resembles BNF, it can succinctly represent structures in natural language — such as 'discontinuous dependencies' in syntax — which are beyond the scope of BNF. SP has at least the expressive power of 'context-sensitive' systems like Definite Clause Grammars (DCGs; Pereira & Warren, 1980).

In the French sentence *Les plumes sont vertes* there are two overlapping sets of discontinuous dependencies. They are shown here by underscores:

Les plumes sont vertes

Les plumes sont vertes

In the first case, the features of the sentence which make it plural are marked. All these parts must agree even though they may be separated by any amount of intervening structure. Likewise, in the second case, the parts of the sentence which express feminine gender must agree.

In the DCG formalism, which is a notational variant of Prolog, these dependen-

128 THE SP THEORY [Ch. 4

cies would be expressed throughout the grammar in a number of rules, including the highest level rule shown here:

$$s(Num,Gen,s(NP,VP)) \rightarrow np(Num,Gen,NP),vp(Num,Gen,VP).$$

In this rule, '*Num*' and '*Gen*' are variables recording number and gender, respectively. Agreement is assured because of the 'meta' rule of Prolog that repeated examples of an instantiated variable within a clause all refer to a single structure. If the first instance of '*Num*' in the rule is instantiated to 'singular' then all the others are too. Likewise for 'plural'. The '*Gen*' variable behaves in the same way for 'masculine' and 'feminine'.

With SP, the same effect is achieved without any need for the meta rule. Fig. 4.10

```
[
(S(NP,_)(VP,_))
(NP(D,_)(N,_))
(VP(V,_){(A,_)((P,_)(NP,_))})
(P{sur,sous,...})
(V{(SING{est,...})(PL{sont,...})})
(D{(SING{(FEM{une,la,...})(MASC{un,le,...})})(PL{les,...})})
(N(NS,_)(SUF1,_))
(NS{(FEM{plume,...})(MASC{papier,...})})
(SUF1{(SING,0)(PL,s)})
(A(AS,_)(SUF2,_)(SUF1,_))
(AS{noir,vert,...})
(SUF2{(FEM,e)(MASC,0)})
(_,D,SING,_,N,_,SUF1,SING,_,V,SING,_{(A,_,SUF1,SING,_)_})
(_,D,PL,_,N,_,SUF1,PL,_,V,PL,_{(A,_,SUF1,PL,_)_})
(_,D,_,FEM,_,N,_,FEM,_{(A,_,SUF2,FEM,_)_})
(_,D,_,MASC,_,N,_,MASC,_{(A,_,SUF2,MASC,_)_})
]
```

Fig. 4.10 — A fragment of French syntax written in SP.

shows a small grammar which can generate the example sentence amongst others. The 'top level' rule is simpler than the top level rule in the DCG formalism because it does not attempt to record discontinuous dependencies at this level. The grammar as a whole is significantly smaller than the equivalent DCG grammar.

Discontinuous dependencies for 'singular'' 'plural', 'feminine' and 'masculine' forms are expressed by the last four rules in the grammar, in that order. The '_' symbol, which will match arbitrarily large amounts of structure, appears wherever there is structure which is irrelevant to the dependencies being expressed. In this way the dependencies can be shown directly and plainly as OAOs.

5.5 Pattern recognition and inductive learning

Perhaps the most interesting aspect of SP is its potential for pattern recognition, for inductive learning and for their integration with other areas of computing.

Computing in SP means searching for patterns which match each other and unifying them; where alternative unifications are possible, which is almost always the case, then the SP system must choose the 'best' one, meaning the one which allows the greatest amount of unification and a correspondingly large simplification of structure.

This and the way SP treats partial matching means that a working SP system is likely to be applicable to practical problems of pattern recognition. It is likely to have the kind of flexibility long recognized in human pattern recognition: the ability to recognize whole patterns from partial patterns and to recognize patterns despite distortion or fragmentation.

The subject of the second paragraph in this section was computing. But essentially the same thing can be said about inductive learning. The inductive learning of a grammar, for example, can be achieved by processes which at heart are pattern matching and unification, with the selection of 'good' (meaning economical) structures in preference to 'bad' ones (see Wolff, 1982, 1987, 1988).

Here is a very simple example to illustrate how an SP system may achieve inductive learning:

[
(*John,runs*)
(*Mary,runs*)
(*John,walks*)
(*Mary,walks*)
]

would be reduced by the SP system to:

({*John,Mary*}{*runs,walks*})

This is functionally equivalent to a grammar which can 'generate' the four sentences from which it was derived.

To infer grammars like those in Figs 4.5 and 4.10, the SP system would need to be able to create new identifiers for structures (e.g. *NP* in (*NP*{*john,mary*})) and *VP* in (*VP*(*V,_*)(*NP,_*))) and introduce them at appropriate points.

The potential applications of a system with inductive learning capabilities include: automation of the process of building natural language grammars; automation of the process of 'knowledge acquisition' for expert systems; optimization of database structures; inductive learning of structures for pattern recognition; automatic programming.

The inductive properties of SP give the added dimension of adaptability to pattern recognition applications. A pattern recognition system based on SP is likely to have the capability to learn new general schemas from unprocessed input. It has long been recognized that much of the power of human pattern recognition in, for example, speech recognition, lies in the dynamic adaptation of the system to changes in the input. Pattern recognition and inductive learning are intimately related.

5.6 Other applications and attributes

There is no space in this article to discuss fully all the possible applications of SP. This section will briefly describe some other areas where SP may be applied and properties of SP which may prove useful.

Configuration management

In software development and many other applications of computers there is a need to control the 'versions' or 'variants' of programs, documents and other information objects. Most such objects come in parts and sub-parts and each such part or sub-part may come in more than one version. The main problem is to keep track of the required combinations of versions and parts. A related problem is to keep track of associations between objects as, for example, between each item of source code and its corresponding object code.

Many of the ideas described in section 5.3 — on the representation of class-inclusion relations, part–whole relations and 'relationships' between entities — may be applied to problems of configuration management.

There is scope here for the *integration* of configuration classes with other classes in a software system: the creation of a new version of a body of software would mean the creation of new sub-class of the appropriate class in the system.

Software re-use

A significant problem in the software industry is the difficulty of incorporating existing software in new developments and the consequent waste of development effort. This difficulty arises from three main sources:

- The diversity of languages and formalisms used in software development makes integration difficult.
- Even when old and new software are written in the same language, many programming languages have only limited means of integrating old with new. In particular, most programming languages lack the OO mechanisms of inheritance which can greatly facilitate the integration of old software with new.
- There are difficulties in identifying and retrieving software to serve a given purpose.

SP may alleviate these problems on all three fronts:

- It has potential as a 'broad-spectrum' language with a wide range of applications. It has potential as a standard for the organization of software systems and may thus promote the integration of old software with new.
- Through the inheritance mechanism which is an implicit part of its organization, SP, like other OO languages, facilitates integration.
- Since SP has potential as a language for information retrieval (see below) it may prove useful in the identification of existing software to serve a given purpose.

Rules for expert systems, probabilistic inference and reasoning with uncertain and incomplete knowledge
'Production rules' of the kind commonly used in expert systems may be expressed directly in SP. For example, a rule to express the common observation that 'Clouds (probably) mean rain' may be expressed as

[[cloud,{black,white}]{rain,hail,snow}]

If this rule is matched with [[cloud,black],_] representing the question '*What do black clouds mean?*', the object [[cloud,black]{rain,hail,snow}] will be returned showing that rain is a possibility.

The rule may work backwards: from the existence of rain may be inferred the certainty of there being clouds. In general SP supports the retrieval of complete patterns from partial patterns. It will also support forwards and backwards chaining.

It should be clear from this example that SP can support the drawing of 'probabilistic' inferences. It would be natural in making these inferences to utilize the 'weights' mentioned earlier, reflecting the frequencies of objects in the raw data.

Uncertainty can be represented directly in SP using OROs. Gaps in knowledge may be represented with variables ('_'). The design of SP accommodates uncertainty and incomplete knowledge without *ad hoc* provision.

The representation of plans and automatic planning
There is a good correspondence between the main constructs of SP and those commonly recognized in project planning:

- An OAO may be used to represent a sequence of activities.
- A UAO may be used to represent activities which are *independent* of each other, where their ordering is not important. This corresponds to the slightly inaccurate use of the term *parallel* in project planning. 'Parallel' activities may be performed in parallel or they may be performed in some arbitrary sequence, depending on the resources available and the required timescales.
- An ORO may be used to represent activities which are *alternatives* in a plan. This is not very common in ordinary projects but the concept is recognized in the term 'contingency planning'.

What is missing from SP as a medium for expressing plans is any explicit concept of 'iteration'. However, an equivalent effect may be achieved by means of recursion.

It is not possible to be very precise at this stage, but it seems likely that the inferential processes embodied in the semantics of SP will lend themselves to the kind of 'automatic planning' which figures in some commercially available systems to support project planning and which has been the subject of extensive research (see, for example, Tate (1985).

Database organization, information retrieval and content-addressable memory
SP provides a framework for organizing information in databases which is similar to, but not identical with the relational model. It would be rash at this stage to claim that

SP were superior to the relational model (although it may be) but it clearly has potential in this area. Amongst the potential benefits of an SP database are:

- Integration of database constructs with 'programming' and software design constructs.
- Integration of databases with expert systems.
- The economy and integration which may be achieved by the use of a single language both for structuring the database and for querying it. The example, above, of querying an expert system rule base illustrates the potential of SP as a flexible 'query-by-example' means of accessing information in a database.
- An SP system may retrieve information using special keys or identifiers but it also provides the functionality of *content-addressable memory*.
- By virtue of the pattern matching and unification mechanisms, an SP database may have capabilities for automatic normalization of the database and removal of redundancies.

Software design and the formal specification of computing systems
The way SP supports OO constructs has already been discussed at length. The benefits of these constructs in software design is in the creation of software which is easy to understand, to modify and to maintain. However, there are other potential benefits of SP in software development.

The simple and regular nature of SP, its close relation to logic (discussed above), and its complete independence of any machine-oriented concepts, means that it should be regarded as a specification language and not a 'programming' language in the conventional sense.

Like Prolog, it has potential as an 'executable' specification language. An SP specification may run immediately without the need for the time-consuming and error-prone processes of 'refining' a specification to become an 'implementation' or 'program' followed by 'verification' that the 'program' conforms to the specification. Of course, it does not eliminate the need to validate the specification against the user's requirements.

Much software design entails the recreation of routines for pattern matching and unification in a variety of guises. By providing powerful and 'universal' methods of processing patterns, SP can save much re-invention of the wheel.

Translation between computer languages and porting of software
SP has potential application in the translation between computer languages which is needed from time to time. SP may also facilitate the porting of software from one machine to another (since porting of software may be regarded as a form of translation).

In any kind of translation (including translation between natural languages) there are advantages in using an 'interlingua' or base form as an intermediary between languages. The main reason for this is that the number of translators which need to be developed may be reduced: for all combinations of N languages the number of two-way translators required is $N!$ without an interlingua but only N with an interlingua.

If SP does indeed capture the essentials of computing in the way which has been claimed then it should be a good choice as an interlingua for translation between existing computer languages.

Integration of diverse kinds of knowledge

A common problem in computing is the need for integration — the need to have simple and uniform methods of storing and using diverse kinds of information. In the preparation of documents, for example, there is a need for an integrated approach to the storage and manipulation of text and diagrams. In databases to support computer-aided design and in integrated project support environments (IPSEs) there is a similar need to be able to integrate the varied kinds of knowledge which are used.

SP has potential to provide the general format which is needed for the uniform storage and use of diverse kinds of knowledge.

It may not always be convenient to map every body of knowledge to the SP syntax. In these cases, SP can serve a useful purpose as a framework within which 'alien' bodies of knowledge may be stored. It can, for example, be used to show (in a UAO) the association between a program written in, say, COBOL, and its corresponding compiler.

The user interface

The usability of any system depends, in part, on simplicity in its organization and consistency across a wide range of applications. The simple syntax of SP and the scope of its semantics can mean a simple user interface which is consistent in a variety of applications.

6. CONCLUSION

SP and the theory on which it is based has potential to integrate and rationalize diverse concepts in computing. The basic conjecture is that the organization and use of all kinds of formal system, knowledge structure or computing system may usefully be seen in terms of the management of redundancy in information.

In this article I have tried to show with examples how a few carefully chosen basic constructs may illuminate a wide range of concerns in computing. No attempt has been made to show how SP would apply to such things as numerical computing, the representation and use of (2D and 3D) geometric information, concepts associated with the interface between a computer and its human user, or the representation and use in computational form of concepts of time.

There is a substantial programme of work needed to explore the adequacy or otherwise of SP constructs in the kinds of areas mentioned. If SP and its underlying theory are sound then they should have something useful to say about areas like these. It should be possible to create 'higher level' constructs from the basic constructs in SP to meet the needs of particular domains.

It may be that the basic constructs in SP will need to be modified or augmented. However, in all circumstances, we should resist the temptation to postulate new basic constructs in an *ad hoc* manner. In accordance with the best scientific traditions, we should try to achieve descriptive and explanatory power with a small range of theoretical devices. In short, we should aim in our thinking for a favourable combination of simplicity and power.

Acknowledgements
Earlier drafts of this article have been circulated quite widely and several people have made useful comments. I am particularly grateful to Simon Tait of Praxis Systems plc with whom I have discussed these ideas extensively. I am also grateful for helpful comments from James Davenport of the University of Bath, Tim Denvir, Anthony Hall, Trevor King, Paul Newman, Martyn Ould and Lynn Robinson of Praxis Systems plc, Robert Kowalski of Imperial College, London, Peter Van Peborg of Plessey Research, James Bond of the Central Electricity Generating Board, Bristol, and Simon Jones of the School of Electronic Engineering Science, University of Wales (Bangor).

REFERENCES

Birtwistle, G. M., Dahl, O.-J., Myhrhaug, B., & Nygaard, K. (1979). *Simula Begin*, New York: Van Nostrand Reinhold.

Bohm, C., & Jacopini, G. (1966). Flow diagrams, Turing machines, and languages with only two formation rules. *Communications of the ACM* 9(5), 366–371.

Cook, S. (1986). Languages and object-oriented programming. *Software Engineering Journal* 1(2), 73–80.

Hinton, G. E., & Sejnowski, T. J. (1986). Learning and relearning in Boltzmann machines. Chapter 7 in D. E. Rumelhart and J. L. McClelland (Eds), *Parallel Distributed Processing*, Vol I, Cambridge, MA: MIT Press, pp. 282–317.

Jackson, M. A. (1975). *Principles of Program Design*. London: Academic Press.

LBMS (Learmonth and Burchett Management Services, London) (1986). *Structure Systems Analysis*.

Peeling, N. E., Morison, J. D., & Whiting, E. V. (1984). ADAM: an abstract database machine. Report No. 84007, Royal Signals and Radar Establishment, Malvern, UK.

Pereira, F. C. N., & Warren, D. H. D. (1980). Definite clause grammars for language analysis — a survey of the formalism and a comparison with augmented transition networks. *Artificial Intelligence* 13, 231–278.

Rumelhart, D. E., & McClelland, J. L. (Eds) (1986). *Parallel Distributed Processing*, Vols I and II, Cambridge Mass.: MIT Press.

Tate, A. (1985). A review of knowledge-based planning techniques. In M. Merry (Ed.), *Expert Systems 85: Proceedings of the Fifth Technical Conference of the British Computer Society Specialist Group on Expert Systems*, Cambridge: Cambridge University Press, pp. 89–112.

Ungar, D., & Smith, R. B. (1987). Self: the power of simplicity. *Proceedings of the Conference on Object Oriented Programming Systems and Languages (OOPSLA '87)*, pp. 227–241.

Winston, P. H. (1984). *Artificial Intelligence*, 2nd edn, Reading, MA: Addison-Wesley (1st edn: 1977).

Wolff, J. G. (1982). Language acquisition, data compression and generalization. *Language & Communication* 2(1), 57–89.
Wolff, J. G. (1987). Cognitive development as optimization. In L. Bolc (Ed.), *Computational Models of Learning*, Heidelberg: Springer-Verlag, pp. 161–205.
Wolff, J. G. (1988). Learning syntax and meanings through optimization and distributional analysis. In Y. Levy, I. M. Schlessinger, and M. D. S. Braine (Eds), *Categories and Processes in Language Acquisition*, New York: Lawrence Erlbaum, pp. 179–215.

APPENDIX: THE CALCULATION OF SIZE, POWER AND EFFICIENCY OF GRAMMARS

The size (s_r), in bits, of a body of raw data may be calculated as

$$s_r = n_r c_r,$$

where n_r is the number of symbols used in the raw data and c_r is the 'cost' (in bits) of each symbol calculated as

$$c_r = \log_2 t_r$$

rounded up, where t_r is the number of symbol types used in the raw data.

The size (s_e), in bits, of a body of data after encoding by a grammar may be calculated as

$$s_e = n_e c_e,$$

where n_e is the number of symbols required to describe the encoded data using the grammar and c_e is the 'cost' (in bits) of each symbol calculated in the same way as c_r.

The size (s_g), in bits, of a grammar may be calculated as

$$s_g = n_g c_g,$$

where n_g is the number of symbols used in the grammar excluding any symbols which are required only for reasons of readability (e.g. some instances of meta-symbols) and c_g is the 'cost' (in bits) of each symbol calculated in the same way as c_r.

The descriptive power (p_g) of a grammar may be defined, with reference to a given body of raw data, as

$$p_g = s_r - s_e.$$

The efficiency (e_g) of a grammar, with reference to a given body of raw data is:

$$e_g = p_g / s_g.$$

5

A prototype of the SP system†

Chapter 4 describes the SP theory and the proposed SP system at a stage before any real attempt had been made to realize the ideas in a concrete form. This chapter is mainly about a prototype of the SP system and includes demonstrations of what the prototype can do.

The process of developing the prototypes, and further thinking about the SP theory has meant some revision of the theory at the abstract level. In particular, we are now working with a simpler and 'cleaner' concept of *power* than was given in Chapter 4. This chapter includes a summary of the SP theory in its up-to-date form with the new definitions of *efficiency* and of *power*.

THE SP THEORY

To understand what the SP theory is about means taking the long view described in Chapter 1, stepping back from those many kinds of things which people talk about in computing — 'data', 'specifications', 'programs', 'grammars', 'symbols', 'tuples', 'logical proposition', 'rules' in 'expert systems' and many more — and viewing them all as *information* or patterns of binary digits ('bits').

The central idea in the SP theory is the conjecture that all kinds of cognition, computing and formal reasoning may usefully be seen as a search for *efficiency* in information, where the concept of efficiency has a precise meaning in terms of the concept of *redundancy* in Shannon's information theory (Shannon & Weaver, 1949).

In the SP theory, the *efficiency* of a body of information, I, is defined as:

efficiency = *power* / *size*.

The *size* of I (which may also be termed its *complexity*) is the information content of I measured in bits. The term *simplicity*, which can be convenient in discussions of these ideas, is defined as $1/size$. *Power* is defined as:

power = *size* − *redundancy*.

The *power* of a body of information is the amount of non-redundant information it contains.

Informally, redundancy is that part of I which is in some sense unnecessary because it repeats information which is already in I. There is a close connection

---

† Part of this chapter is based on the paper by J. G. Wolff and A. J. Chipperfield called 'Unifying computing: inductive learning and logic' presented at the Expert Systems '90 conference in Reading, England, September 1990, and published in T. R. Addis and R. M. Muir (Eds), *Research and Development in Expert Systems VII*, Cambridge: Cambridge University Press, 1990, pages 263 to 276. The material is reproduced here with the kind permission of the publishers.

between the notion of redundancy and the intuitive concept of 'structure': wherever there is structure in information there is redundancy; information is structured to the extent that it contains redundancy.

Searching for efficiency
Searching for efficiency in information means, for the most part, searching for redundancy in information and removing it wherever it is found:

(1) Redundancy means repetition of information and repetition of information means redundancy. More strictly, there is redundancy when a pattern of information repeats more often than other patterns of the same size.
(2) Finding the repeating patterns which represent redundancy means comparing or *matching* patterns. Where two or more patterns, or parts of patterns, are the same, there is likely to be redundancy.
(3) Redundancy may be reduced by merging or *unifying* patterns or parts of patterns which are the same, making one copy instead of two or more.
(4) This sounds simple enough but it can be complicated because there are often many alternative ways in which a given pattern or part of it may be unified. Finding a good set of unifications for the repeating patterns in a body of information amongst all the many other possible sets of unifications means a process of searching. Because the search space is usually very large, often infinite, it is necessary to use a hill climbing technique — or something equivalent — to achieve an effective search in a reasonable time.

In short, extracting redundancy means searching for patterns which match each other and unifying them. To find and extract as much redundancy as possible means searching for the largest possible value of R:

$$R = \sum_{i=1}^{i=n} (f_i - 1)s_i ,$$

f is the frequency of the ith member of a set of n patterns and s is its size in bits.

In this summary of the SP principles, the word 'unifying' has been used to mean the merging of matching patterns. This word has been chosen to describe the idea because there is a clear similarity with the concept of 'unification' as it is used in logic programming systems like Prolog. But the two ideas are not exactly the same — unification in logic is a more complicated idea than unification in SP.

The SP search space
The SP search space is illustrated in Fig. 5.1.† Each point in the diagram represents a body of information or a knowledge structure with its own measure of simplicity and power. Each curve in the diagram illustrates the tradeoff between simplicity and power: big knowledge structures are usually more powerful than little ones and *vice*

---

† Figs 2.2, 4.2 and 5.1 are similar but not identical. Despite their similarity it has seemed best to present them separately rather than merge them into a single diagram.

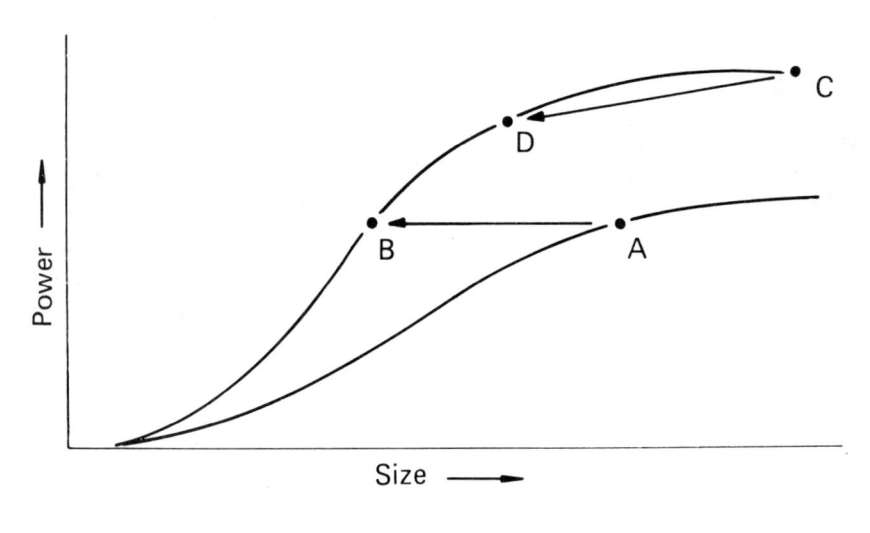

Fig. 5.1.

versa. The upper curves represent sets of relatively efficient knowledge structures at varying levels of simplicity and power while the lower curves represent relatively inefficient knowledge structures varying in a similar way.

Kinds of search

The process of searching for efficiency in information can take several different forms. There are at least four dimensions which can be used to classify the various search methods. Here is one of the choices which can be made:

(1) *Preserving power*. The search may be constrained to preserve all the power in the body of information, *I*. A search for efficiency in this case means a search for a minimum size consistent with preserving the power in *I*. This in turn means searching for redundancy in *I* and extracting redundancy wherever possible. In the diagram, a transformation in a knowledge structure which moves it from A to B means increasing its efficiency without reducing its power.

(2) *Sacrificing power*. The constraint in (1) may be relaxed. A search for efficiency in this case means extraction of redundancy, as in (1), but it also means that, if the circumstances are right, the knowledge structure may be moved 'down market' by sacrificing power in order to gain an overall increase in efficiency. In the diagram, a transformation in a knowledge structure which moves it from C to D reduces its power but increases the ratio of power to size and thus increases efficiency.

Independent of these two modes are two other options:

(1) *Exhaustive search*. In the case of small knowledge structures which have a correspondingly small search space, the space may be searched exhaustively.
(2) *Hill climbing search*. In all other cases, the search spaces are so large that it is

necessary to apply hill climbing techniques in order to do a reasonably effective search with a realistic amount of computational effort.

Within the scope of the hill climbing concept, there is another dimension:

(1) *Broad searching* means searching which is relatively thorough. The cost of a thorough search is that it is hungry for computing resources and is likely to need high levels of parallelism in processing to achieve adequate speed. The benefit of thorough search in a computing system is that the system can be relatively flexible and intelligent.
(2) *Narrow searching*. Where computational resources are limited — as they are in ordinary computers — the search process may be constrained in various ways so that relatively large portions of the search space can never be reached. This kind of constraint reduces computational costs but means that the computing system has less flexibility and more of that 'brittleness' and stupidity which characterizes current systems.

Amongst existing computer languages, those classified as 'declarative' seem to provide a relatively broad search compared with those classified as 'procedural'. Procedural languages seem to have been developed as a response, at least in part, to the limited power of present-day computers. The greater power of computers in the future should allow the declarative style to flower.

The fourth choice which we have in creating search mechanisms is related to the distinction between broad and narrow searching but is distinct from it:

(1) *One path and one answer*. The search process may thread one path through the search space and give one 'best' answer.
(2) *Multiple paths and multiple answers*. Alternatively, the search process may follow two or more paths through the search space and give a set of answers, graded in terms of the efficiency they represent. These parallel paths may be followed in sequence — in which case we have the effect of 'back-tracking'. If there are sufficient resources, these alternative paths may be explored in parallel.

Related work

This sub-section summarizes the main affinities of the SP concepts, apart from the origins of the ideas in autonomous inductive learning, which I described in Chapter 1.

The idea of searching for economical structures, which is a central part of the theory, features in some research on 'neural' computing (see, for example, Campbell *et al.* (1989), and Hinton & Sejnowski (1986)) and it has been recognized for many years in research on cluster analysis and numerical taxonomy (e.g. Boulton & Wallace, 1970). The SP theory presents a view of computing which is not tied to any particular architecture (such as neural networks) and which is in several other respects different from work on neural computing or cluster analysis.

The probabilistic nature of the SP system provides a link with work on the probabilistic analysis of English (Garside *et al.*, 1987) but there are many differences in objectives, methods and results between that work and the SP programme of research.

The idea of viewing all kinds of formal system and computing system in terms of information has been developed as 'algorithmic information theory' (see, for example, Chaitin (1987, 1988)). That work focuses on issues of completeness and decidability in formal systems whereas the SP theory focuses on how an analysis of formal systems in terms of information and redundancy may illuminate issues in knowledge representation and the process of computation itself. As was said in Chapter 1, Chaitin's ideas about the nature of redundancy appear to enhance rather than replace Shannon's ideas on which the SP theory is based.

The SP language, to be described below, owes its greatest debt to Prolog (see, for example, Clocksin & Mellish (1981)) but differs from Prolog in several ways. There is some resemblance between SP and 'unification grammars' (see, for example, Shieber (1986)) but also significant differences. The most important difference between SP and these systems is that the pattern matching and unification processes in SP are much more general and they are set within a broader theoretical frame. This generalization gives SP capabilities — like a capacity for autonomous inductive learning — which are not exhibited by Prolog or by other systems of that type.

Although, as explained earlier, *unification* in SP is distinct from and simpler than the concept of unification in logic, there is enough similarity to justify using the same term in both cases. The uses of unification in its traditional sense have been reviewed by Siekmann (1989) and by Knight (1989). The wide scope of the concept is recognized, particularly in the second of these reviews. As noted in Chapter 1, Muggleton & Buntine (1988) have shown how an 'inversion' of Robinson's (1965) 'resolution principle' (which uses unification) can serve as a learning mechanism with error correction by a human teacher.

Seen as a 'universal' abstract machine, SP has some similarity with the Ten15 system (Foster, 1989). However, the principles underlying SP are quite different from Ten15 and there are many differences in design objectives and expected capabilities of the two systems.

SP incorporates many of the concepts associated with object-oriented design (see, for example, Birtwistle *et al.* (1979) and Cook (1986)).

Although extraction of redundancy in information is a key part of the SP theory, the SP system is not a *reduction* system in the technical sense of that word (see, for example, Robinson (1988)). Although SP can imitate the effect of a *rewrite* system it does not use any rewriting technique in the technical sense of that term (see, for example, Baeten *et al.* (1987)).

The SP system may be loosely classified as a 'knowledge manipulation engine' like the FACT database system (e.g. McGregor *et al.*, 1987), the 'Intelligent File Store' (Lavington, 1988) or the integrated database and expert system described by Risch and others (1988) but there are many differences between SP and these systems in orientation and expected capabilities.

Is computing really about extraction of redundancy?
The proposition that computing is largely a matter of extracting redundancy from information looks implausible if you consider how easy it is to write a computer program which creates redundancy and the usefulness of redundancy in some aspects of computing. Here are some general points which are relevant to any discussion of this issue:

- The creation of redundancy by computing may be achieved by the use of commands like *copy*(X,Y) or commands which have an equivalent effect like *print*(X). Such commands do not, perhaps, represent the kind of inferential process which appears to be the essential 'core' of computing.
- The use of redundancy to reduce errors — in data transmission, for example — is compatible with the basic proposition: processes which correct errors in a stream of information containing redundancy appear to work by extracting that redundancy from the information.
- The use of redundancy to increase processing speed — in the indexing of a database, for example — reflects limitations in the search capability of the current generation of computers and does not, in itself, invalidate the basic proposition.
- The use of redundancy to increase the readability of computer programs, for example, is also compatible with the basic proposition if it is accepted that the SP principles apply to human cognition as well as computers. If brains, like computers, work by extracting redundancy from information then they need to have redundancy in incoming information in order to work properly.

But these points do not meet the apparent contradiction in the idea that extraction of redundancy can be the mechanism both for abstracting a grammar from a language sample and also for creating samples of the language from the grammar.

The answer seems to lie in the idea that the search process may take more than one path through the search space and may offer more than one solution to any problem. In general terms, an SP system can, in effect, create redundancy by showing a variety of different 'good' answers to the unification search. Here is an example, using the SP notation described in Chapter 4, to show how this might happen:

```
[([N _][V _][ADV _])
[N john]
[N mary]
[V walks]
[V runs]
[ADV fast]
[ADV slowly]]
```

→

```
[([N john][V walks][ADV fast])
[N mary]
[V runs]
[ADV slowly]]
```

OR

```
[([N mary][V walks][ADV fast])
[N john]
[V runs]
[ADV slowly]]
```

OR

```
           [([N john][V runs][ADV fast])
            [N mary]
            [V walks]
            [ADV slowly]]

            etc.
```

(The symbol '→' is not part of the SP language. It is used to show how the SP system may transform one SP object into another.)

The example does not use any OROs although it contains word classes (e.g. {*john mary*}) for which OROs have been used previously (e.g. in the examples in Chapter 4). There may be a case for dropping the ORO construct from the SP language. The idea of alternatives may best be handled within the search process.

Context and meaning in SP

A feature of SP which is sometimes misunderstood is how it handles notions of 'context' in the interpretation of data and the 'meanings' of symbols or other structures used in the system.

In many systems, the information which is visible to the user is a relatively small sub-set of the information which is relevant to understanding how the visible information will be used or what it means in the system. For example, most computing systems provide a square root function called something like *sqrt(X)*. A function like this may be used in computer programs but, typically, the user does not see the code which lies behind it and which gives it its meaning.

In SP, there are no hidden meanings, apart from the interpretive framework provided by the SP system itself. All kinds of knowledge are visible and are represented in one simple notation. This is true of 'data' and it is also true of any semantic structure or 'schema' which provides an interpretive context for those data. Any structure may be given a meaning by the user by associating it with the relevant semantic structure within a UAO or an OAO.

SP6

SP6 is a software simulation of SP, written in C, which runs on a Sun workstation. The following sub-sections describe the visible features of this prototype and some of its internal workings.

The SP language

In the SP system, all kinds of information or knowledge — 'data', programs', 'results' — are expressed in one simple language. The formal syntax for this language is given in Chapter 4 with a first informal description of the semantics. The semantics of the SP language, represented by parts of the SP6 simulation, is now much more precisely defined than the description in Chapter 4 but there are still some issues to be resolved. A goal of the development is the formal specification of the semantics of the SP language, perhaps using SP itself.

In the SP language, any item of information or knowledge is represented as an *object*. SP objects come in four main types:

- (...). Zero or more objects enclosed in round brackets are an *Ordered AND Object* (*OAO*). In an OAO, the order or sequence of the constituent objects is significant.
- [...]. Zero or more objects enclosed in square brackets are an *Unordered AND Object* (*UAO*). In a UAO, the order or sequence of the constituent objects is not significant. The concept of a UAO is similar to the concept of a 'set' in logic or, more accurately, a 'bag' because two or more of the constituents of a UAO may be identical.
- { ... }. Zero or more objects enclosed in curly brackets are an *OR Object* (*ORO*). In an ORO, the constituent objects are treated as alternatives in the context in which the ORO is found.
- Simple objects come in two sub-types:
  - A *symbol* is one or more alphanumeric characters. For the purpose of pattern matching, a symbol is an indivisible unit which matches in an all-or-nothing manner with other symbols. If the symbols are always one fixed length, boundary markers are not needed. In the SP6 version of the SP language, the symbols can vary in length which means that boundary markers (spaces or commas) are needed.
  - A *variable*, represented by an underscore ('_'), is similar to an unnamed variable in Prolog. It functions as a place marker which, in SP6, will match and unify with any one object and only one object. Future versions of SP will probably be designed so that a variable will match and unify with zero or more other objects.

Unlike Prolog, and most other systems of that kind, SP does not have named variables. The effect of naming can be achieved in SP by bracketing a 'name' with an object to be named inside a UAO or OAO, e.g. [Fred _]. Normally, a name will be a SP symbol but other kinds of objects may be used as names.

Every symbol in an SP object has a frequency value which shows how many identical copies of that symbol were unified to create the given symbol. In the examples presented later, frequency values are not shown in full because this makes the examples difficult to read. Instead, symbols with a frequency of 1 are shown in plain type and symbols with any frequency greater than 1 are shown in bold type.

Sets of symbols used in versions of the SP language may vary from large sets of variable-length character strings down to the familiar binary set of single characters, 0 and 1. The symbol set used in any given SP object controls the 'granularity' of the operations in SP. Where fine-grained pattern matching is required, information should be encoded using binary symbols or something similar. Where a coarser grain of matching is appropriate (as, for example, when there is a need to save on processing costs) then larger symbols should be used.

At some stage, it is likely that the OAO construct will be generalized to two-dimensional, three-dimensional or even four-dimensional structures as well as simple sequences. This will mean that the SP language can be used to represent such things as maps, three-dimensional models of real-world objects or a space–time continuum!

144 A PROTOTYPE OF THE SP SYSTEM [Ch. 5

The user interface
The user interface for SP6 exploits the interactive graphics facilities of the Sun workstation: bit-mapped screen, mouse, keyboard and window management software. Using two windows, SP6 displays an SP object to the user like this:

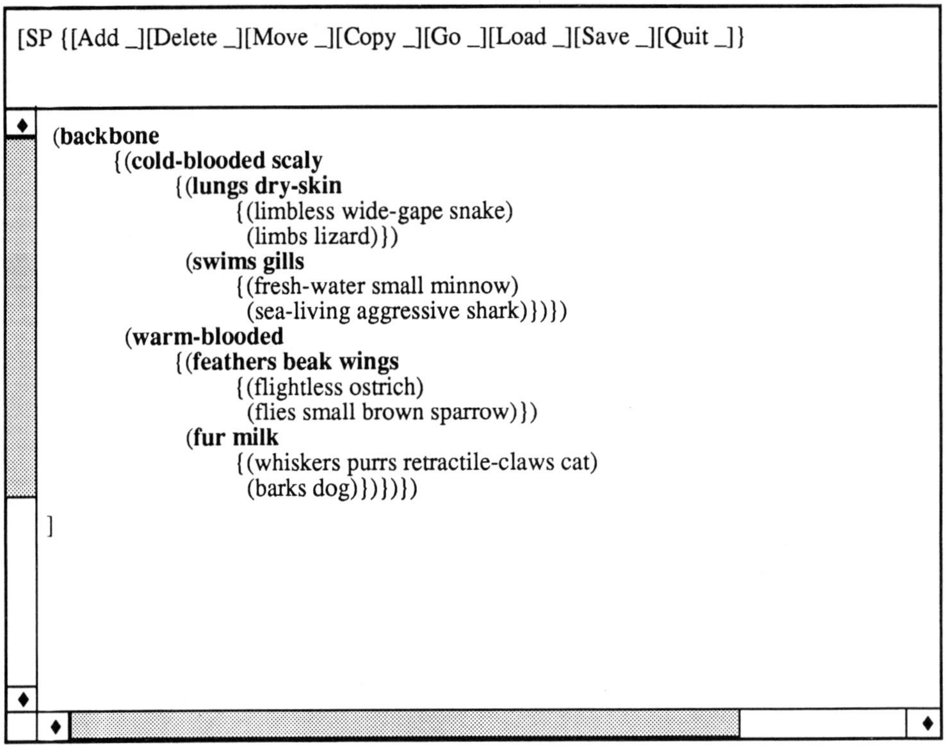

```
[SP {[Add _][Delete _][Move _][Copy _][Go _][Load _][Save _][Quit _]}


    (backbone
        {(cold-blooded scaly
            {(lungs dry-skin
                {(limbless wide-gape snake)
                 (limbs lizard)})
             (swims gills
                {(fresh-water small minnow)
                 (sea-living aggressive shark)})})
         (warm-blooded
            {(feathers beak wings
                {(flightless ostrich)
                 (flies small brown sparrow)})
             (fur milk
                {(whiskers purrs retractile-claws cat)
                 (barks dog)})})})
    ]
```

Fig. 5.2 — The user interface for SP6.

The parts of this object which are in the top window are used like a menu bar to initiate functions and to control the system. This 'control panel' for the prototype does not have the semantics of SP. It is shown like this as a cosmetic arrangement to convey the idea that, in a fully developed SP system, SP may be written in SP and the SP language may provide a complete environment which supports all functions and all kinds of interaction with the system.

The lower window shows the 'user object' or 'corpus': an object which represents all knowledge which is under the control of the user. Amongst its constituent objects there may be an object which is analogous to 'data' in a conventional system and another which is analogous to 'program'. The user object or corpus has the full semantics of SP as currently understood.

The functions which are provided for the user include:

- Loading a new user object from a text file.
- Writing a user object to a text file.
- Structure editing functions — add, delete, copy, move — for the user object.

These are provided as 'buttons' on the control panel and also as single-character keyboard commands.
- A 'search' function which searches for efficiency in the user object. When this function is applied, the resulting form of the user object is displayed. The function may be applied as one operation or the user may step through the stages of compression, seeing intermediate results on the way.

Processing in SP6

The 'search' function, just mentioned, provides the semantics of the SP language and expresses the SP theory of computing, as currently understood.

In terms of the 'dimensions' described earlier, the search process in SP6 works like this:

- The search for efficiency in SP6 means searching for redundancy in the corpus and extracting it wherever possible but without removing any non-redundant information. In other words, the search process is designed to preserve all the power in the corpus. Exploring how power may be sacrificed to improve efficiency has not been attempted yet in developing the SP system.

    Although the intention has been to preserve all non-redundant information in the corpus some gets lost with certain kinds of structures. This defect should be cured in future versions of SP.
- The search process is systematic but not totally exhaustive. There are some kinds of redundancy which it cannot detect.
- A relatively unsophisticated kind of hill climbing technique is being used. In future versions of SP, there is scope for substantial improvements in the efficiency of the searching process (using 'efficiency' here in the sense of cutting out unnecessary repetition of operations).
- SP6 follows one path through the search space and gives one answer when it has extracted all the redundancy it can find.

Finding redundancy

SP6 searches for redundancy by searching for patterns which match each other. To do this, it makes systematic comparisons between all the constituent objects of the corpus and all sub-sets of the OAOs in the corpus, where the members of each sub-set are contiguous within the OAO from which they are drawn. SP6 does not compare sub-sets of UAOs although it would be relatively easy to extend the search in this way.

SP6 records all cases where two patterns match exactly. With two exceptions, a successful match between two objects means that they are the same type and that there is a one-to-one matching of the constituents. For OAOs, there is the additional constraint that the ordering of the matching constituents must be the same.

The two exceptions are:

- When a child of an OAO which is not an ORO is matched with a child of another OAO which is an ORO, the match succeeds if the first child matches any one child of the ORO.
- A variable will match any other object.

This treatment of OROs and variables is not wholly satisfactory. Later versions of SP will aim for a more streamlined method for handling these objects: it seems that the meanings of these constructs should be realized in the unification process and not in the matching process. Notice that, although the matching process gives a simple all-or-nothing result, *SP6 detects partial matches between objects*. This is because the all-or-nothing matching process is applied to sub-sets of OAOs as well as whole OAOs.

The unification process

Where two patterns match, they may be unified. This is achieved in four main ways:

- Where two objects match and are siblings within a UAO or ORO, they may be unified to give an object which replaces them within the parent. For example:

    [A A B] → [**A** B]

- Where two objects match and have an 'uncle/nephew' relationship within a UAO (or grand-uncle/grand-nephew relationship, etc.), they may be unified and replaced by an object in the location of the nephew. In effect, the uncle 'moves' to merge with its nephew. Here is a simple example:

    [A (A B) C] → [(**A** B) C]

    The argument here is that if the uncle moves to join the nephew then there is no loss of non-redundant information because the uncle is merely 'associated' with the other objects and this association is not destroyed by the unification. But if the nephew moves to join the uncle then there is loss of non-redundant information about its position relative to other objects: the fact that it precedes B within (A B) in the example.

- Where there is a partial match between two OAOs which are siblings within a UAO, the parts which match are merged to make one pattern and the parts which do not match are formed into an ORO. For example,

    [(A B C D E F) (A B C X Y Z)]
    →
    (**A B C** {(D E F)(X Y Z)})

    In SP6, there are constraints on when this kind of unification can be done which are designed to ensure that there is no loss of power in the corpus.

- In cases where the other three kinds of unification cannot be applied, SP6 may achieve unification by the creation of 'references' and 'definitions'. A reference is a UAO containing a 'reference tag' and a variable like this: [%1 _]; the corresponding definition is a UAO containing the same reference tag and another object — the 'body' of the definition — which is typically an OAO. The following example illustrates how references and a definition may be used to effect the extraction of redundancy in an object:

    (A B C D E F G H I J K L X Y Z A B C D E F G H I J K L)
    →
    ([%1 (**A B C D E F G H I J K L**) X Y Z [%1 _])

The general idea is to record the repeating pattern once within the body of a definition, leaving references to mark all other locations where the original patterns came from. With this mechanism, redundancy may be extracted without losing the non-redundant information about where the original patterns were located within the corpus.

References and definitions are only created where the redundancy which is extracted is greater than the information 'cost' of the symbols which are introduced by the transformation. With one qualification, references and definitions do not have any formal status in the SP theory. A reference tag is simply a 'pattern' with the same status as any other pattern. The mechanisms in SP for pattern matching and unification may be used to bring the body of a definition back into the context whence it came.

The qualification, just mentioned, is that the SP system knows that the reference tags are information which has been added by the system and that they are distinct from information supplied to the system by the user. For this reason, the system can undo references and definitions which it has created at one stage in the search for efficiency if, at a later stage, they are no longer needed.

Scheduling of processes

The search function of SP6 extracts redundancy in an iterative way like this:

> While no more extractable redundancy in the corpus do
> BEGIN
> > 1 Search for redundancy in the corpus by identifying matching patterns.
> > 2 Select the pair of matching patterns which represents the greatest amount of redundancy.
> > 3 Unify the selected pair of matching patterns.
> END

The iteration of these three operations constitutes a simple form of hill climbing search. SP6 follows one path to the best result it can find. Future versions of SP should be able to follow more than one path and thus to be able to show a set of alternative results for any given object.

EXAMPLES

The examples described in this section are intended to illustrate some of the scope of the SP concepts and some of the variety of capabilities and potential applications of a fully developed SP system.

I stress that *the variety of capabilities illustrated in this section are the product of one unifying concept — the search for efficiency in information*. Any one of the functions described can be done more effectively by some existing computing system or program but, as far as I know, there is no existing system which embraces all these capabilities as a product of one organizing principle.

Most of the examples are small, partly to make the concepts easy to understand and partly because the search processes in SP6 are relatively inefficient and this can mean lengthy processing with larger examples. Although the examples are small, the processes which they illustrate seem to be general and can probably be scaled up to handle realistically complicated problems.

As already mentioned, bold type is used in the examples to highlight symbols which have been created by unifying two or more other symbols.

Remember that the symbol '→' used in the examples is not part of the SP language but is used to show how one SP object is transformed into another in the course of computing.

Inductive learning

I am using the term inductive learning to mean a process of organizing knowledge which is done without explicit instruction or intervention from a (human or non-human) 'teacher' and without recourse to any additional knowledge apart from the learning techniques themselves. Children seem to learn the grammar of their mother tongue in this kind of way (although that is a debating issue). People — in contrast to ordinary computers — are rather good at creating new abstract concepts by observing concrete examples.

As I described in Chapter 1, research in inductive learning and, more specifically, research into how children learn language was where many of the ideas for SP originated.

Discovering word segments, classes and shared structure

[
    (p e t e r m e e t s j a n e)
    (p e t e r a d m i r e s j a n e)
    (p e t e r m e e t s p e t e r)
    (p e t e r a d m i r e s p e t e r)
    (j a n e m e e t s p e t e r)
    (j a n e a d m i r e s p e t e r)
    (j a n e m e e t s j a n e)
    (j a n e a d m i r e s j a n e)
]

→

([%1 {(**p e t e r**)(**j a n e**)}] {(**m e e t**)(**a d m i r e**)} **s** [%1 _])

Fig. 5.3.

The first example (Fig. 5.3) illustrates how, from a simple sub-set of English, the SP system infers a structure which is equivalent to a grammar for the sub-set.

The OAOs in the first SP object may be seen as 'sentences'. By analogy with the way people normally talk, there is no explicit marker for the end of one word within a sentence and the beginning of the next. Likewise, there is nothing explicit in the example sentences to mark classes of syntactically equivalent words.

SP6 transforms the first object into the second by searching for redundancy and removing it wherever possible. The effect of this search is to identify the words within the sentences as discrete entities and to group the words into syntactic classes. The search process also has the effect of isolating the terminal 's' in 'meets' and 'admires' rather in the same way that a linguist would identify that terminal 's' as a distinct substructure ('morpheme') within these words.

SP6 recognizes that the ORO {(p e t e r)(j a n e)} occurs in two contexts, at the start of each sentence and at the end. It removes the redundancy by placing the structure arbitrarily in one of the two locations (first in the example) giving it a label ('%1') and leaving this label as a 'reference' at the other location (last) where the structure can occur. A tag like '%1' is equivalent to a label like 'NP' used in conventional grammars.

Discovering phrase groupings

>   [
>   (the tall lady with long hair owns the little dog)
>   (the little dog with long hair follows the tall lady)
>   (the tall lady pats the little dog with long hair)
>   (the little dog likes the tall lady with long hair)
>   ]
>   →
>   [
>   ([%2 ([%5 **(the tall lady)**][%4 **with long hair**)])] owns [%3 **(the little dog)**])
>   ([%1 ([%3 _] [%4 _])] follows [%5 _])
>   ([%5 _] pats [%1 _])
>   ([%3 _] likes [%2 _])
>   ]

Fig. 5.4.

The example in Fig. 5.4 shows how SP6 may identify 'phrase structures' within 'sentences' in a simple language and how hierarchical relationships amongst phrase groupings may be discovered. To save on processing time, the granularity of the examples has been increased by representing words as atomic symbols.

Repeating patterns like 'the tall lady' and 'with long hair' are recognized and reduced to single instances. Each such instance is made into a 'definition' by bracketing it with a 'reference tag' within a UAO. A corresponding 'reference' is left in every location where the pattern was deleted. Notice how the system can embed one phrase within another. In general, it can create arbitrarily complex grammars with an arbitrarily large number of 'levels'. As can be seen in Fig. 5.3, SP6 is quite capable of mixing OROs and 'references' freely within an object if that is called for by the input.

Amongst the many differences between these two examples and how children learn a language, there is one which deserves comment here. A prominent feature of 'natural' grammar induction, which is missing from these examples, is the phenomenon of generalization.

In learning a language, people very quickly create or infer rules which are more general than the linguistic evidence on which they are based. This can be interpreted

150 A PROTOTYPE OF THE SP SYSTEM [Ch. 5]

in terms of the SP theory as a deliberate loss of power in the grammars in order to gain efficiency, as was described earlier. These issues are discussed in Chapter 2. Exploring how the SP system may gain efficiency by sacrificing power and thus create generalizations is something for the future.

Induction of a class hierarchy

[
(backbone cold-blooded scaly lungs dry-skin limbless
   wide-gape snake)
(backbone warm-blooded fur milk whiskers purrs retractile-claws cat)
(backbone cold-blooded scaly lungs dry-skin limbs lizard)
(backbone warm-blooded feathers beak wings flightless ostrich)
(backbone cold-blooded scaly swims gills fresh-water small minnow)
(backbone warm-blooded fur milk barks dog)
(backbone warm-blooded feathers beak wings flies
   small brown sparrow)
(backbone cold-blooded scaly swims gills sea-living aggressive shark)
]
→
(backbone
   {(cold-blooded scaly
      {(lungs dry-skin
         {(limbless wide-gape snake)
         (limbs lizard)})
      (swims gills
         {(fresh-water small minnow)
         (sea-living aggressive shark)})})
   (warm-blooded
      {(feathers beak wings
         {(flightless ostrich)
         (flies small brown sparrow)})
      (fur milk
         {(whiskers purrs retractile-claws cat)
         (barks dog)})})})

Fig. 5.5.

The example in Fig. 5.5 illustrates how SP6 may create a class hierarchy or taxonomic hierarchy in the manner of numerical taxonomy or cluster analysis. The example also illustrates how SP6 can create a 'discrimination net' like the the ones produced by Quinlan's ID3 (1983). The first object shows a set of animals, each with some distinctive attributes. OAOs have been used rather than the more appropriate

UAOs because SP6 has been constrained to look for patterns and sub-groupings only within OAOs and not within UAOs. Future versions of SP will plug this gap.

The second object is, in effect, a class hierarchy or discrimination net with attributes at appropriate levels. In the spirit of object-oriented design (discussed below), redundancy is minimized by placing each attribute at a level in the hierarchy where it applies to all the lower levels and none of the higher levels.

Logic and logical inferences
The two examples in this section illustrate how the SP language may be used to express logical propositions and how, as a by-product of its search for efficiency in information, the SP system may do the kinds of things which are normally regarded as logical inference.

In this area, SP6 has a weakness which should be cured in future versions. SP6 is designed so that variables (shown with the symbol '_') will match and unify with one SP object and only one object. It looks now as if the number of objects to be matched and unified with any given variable should not be set at an arbitrary value but should be determined by the search for efficiency. This would mean that any given variable would match and unify with zero or more SP objects.

A simple syllogism

    [[mortal [man _]] [man Socrates]]
    →
    [mortal [**man** Socrates]]

Fig. 5.6.

The example in Fig. 5.6 (which was also given in Chapter 4) is modelled on the well-known syllogism: 'All men are mortal. Socrates is a man. Therefore, Socrates is mortal'. In logical notation the syllogism may be written like this:

$$\forall x \in \text{man} . \text{mortal}(x) \land \text{Socrates} \in \text{man} \Rightarrow \text{mortal (Socrates)}.$$

Given the current meaning of '_' as 'one and only one', the object [man _] may be unified with any UAO which contains the symbol 'man' and one other object. Thus it may be read as 'any man with one attribute' rather than the more general 'any man' or 'all men'. If we ignore the restriction on the meaning of [man _] then [mortal [man _]] should be read as, 'Any man is mortal' or 'All men are mortal'.

[man Socrates] should be read as 'Socrates is a man'.

The object created by SP, [mortal[man Socrates]], should be read as 'Socrates is a man and he is mortal'. This covers the meaning of the conventional conclusion ('Socrates is mortal') and also includes one of the premises of the syllogism — that 'Socrates is a man'. There are two points here which deserve comment:

- The first point is that any version of SP which is designed to preserve power in a

knowledge structure — like SP6 — should preserve logical premises along with any inferences which may be drawn. The apparent difference between this style of working and the conventional style (where only the inference is given) is more cosmetic than real. Conventional systems for logic do normally preserve logical premises but only display the inferences. The display mechanisms in SP could, perhaps, be designed to picked out inferences for attention in a similar way.
- The second point is that this version of SP6 has actually failed to preserve one of the premises in this example (that 'All men are mortal') although, in designing the system, it was intended that it should not lose power in its knowledge structures. This weakness in SP6 should be cured in later versions of SP when the meaning of '_' is changed to become 'zero or more objects'. In this case, the SP system should work like this:

>[[mortal[man _]][man Socrates]]
>→
>[mortal[**man** Socrates _]]

The variable remains in the final object because unification with 'Socrates' does not exhaust the 'or more' part of its meaning. The result should be read as 'Socrates, and all other men, are mortal', a conclusion which covers the meaning of 'Socrates is mortal' and preserves the meaning of both of the original premises.

Transitive relations

>[[equals A B _ _] [equals B C _ _] [equals C D _ _]]
>→
>[**equals C D A B**]

Fig. 5.7.

The example of Fig. 5.7 illustrates how, from the premises that 'A equals B and B equals C and C equals D', the SP system can infer that A, B, C and D are all equal. Like the previous example, this example is not completely accurate because the variable ('_') means 'one and only one' instead of 'zero or more'. Given the current meaning of the SP variable, an object like [**equals A B _ _**] means 'A and B and two other unspecified objects are all equal'. The two instances of '_' are needed for unification with the other objects.

If '_' had its proper meaning then a transitive relation like 'A equals B' would be represented in SP as [**equals A B _**] which may be read as 'A equals B and there may be other objects which are equal to A and B'. The variable shows that unification may add other objects to the relationship and thus marks the relationship as transitive. By contrast, an intransitive relationship such as 'likes' may be represented as (**likes A B**). This is an ordered relationship because the fact of A liking B does not mean that B likes A.

Notice that this example would not give a valid conclusion if the relationship were, say, 'not-equals'. This and other examples point to the conclusion that negation will require special treatment in SP, a point discussed below.

A comparison with Prolog

To represent a transitive relationship like 'equals' in an established logic programming system like Prolog, it is necessary to include a rule like this:

equals(X,Z) :- equals(X,Y), equals(Y,Z).

This rule means 'X equals Z if X equals Y and Y equals Z'; X, Y and Z are all variables. The inclusion of this rule along with 'facts' like equals(a,b) and equals(b,c) allows the system to infer that equals(a,c) is true.

This way of representing the transitive nature of 'equals' works well enough but is distinctly more cumbersome than what is needed in SP. In addition, a rule like the one just shown needs to be generalized to cope with other transitive relations like 'ancestor', 'before', 'above', 'bigger' etc. and the generalization is relatively complicated. SP seems to have an advantage over established systems in this area.

TRUE and FALSE in SP

At present, SP has no explicit concepts of TRUE and FALSE. As with systems like Prolog, we may adopt the 'closed world hypothesis' and suppose that truth is whatever the system knows about and everything else is false. In this case, the answer to a 'query' is 'true' if the query unifies with an object in a given knowledge structure, otherwise it is 'false'.

In SP it is natural to generalize this model of TRUE and FALSE to take advantage of the fact that SP can recognize partial matches between structures as well as full matches. Given this feature of SP, we may recognize degrees of truth and falsehood. If a query unifies completely with an object in the knowledge base then it is unequivocally true in terms of that knowledge base. If it does not unify with anything in the knowledge base then it is unequivocally false. In all other cases, it has some degree of truth corresponding to the amount of unification which has been achieved.

Does SP need a negation operator ('not') and, if so, what is its status within the SP theory? In the spirit of 'simplicity and power' it would be nice if negation in SP could be a by-product of mechanisms which are already established in the system.

One possibility is that 'not' is simply a symbol (with the same status as all other symbols) which may used as a 'spoiler' to prevent a given object unifying with any identical copy of that object. Thus [not TRUE] would not unify with TRUE and would therefore be 'false' in the terms which I have sketched.

One difficulty with this idea is that the 'spoiler' would never eliminate partial unification and would thus never have the meaning 'unequivocally false' as one would wish. Another problem is that [not [not TRUE]] would not mean the same as TRUE as one would wish. There may be a case for creating a special negation operator in SP. This and related questions are issues to be explored in the future.

Knowledge-based systems and probabilistic inference

This section presents two examples showing how SP may be used in knowledge-intensive applications.

154   A PROTOTYPE OF THE SP SYSTEM   [Ch. 5

A database

[
    [[Name (John _)] [Address (_ New Street _)]]
    [Database
        [[Name (John Smith)] [Address (10 New Street Thistown)]]
        [[Name (Mary Jones)] [Address (22 Old Street Thatcity)]]
        [[Name (Bilbo Baggins)] [Address (Bag End The Hill Hobbiton)]]
    ]
]
→
[Database
    [[Name (**John** Smith)] [[%1 **Address**] (10 **New Street** Thistown)]]
    [[Name (Mary Jones)] [[%1 _] (22 Old Street Thatcity)]]
    [[Name (Bilbo Baggins)] [[%1 _] (Bag End The Hill Hobbiton)]]
]

Fig. 5.8.

The sixth example (Fig. 5.8) is intended to show how the SP language may be used to represent the kind of information that might appear in a conventional database management system. It is also intended to show how the SP language may be used in a 'query-by-example' style to retrieve information from the database.

The object labelled 'Database' is like a table of names and addresses in a relational DBMS. It is bracketed with another object representing an incomplete record of one person's name and address. The result of matching and unification in SP is that this incomplete record is unified with the complete record within the database which is most similar. In this way, the missing parts of the record are found.

What happens when there is more than one record in the database which 'fits' the query? SP6 only shows one result (the best one it can find) but I expect future versions of SP to be able to show a set of alternative results, each with a measure of its efficiency (or, more strictly, an estimate).

In this example, the 'database' actually contains redundancy in the form of repeated occurrences of the words 'Name' and 'Address'. SP6 has removed some of this redundancy by creating a reference to 'Address'. It has not created a reference to 'Name' because it does not represent enough redundancy to warrant the 'expense' of the references. Eliminating the kind of redundancy represented by repeated instances of 'Name' and 'Address' may be done more effectively by recasting the database in a form something like this:

[Database
    ([Name _][Address _])
    ([_(John Smith)][_ (10 New Street Thistown)])
    ([_(Mary Jones)][_ (22 Old Street Thatcity)])
    ([_(Bilbo Baggins)][_ (Bag End The Hill Hobbiton)])
]

However, this raises some questions about how matching and unification should be done which have not yet been answered.

An expert system

```
[
    [cloud [black [cold _]]]
    [cloud
        {[black
            {[warm {rain #}]
            [cold {hail snow #}]}]
        [white dry]
        [clear-sky
            {[warm {drought #}]
            [cold {frost #}]}]}]
    [March [wind strong]]
    [{June July August} warm]
    [{October November} fog]
]
→
[
    [**cloud**
        {[**black**
            {[warm {rain #}]
            [**cold** {hail snow #}]}]
        [white dry]
        [clear-sky
            [warm {drought #}]
            [cold {frost #}]]}]
    [March [wind strong]]
    [{June July August} warm]
    [{October November} fog]
]
```

Fig. 5.9.

Fig. 5.9 is intended to show how the SP language may be used to represent rules of the kind associated with 'expert systems'. The hash symbol ('#') in this example should be read as a 'null' alternative to other objects in any ORO where it appears.

As with Fig. 5.8, the knowledge in the system can be accessed by bracketing the 'knowledge base' with an SP object which represents a 'query'. In this example, the object [cloud [black [cold _]]] may be read as 'What do black clouds mean when the temperature is cold?' This query unifies with the object [cloud {[black {[warm {rain #}][cold {hail snow #}]}] showing that hail or snow is likely but not certain and that, if the temperature were 'warm', then rain would be a possibility.

Probabilities

Every symbol in an SP object has a frequency value. If the knowledge-base has been 'tuned' to the real world then these frequencies will reflect the frequencies of corresponding objects and events in the world. Given this kind of information, it should be possible to derive conditional probabilities for SP predictions but this has not been given any serious attention yet.

Object-oriented concepts: class hierarchies with cross classification, inheritance and part–whole relations

```
[
    [person [name Tom] _ _ [profession [tinker _]][gender [male _]]]
    [person [name _]
        [anatomy ([head ([eyes ...][nose ...] ...)]
                  [body ...][ legs ...])]
        [functions [eats ...][sleeps ...][breathes ...]]
        [profession
            {[ tinker ...]
             [tailor ...] ...}]
        [gender
            {[male ...]
             [female ...]}]
    ]
]
→
[person [name Tom]
    [anatomy ([head ([eyes ...] [nose ...] ...)][body ...] [legs ...])]
    [functions [eats ...] [sleeps ...] [breathes ...]]
    [profession
        {[tinker ...]
         [tailor ...] ...}]
    [gender
        {[male ...]
         [female ...]}]
]
```

Fig. 5.10.

Fig. 5.5 showed how SP6 can derive class hierarchies from appropriate input. The example of Fig. 5.10 shows cross-classification in SP and the way SP supports a notion of 'inheritance of attributes' which is comparable with the notion of inheritance in computer languages like Simula or Smalltalk. In the example, sets of three dots ('...') have been used to show where more information would go in a more fully developed description.

The second part of the first object in Fig. 5.10 is a schema for the concept of 'person' showing how, using UAOs and OAOs, a person has a name, an anatomy, a set of functions, a profession and a gender. These are components or parts of the schema and can be divided into sub-parts down to any desired level of detail. In short, they represent part–whole relations in the schema.

The sub-divisions of the profession and gender categories are orthogonal sub-classes of the class person. Classification and cross-classification can be expressed quite straightforwardly in the SP language down any number of levels using OROs. Notice how SP integrates the notions of part–whole hierarchy and class-inclusion hierarchy. To my knowledge, no other OO language integrates these two ideas as fully as SP.

Inheritance and the description of an 'instance' using SP

This schema for the class 'person' is bracketed with an SP object representing one particular person, 'Tom'. This description of Tom identifies him as a person and gives his profession and his gender but leaves out all the general information about anatomy and functions.

The SP system unifies the description of 'Tom' with the schema for 'person'. What this means, in effect, is that all the general information about people becomes available for use within the description of Tom. In 'object-oriented' terms, the description of Tom inherits the attributes of 'person' together with the attributes of 'tinker' and 'male'. We do not need to say that Tom has a head, body and legs etc. because this is implied by saying that he is a person. Likewise, we do not need to spell out in detail what it means for him to be a tinker and to be male.

There is more discussion in Chapter 4 of how SP can support object-oriented concepts, including such ideas as the passing of 'messages' between objects.

Pattern recognition

```
[
    (i n f a r m a t i o n)
    (t a b l e)
    (y e l l o w)
    (i n f o r m a t i o n)
]
→
[
    (t a b l e)
    (y e l l o w)
    (i n f {a o} r m a t i o n)
]
```

Fig. 5.11.

Conventional computing systems often fail catastrophically as a result of small errors in data or programs. The example in Fig. 5.11 shows how SP can make an 'intelligent' guess about the probable identity of 'infarmation' despite the error which it contains. What happens is that the 'mis-spelled' pattern (i n f a r m a t i o n) is unified with (i n f o r m a t i o n), the OAO which is most similar to it in the example.

Means–ends analysis

The technique of 'means–ends analysis', used in some AI programs for solving problems, means finding a 'path' from a problem state to a solution state using available information. Working out a route between two places is an example of the kind of problem which can be solved using this technique.

Fig. 5.12, shows how SP can achieve this effect as a by-product of its search for efficiency in information. Like the examples of logic given earlier, this example will be improved when the SP variable has the meaning 'zero or more' rather than its present meaning of 'one and only one'. When the variable has the new meaning, multiple occurrences of '_' may be replaced by one.

158 A PROTOTYPE OF THE SP SYSTEM   [Ch. 5

Inferring a route

    [
        [before (_ Chester Crewe _ _)]
        [before (Bangor Chester _ _ _)]
        [before (_ _ _ Watford London)]
        [before (_ _ Crewe Watford _)]
    ]
    →

[before (Bangor **Chester Crewe Watford** London)]

Fig. 5.12.

In the example in Fig. 5.12, SP6 is supplied with a collection of 'facts' about the relationship between stations on the railway route from Bangor to London. From these separate facts it creates an OAO representing the sequence of stations on the route.

The variables are needed in facts like [before(_ _ **Crewe Watford** _)] to show that the line from Crewe to Watford is part of a longer line with other stations earlier and later. This example is similar to the example of Fig. 5.7 (transitive relations) and, like that example, more variables are needed than when the meaning of ' _ ' is changed to 'zero or more'.

The example may seem trivial but it appears to capture the essence of what is meant by means–ends analysis and is likely to generalize to more ambitious cases. Unlike conventional means–ends analysis, the system works out the route immediately and does not wait to be set a problem like 'Is there a route between Bangor and London?' However, a question like that can be expressed as [**before(Bangor _ London)**] (with the preferred meaning of ' _ ') and unification with the available knowledge will supply an affirmative answer.

Plans and automatic planning

Three of the key constructs in the SP language — OAOs, UAOs and OROs — map onto key concepts in the representation of plans:

- A sequence of tasks, activities or events in a plan may be represented with an OAO.
- Where two or more activities may run in parallel or where their order is unimportant they may be bracketed together within a UAO.
- Where two or more activities are alternatives within a plan, this may be shown using an ORO. Alternatives are not often shown in project plans but the concept is recognised in the term 'contingency planning'.

Apart from representing plans, SP seems to have potential for creating plans automatically. In its simplest form, automatic planning is very much like means–ends analysis. Fig. 5.12 illustrates the point if the names of stations are replaced by the names of activities in a project plan.

Natural language processing

The syntax of the SP language is similar to that of systems like BNF or unaugmented context-free phrase-structure grammars. This may suggest that the SP language suffers from the same limitations as BNF or unaugmented CF-PSGs in expressing the kinds of structures found in the syntax of natural languages.

The section of Chapter 4 entitled 'Context-sensitive power in SP' describes how the SP language may be used to represent the syntax of a fragment of the French language and, in particular, how it may provide an elegant alternative to existing mechanisms which have been developed to handle 'context-sensitive' features in natural language syntax. In this section, I give another, simpler example to show how the SP system may, in the future, handle discontinuous dependencies in syntax.

Consider these two sentences:

The man with red hair is tall.
The men with red hair are tall.

They illustrate the dependency which exists in English between the first noun of each of the two example sentences and the verb in each sentence. A singular noun in that position must be followed by a singular verb and likewise for plurals. This dependency is 'discontinuous' because the noun and the verb are not contiguous; the intervening structure ('with red hair' in the examples) can be arbitrarily large.

In SP, the relevant dependencies in these two sentences may be shown quite simply and directly like this:

```
[(The [N _] with red hair [V _] tall)
(_ [N man] _ [V is] _)
(_ [N men] _ [V are] _)].
```

The singular dependency is shown in the second OAO and the plural dependency in the third. To make sense of this and similar examples, the SP system will, in the future, need two capabilities which are not provided in SP6:

- The system should be able to detect the redundancy represented by the discontinuous N ... V pattern, in the three OAOs. SP6 can only detect the redundancy represented by groupings of contiguous symbols.
- The SP system should then be able to create *both* of the two possible unifications:
  - (The [N man] with red hair [V is] tall) from the first two OAOs.
  - (The [N men] with red hair [V are] tall) from the first and third OAOs.

The second capability means an ability in SP to follow more than one path through the space of possible unifications and an ability to find alternative solutions to a problem. For any one corpus, SP6 follows one path through the search space and presents only one answer.

If this kind of mechanism can be made to work it will provide a means of representing the structure of natural language which is apparently simpler and more direct than existing systems.

CONCLUSION

This early version of the SP system demonstrates several of the possibilities described in Chapter 4. There is a lot more work to be done in each of the areas which have been illustrated. For example, the demonstration of how an SP system may be used for logical inference is tentative and there are many unanswered questions. In particular, there is a need to understand whether and how a negation operator should be introduced into the system. The proposal for how discontinuous dependencies in syntax and other knowledge structures may be represented cannot yet be shown to work.

The work which we are doing now and which is planned for the future is of two kinds:

- We are continuing to study existing concepts in computing and trying to understand whether and how they may be mapped into the SP framework of ideas. A particular interest at present is number theory (including the familiar arithmetic operators) and how it may be accommodated in an SP system without ad hoc provision.
- In parallel with this work, we are developing new versions of the SP system exploring basic issues and trying to remedy weaknesses in SP6.

Here are some of the questions and issues which we are looking at in developing the system:

- Understanding more fully how 'broad' hill climbing search may be done. More specifically, there is a need to understand how the search can be done without repeating operations unnecessarily and how the search process can be designed so that all parts of the search space can be reached. The last point is closely related to the question of how 'discontinuous dependencies' may be represented in natural language syntax.
- There is a need to understand how the search process can follow more than one path through the search space and can offer alternative answers to problems. This is closely related to issues in logic, retrieval of information from knowledge bases and the parsing and interpretation of natural language.
- There is a need to explore the several ways in which the search for efficiency in SP may be constrained to become more 'narrow'. This is related to understanding how SP may imitate the effect of 'procedural' programming languages.

REFERENCES

Baeten, J. C. M., Bergstra, J. A., & Klop, J. W. (1987). Term re-writing systems with priorities. *Proceedings of the Conference on Re-writing Techniques and Applications, Bordeaux, France, May* 1987, pp 83–94.

Birtwistle, G. M., Dahl, O.-J., Myhrhaug, B., & Nygaard, K. (1979). *Simula Begin*, New York: Van Nostrand Reinhold.

Boulton, D. M., & Wallace, C. S. (1970). A program for numerical classification. *Computer Journal* 13, 63–69.

Campbell, C., Sherrington, D., & Wong, K. Y. M. (1989). Statistical mechanics and neural networks. In I. Aleksander (Ed.), *Neural Computing Architectures*, London: North Oxford Academic.

Chaitin, G. J. (1987). *Algorithmic Information Theory*. Cambridge: Cambridge University Press.

Chaitin, G. J. (1988). Randomness in arithmetic. *Scientific American* **259**(1), 80–85.
Clocksin, W. F., & Mellish, C. S. (1981). *Programming in Prolog*. Heidelberg: Springer-Verlag.
Cook, S. (1986). Languages and object-oriented programming. *Software Engineering Journal* **1**(2), 73–80.
Foster, J. M. (1989). The algebraic specification of a target machine. In C. G. Sennett (Ed.), *High Integrity Software*, London: Pitman, pp. 198–225.
Garside, R., Leech, G., & Sampson, G. (1987). *The Computational Analysis of English: a Corpus-Based Approach*, London: Longman.
Hinton, G. E. & Sejnowski, T. J. (1986). Learning and relearning in Boltzmann machines. Chapter 7 in D. E. Rumelhart and J. L. McClelland (Eds), *Parallel Distributed Processing*, Vol I. Cambridge MA: MIT Press, pp. 282–317.
Knight, K. (1989). Unification: a multidisciplinary survey. *ACM Computing Surveys* **21**(1), 93–124.
Lavington, S. H. (1988). An overview of knowledge manipulation engines and the Intelligent File Store. *Proceedings of the IEE Colloquium on Knowledge Manipulation Engines*, London. pp 1–4.
McGregor, D., McInnes, S., & Henning, M. (1987). An architecture for associative processing of large knowledge bases (LKBs). *Computer Journal* **30**(5), 404–412.
Muggleton, S., & Buntine, W. (1988). Machine invention of first-order predicates by inverting resolution. *Proceedings of the Fifth International Conference on Machine Learning*, Michigan. pp. 339–352.
Quinlan, J. R. (1983). Learning efficient classification procedures and their application to chess end games. In R. Michalski, J. G. Carbonell and T. Mitchell (Eds), *Machine Learning: an Artificial Intelligence Approach*, Palo Alto: Tioga.
Risch, T., Reboh, R., Hart, P., & Duda, R. (1988). A functional approach to integrating database and expert systems. *Communications of the ACM* **31**, 1424–1437.
Robinson, J. A. (1965). A machine-oriented logic based on the resolution principle. *Journal of the ACM* **12**(1), 23–41.
Robinson, J. A. (1988). Beyond Loglisp: combining functional and relational programming in a reduction setting. *Machine Intelligence*, **11**, 57–68.
Shannon, C. E., & Weaver, W. (1949). *The Mathematical Theory of Communication*. Urbana: University of Illinois Press.
Shieber, S. M. (1986). *An Introduction to Unification-Based Approaches to Grammar*. Stanford, CA: Center for the Study of Language and Information.
Siekmann, J. H. (1989). Unification theory. *Journal of Symbolic Computation* **7**(3-4), 207–274.

6

The expected benefits of a mature SP system

When the SP system is fully developed, I believe it will provide answers to several current problems in the application of computers and new opportunities in the use of computers. The purpose of this chapter is to focus on what the system may be good for and the practical problems it may solve. I have tried to paint a picture of the benefits and advantages which I expect from the system when it is mature.

Although there are issues to be resolved in this programme of research, both at an abstract level and in the more concrete details of how the system will work, I feel that enough progress has been made in developing the theory and in developing prototypes of the system to feel confident that the possibilities which I describe can be realized.

Even if the SP system itself fails to live up to expectations, the ideas described in this chapter provide a new perspective on current problems and, perhaps, a useful vision of new possibilities in the application of computers in the future.

SP concepts and conventional computing

The SP view of computing sees pattern matching, unification and search as fundamental operations. In current computing systems, these operations appear in a variety of guises and they are often not seen in those terms. They are often recreated repeatedly in different forms, both in the design of computing hardware and, more significantly, in the design of software systems.

Existing computing systems have developed piecemeal without a sufficiently comprehensive theory to guide their development. The result is a large range of different kinds of system with many problems of compatibility between systems and a confusing variety of concepts, philosophies and sub-cultures.

Although many existing concepts may be understood in terms of the SP theory, no existing system comes near to expressing the theory fully. The main aim in developing the SP system is to plug this gap. There are many potential advantages in designing a computing system which expresses the theory as accurately as possible and which is designed to perform the fundamental operations as efficiently as possible.

Evolution, not revolution

An issue which needs to be considered whenever new developments in computing are on offer is: what are people supposed to do with their existing systems and, in particular, what is to be done with existing software, which often represents a large investment? Any new development must provide a smooth transition from existing systems and should allow existing software to be used until it has become obsolete and would have to be rewritten anyway.

This is where the SP system should score. The SP computer may serve as a front end to existing systems and the SP language may serve as a framework for existing software, rather like a hierarchical system of directories. As old systems become obsolete they may be replaced progressively by software written in the SP language, running on the SP computer.

There is a second way in which the process of transition may be eased. If the SP language is indeed a universal medium for representing all kinds of knowledge, then it should be possible to represent the syntax and semantics of existing computer languages in SP. Given that knowledge, programs written in existing languages may be run on an SP computer. In this way, old software may run alongside new software; old and new software may be integrated; an existing investment in software may be preserved whilst gaining the advantages of the new system.

Universal language

Another thing which deserves some preliminary comment is the notion of SP as a 'universal' language. In the last sub-section and at several points below, I have suggested that the SP language may replace a variety of the more or less specialized languages which are currently in use.

The functionality of all computer languages can be extended easily by the addition of supplementary libraries. A programming language like C is typically extended with a library of functions like 'printf'. Smalltalk is normally supplied with an extensive library of classes. In this sense, all computer languages can be universal. Most things can be done with most languages provided that enough code is written to achieve what is needed in each case.

The SP language has been designed to be extensible in the same kind of way. The suggestion that the mature SP language may be universal should be translated into the more precise idea that, by comparison with other computer languages, the SP language is intended to provide a favourable combination of simplicity and power. The aim of the research programme is to create a language which can do a relatively wide variety of things with relatively little code, complexity or mechanism.

THE POTENTIAL BENEFITS OF SP

In general terms, the expected benefits of a mature SP system lie in a global simplification and streamlining of computing applications, better integration amongst applications, less re-invention of the wheel, simplification of the ways in which people interact with computers and more overall 'intelligence' in computers. The more specific benefits are described later in this chapter.

One of the potential benefits of the SP theory is to provide a unifying framework of ideas within which existing systems and concepts may be understood. Examples are described and discussed in Chapters 4 and 5. The theory may simplify thinking and discussion about existing systems and it may lead to better solutions to computing problems.

In the sections which follow, I describe the expected benefits of the SP system in terms of traditional categories but it should be born in mind that the SP theory breaks down traditional distinctions and attempts to replace them with an integrated view of different kinds of computing. There are many expected capabilities and advantages of the SP system in areas associated with the term *software engineering* but these benefits are married in a seamless way with expected capabilities and advantages in areas of computing associated with the terms *database*, *expert system* and *artificial intelligence*.

Knowledge management

The first area of application to be discussed is the storage, retrieval, organization and use of knowledge. The SP system should, *inter alia*, combine the functions of a database and an expert system. Its potential advantages over existing systems are described in the following sub-sections.

One simple language instead of several

In database systems like Ingres and Oracle there are three or more languages or representational schemes which users need to know:

- The format for representing knowledge — meaning tables in the case of relational databases or networks or trees in other cases.
- The language — like SQL or QUEL — for adding knowledge or retrieving knowledge from the database and for expressing constraints on knowledge within the database (e.g. the fact that the start date of some event cannot be later than the end date).
- A 'report writing' language for describing the layout of reports.
- A programming language like C or COBOL for writing the functions which cannot be expressed in any of the other languages and which is often needed as an environment in which the other languages may be embedded.

In the SP system, I envisage that all these different schemes, notations or languages will be replaced by the one simple SP language. The SP language may be used for describing the knowledge in the system. It may be used also as a query language in the manner of 'query-by-example' (as explained more fully below). The SP language may be used also for expressing constraints, as a report-writer language and for any other functions which are required.

The main advantage in this context of using one simple language instead of several different languages is that users of the system have less to learn. If, as proposed below, the knowledge-base language can be the same as the language used for 'programs', then database functions can be fully integrated with other kinds of software.

Expressive power and integration of knowledge

In the same spirit, I envisage that the SP language will be a 'universal' medium to store a wide variety of kinds of knowledge in a knowledge base in an efficient manner: logical propositions, the syntax and semantics of natural languages, speech, two-dimensional maps, text (including information about fonts and layout), rules of the kind used in expert systems, engineering design information (including three-dimensional models) — and other kinds of knowledge.

This is, admittedly, a bold claim for a language with an exceptionally simple syntax and it cannot yet be fully justified. I believe the expressive power of the language will derive from the flexible processes for pattern matching and unification in the semantics of the language. Amongst other things, these mechanisms will provide a capability for inheritance (similar to that provided in 'object-oriented' languages) which supports succinct expression of complex structures.

Whether or not the SP language lives up to expectations, I believe the objective is worthwhile. If a language can be found which combines simplicity with sufficient expressive power to represent, in an economical way, all the different kinds of knowledge one might wish to store in a computer, this will bring great benefits.

One advantage, as in the previous section, is that users of the system need learn just one simple language instead of several relatively complex languages. The more important benefit in this context is achieving seamless integration of many different kinds of knowledge without the many problems of compatibility which plague current systems.

Information retrieval

I expect the pattern matching and search capabilities of SP to support flexible and efficient retrieval of information from a knowledge base. This mode of retrieval is a generalization of the 'query-by-example' method often used in relational databases. Pattern matching allows information to be retrieved by identifier or 'key'. It also allows a database to function more flexibly as 'content addressable memory': any sub-set of a body of knowledge may be used to retrieve the whole body of knowledge.

Automatic organization of knowledge

I expect an SP knowledge base to have the kind of intelligence which is missing from conventional databases and which is partly realized in current expert systems. The main discussion of SP's potential for artificial intelligence is reserved for a later section. Here I describe one facet which is particularly relevant to the efficient management of knowledge-based systems.

An ability to learn new concepts from experience and to create class hierarchies automatically with cross-classification where appropriate means automatic normalization of databases and automatic organization of knowledge for efficiency. In the future, I envisage database systems which can derive efficient structures automatically from any knowledge with which they are supplied. This saves the labour of having to design knowledge structures by 'hand'. It has the potential to produce a more accurate result than any person. And it can mean much greater speed in achieving good structuring without the delays and expense of committees, reviews and discussion.

This is not science fiction. The SP6 prototype already demonstrates significant abilities of this kind. Some other relevant work is reviewed by Partridge (1989).

Software engineering

In spite of 'fourth generation' languages and the slowly maturing CASE tools and IPSEs, the process of developing new software and maintaining or upgrading existing software still has problems:

- Software development is often *slow*. If there is a pressing need for a given software system, delays mean costs and inconvenience.
- Software development is *labour-intensive* and correspondingly expensive.
- *Incompatibilies* between machines, operating system and languages means difficulties in re-using software in new contexts and difficulties in integrating software systems. The resulting need to translate software or adapt it, or develop interfaces to translate information from one system to another, means complexity, delays, costs and new sources of bugs.
- Software developers need extensive (and expensive) *training*.
- *Verification*. Notwithstanding the use of formal methods in software development, it is impossible to be sure that any significant piece of software is totally correct in the sense that it does exactly what its designers intended in all circumstances. Any significant body of software is likely to contain bugs.
- *Validation*. System designers can, and often do, fail to understand fully what the users want and, consequently, fail to capture the users' requirements in the system.

In the following sub-sections, I outline some of the causes of these problems and how they may be solved or at least alleviated by the SP system.

One simple language and one model of computing for all purposes

There are several different computer languages, specification formalisms and design notations in common use today — including diagrammatic notations and formalisms — and there are many other systems which are less commonly used.

Associated with these various languages and notations are several different perspectives or 'philosophies' about how software and related knowledge should be organized: 'entity-relationship models', 'data flow models', 'entity life histories', 'object-oriented design', 'logic programming', functional programming' and others.

Training software developers in these different languages, notations and perspectives takes time and money. The lack of clear guidelines about which formalism or perspective is appropriate in which contexts, and how they should be related, if at all, causes confusion and wasted effort.

In keeping with what I said earlier about the SP system in the management of knowledge, I believe that the SP language may serve as a wide spectrum language in software engineering with a wide range of potential applications. It may be used for systems analysis (describing entity-relationship models, entity life histories and data flows), it may be used for the 'formal' specification of software, for 'programming' in addition to the kinds of knowledge engineering applications discussed in the previous section.

Using one simple language for all types of software means less training and less confusion about how software development should be done. Carried to its logical conclusion it can eliminate all problems of compatibility between systems.

SP as an IPSE

Continuing the theme of the previous sub-section, the SP language may also serve as a general-purpose 'command language' for an operating system. In SP, the distinction between an operating system and other kinds of software disappears. The SP language may be used like an hierarchical directory and it may be used to represent the main elements of a project plan. Given its potential, already described, for storing the several kinds of knowledge generated in a typical development project — text, speech, diagrams etc. — the SP system may function as a conceptually simple and highly integrated IPSE. Its possible uses in project management are described in Chapter 7.

No refinement, verification or compiling

In a typical development project, two, three or more different formalisms, languages or notations will be used in different stages or parts of the development. There may be two or three translations between formalisms — from analysts' models to formal specifications and from formal specifications to program code. There is always some kind of compiling of the code into a form which the machine can use. If proper standards of quality are to be maintained, it will be necessary to check rigorously or 'prove' that each of these translations have been done correctly. The correctness of compilers must also be verified.

The whole process of translating between formalisms and proving the correctness of translations is labour-intensive and expensive. The complexity of the process means there is plenty of scope for making mistakes and there are corresponding problems in maintaining the quality of the final product.

In some CASE tools, some of this process of translation and checking has been automated. This is really an extension of the idea of compiling a programming language and it can give useful gains in speed and accuracy in the development process. But the process is still complicated and it still gives scope for errors.

The SP language has the potential to simplify the process of developing software dramatically. As a universal language it may be used in all stages and phases of development. An SP data model prepared during systems analysis may be incorporated directly in a software system without modification. A formal specification of a software system expressed in SP may be run immediately without translation into a programming language. All translations and all compiling may be eliminated. Since SP code is intended to be executed 'directly' without translation or compiling, there should be no need for 'verification' or proof that an implementation conforms to a specification.

The use of the SP language as an executable specification language, eliminating all translation between formalisms and all verification that translations have been done correctly, can bring four major benefits:

- It can save large amounts of manpower and corresponding expense.
- It can shorten the time needed to produce a working system. This is useful in itself and
- It means that iterative prototyping techniques can be used, giving prospective users good opportunities to validate the developing system and ensure that it meets their needs (Hekmatpour & Ince, 1986).

- It eliminates all errors arising from translation between formalisms, i.e. all errors arising from refinement and verification. This is a major source of errors in software and its total elimination would mean a dramatic improvement in the quality of software products.

Software re-use
The variety of languages and systems in use and the fact that they rarely integrate properly, one with another, means significant difficulties in re-using software in more than one context. Significant resources go into translating between languages, porting software between machines and operating systems or simply rewriting functions from scratch. It should never again be necessary to rewrite the standard arithmetic functions but this does still happen.

The SP language may facilitate software re-use in three main ways:

- It supports the notions of 'classes' and 'inheritance' which feature in 'object-oriented' languages like Simula, Smalltalk, LOOPS, Objective-C and C++. For this reason, it facilitates the re-use of software.

    The concepts of classes and inheritance provide a means of avoiding unnecessary repetition of structures in a program whilst preserving proper modularization in the program. In any situation where two or more modules within a program are similar in the sense that they have data structures or procedures which are the same, they may be partially merged by extracting the shared parts, declaring them once within a super-class and declaring the unshared parts within two or more sub-classes.

    Re-using software with this kind of system is easy. Any new class may re-use an existing class by declaring the old class as a super-class of the new class. In this way, all the data structures and procedures in the old class are inherited by the new class.
- A significant problem in re-using software is finding what is needed within a library of existing modules, functions or classes. The use of meaningful names for functions can help as can indexing and cross-referencing of functions. SP provides the additional facility of powerful pattern matching and searching. This can mean flexible retrieval capabilities comparable with what is provided in the best systems for bibliographic search.
- If the SP language does indeed prove to be a 'universal' language, suitable for all purposes in computing, there will be a case for adopting it as a standard. Standardization on one universal language would facilitate the integration of software from diverse sources or written for diverse purposes and would thus facilitate re-use of software.
- Even without the adoption of the SP language as a standard, the potential of the system, already noted, to integrate software written in different languages will obviously facilitate the re-use of software.

Configuration management
A significant problem in system development is the 'configuration management' problem, meaning the problem of keeping track of and managing the several versions of a software system which are typically produced in the course of

development. What gives the problem spice is that most systems of any size come in parts, sub-parts and so on and each component at any level may come in several versions. Furthermore, associations must be maintained between source code, object code, requirements specifications, designs and other documentation for all the versions and at all the different levels within each version. There is a close relation between the idea of a class in object-oriented design and the notion of a version in configuration management. Although this is not widely recognized, the two ideas are essentially the same.

Writings about object-oriented design usually make no mention of configuration management and *vice versa*. But in SP the two sets of ideas are unified. The mechanisms which allow SP software to be designed in terms of classes, sub-classes and inheritance may also serve for maintaining a disciplined system of versions and sub-versions in the course of system development. As a by-product of its design, we expect the SP system to have all the mechanisms needed to control versions within the parts and sub-parts of a system and to keep track of associations between structures at all levels within a system.

Automatic programming
There is a well-established principle in software engineering that a well-designed software system should model the domain which it is designed to serve. This principle was cogently argued by Michael Jackson (1975) for data processing, it underpins the practice of using entity-relationship models, data-flow models and entity life histories as a basis for software design and it is a key part of the philosophy of object-oriented design. SP's ability to learn new concepts from experience means that, given appropriate data about a domain, an SP system may create a model of that domain automatically. Given a stream of data, an SP system may derive a well-structured Jackson diagram or grammar for the data. Information may also be organized into class hierarchies with inheritance of attributes in the manner of object-oriented design.

This ability to infer efficient modularization and structuring for software should greatly accelerate the process of designing new software systems.

Modifiability
Most software is far too inflexible. Although most packages give the end-user some scope to set parameters or tailor the package to their individual requirements, this flexibility is usually very limited. In general, a software package is a take-it-or-leave-it item. Buying software can mean a lot of effort in evaluating packages which are nearly but not exactly what one needs. Short cuts in evaluation often mean discovering shortcomings after a package has been bought. The same kinds of problem apply to bespoke software: it is too difficult to modify software to meet changing needs even when that software was originally designed to fit one's specific requirements. All these problems would be reduced if it were easier to modify software to meet one's needs or changes in one's needs.

It should be relatively easy to make changes to SP software for three main reasons:

- *Simplicity* in use. As described earlier, all the processes of translation, compiling

and verification have been eliminated. This greatly simplifies the process of changing software.
- *Minimal redundancy* in software. SP avoids one of the main difficulties in making changes to conventional programs: a change made in one part of the program often means that corresponding changes must be made in other parts; it can be troublesome finding all the parts which must be kept in step and errors can easily creep in. As with other object-oriented systems which support class hierarchies and inheritance, SP allows software to be designed with a minimum of redundancy; this means that any given change to a program can be made in only one part of the program without risk of inconsistencies.
- SP's potential, already noted, for *automatic programming* should assist the process of modifying software. Any inefficiencies in a modified software system may be corrected automatically.

The user interface

There are potential benefits in the SP system and its underlying concepts in the design of the user interface for applications and in the usability of those applications:

- The SP language is not merely a language for system developers. The language may serve as an exceptionally simple command language, easy to learn and easy to use. It may be used in traditional textual mode or it may be used in a structure-editing mode, much like the system of menus, forms and dialogue boxes which are a now-familiar part of the WIMP style of user interface.
- The use of one simple language and one model of computing for all purposes means that a uniform, simple style of interface can be provided for diverse applications. Once a user has learned to use one SP application, there is relatively little to learn in transferring to other applications.
- If SP's potential for natural language processing is realized (see below) then it should provide a vehicle for natural language interfaces to applications, either text or speech.

Artificial intelligence

In spite of optimism about the possibilities in artificial intelligence, expert systems and 'neural' computing, we are still a long way short of that kind of human-like intelligence in computers which is the stuff of many sci-fi novels. Computers usually depend on instructions and data in precise forms. In conventional systems, there is little or no ability to learn from experience or to draw 'intelligent' inferences when there is insufficient information for purely logical deductions to be made.

Although more research is needed to substantiate the claim, there is every sign that the SP system will have a significant measure of the human-like flexibility and adaptability which is missing from the current generation of computers. The processes of pattern matching, unification and search built into the system provide the key to several useful capabilities.

Learning

We have already described how the kind of ability to learn new concepts from experience demonstrated in the SP system can bring advantages in database applications and in software development.

An ability to learn automatically is valuable for any expert system. At present, expert systems are normally built laboriously by interviewing human experts, analysing and organizing what they say and translating the knowledge into a form which is appropriate for loading into the expert system. In the future, expert systems may build their expertise from experience in a way which is comparable with how human experts acquire their knowledge.

I expect the SP system to be able to learn grammars for natural languages. Such grammars are needed in systems for machine translation and in other applications which interpret or produce natural language. Current 'manual' methods of preparing such grammars are slow, labour-intensive and not very accurate. If the full potential of the SP system is realized, grammars may be created more quickly and cheaply than at present and the results can be more accurate and more comprehensive than hand-crafted grammars.

Logic and logical inference

The SP prototype which has been developed demonstrates an ability to make logical inferences which is comparable with the capability of systems like Prolog. There are still problems to be solved but the mature SP system should be able to store logical propositions and to make logical inferences at least as well as existing systems for theorem proving and logic programming.

Uncertainty and probabilistic inference

The SP language provides for the representation of knowledge which is uncertain or incomplete. When inferences are made by the SP system using this kind of knowledge, the clockwork certainty of logic gives way to judgements of probabilities. The probabilities associated with any inference may be derived in a straightforward way from the measures of simplicity and power which are basic in SP processing.

Natural language processing

As implied in the previous remarks about grammars, it is expected that the SP language will provide an efficient medium for expressing the syntax and semantics of natural languages. Knowledge of natural languages may be integrated with other kinds of knowledge and used in systems for the creation or understanding of natural languages or for translating between natural languages.

Pattern recognition

Conventional computing systems are usually 'brittle' in the sense that commands, data or programs have to conform to precise formats and they give error messages or fail catastrophically when these precise needs are not met. I expect the SP system to be less temperamental, to guess what was intended if what it is given is not precisely right and to make 'fuzzy' matches on patterns to determine what they are. SP prototypes already demonstrate some capability of this kind.

Problem solving and automatic planning

Key concepts in SP (ordered AND relations, unordered AND relations and OR relations) map directly to established concepts in planning. Processing in SP can reproduce the kinds of inference processes which have been developed in systems for the automatic generation of plans. These processes are themselves rather similar to 'means–ends analysis' which has been established for some time as a problem solving technique in AI. I believe that automatic planning and problem solving will be part of the repertoire of capabilities in the mature SP system.

CONCLUSION

The SP theory is quite radical in the sense that it can provide a framework and interpretation for a wide range of concepts in computing. In another sense, the theory is very conservative, based as it is on the well-established and uncontroversial theory of information proposed by Claude Shannon.

Either way, there is potential in the SP theory and in the SP system to sweep away many of the problems in software engineering and computing which have dogged the industry for many years and to realize new capabilities and benefits which currently exist only in embryo form.

If the SP system lives up to expectations, much of the money which is currently spent trying to solve software engineering problems may be saved. Solving those problems means saving much larger sums of money in the many organizations which use computers and in the many applications of computers. Compared with these potential savings, only tiny resources are needed to develop the SP system.

REFERENCES

Hekmatpour, S., & Ince, D. (1986): Rapid software prototyping. Open University Technical Report 86/4. Milton Keynes: The Open University.

Jackson, M. A. (1975). *Principles of Program Design*. New York: Academic Press.

Partridge, D. (1989). Databases that learn. In R. Forsyth (Ed.), *Machine Learning*, London: Chapman & Hall, pp. 207–218.

7

The SP language in project management

The main subject of the article reproduced in this chapter — how to manage or, more precisely, minimize the level of risk in developing new systems — is not directly related to the SP theory. The article has been included in the book because it shows how an informal version of the SP language may be used to keep track of the knowledge associated with a development project and can help to highlight areas of uncertainty and corresponding risk.

Even when it is used in the purely 'textual' way described in the article, the SP language can be quite useful. It is not hard to imagine how a computational version of SP, supported by the processes of pattern matching, unification and search described in Chapters 4 and 5, could become a valuable tool in system development. If the language lives up to expectations — if it can be used to represent the wide range of kinds of knowledge which are used in a typical development project, and can be used as an efficient, executable specification language — then the SP system should be a good basis for a highly integrated and conceptually simple IPSE.

THE MANAGEMENT OF RISK IN SYSTEM DEVELOPMENT: 'PROJECT SP' AND THE 'NEW SPIRAL MODEL'[†]

ABSTRACT

The article discusses the development of complex products, with a particular emphasis on software, and focuses on the problem of how to manage the risks in the development process.

A number of models of the development process are described including Boehm's Spiral Model, which has risk management as a central theme. An example is described where Boehm's Spiral Model has been tried. The strengths and weaknesses of the model are discussed in the light of this experience. In the last part of the article, a notation called 'Project SP' is presented as a means of recording the progressively growing knowledge base of a project and the areas of uncertainty and

---

[†] From the article with the same title by J. G. Wolff, 1989, *Software Engineering Journal* **4**(3), pp. 134–142, Copyright 1989 by the Institute of Electrical Engineers. Reprinted by permission.

associated risk. Also described is the 'New Spiral Model', derived from Boehm's model and designed to be used in conjunction with Project SP. The New Spiral Model appears to preserve the advantages of the previous model and appears to remedy its weaknesses. Associated issues are described and discussed.

1. INTRODUCTION

Many products of modern technology — cars, aeroplanes, computing systems — have proved to be very useful. But the development of products like these is complicated — and there are risks (Wingrove, 1986). There are many examples — from Concorde to Nimrod — to illustrate the hazards in the development of new complex systems. In the software industry — which is what I know best — cost overruns and the wasted effort represented by projects which are abandoned at a late stage, or whose deliverables are never used, are notorious.

This article considers the process of designing and developing complicated systems, especially software, and discusses how the risks in development and the overall cost of development can be minimized.

In many ways, software provides a paradigm for all kinds of design and development. Software is pure information and, as such, it captures the essence of all kinds of design. Software systems are often very complicated (although the same is increasingly true of integrated circuits). The main difference between software and hardware systems is that, with software, there is no significant process of 'production'. Once the design is complete, multiple copies may be made very easily. This difference has some bearing on the design process — and this will be briefly discussed. But the model of design and development proposed in this article is general enough to cover all kinds of system.

In the next section I briefly examine a small range of models of design and development giving special attention to Boehm's 'Spiral Model' and its approach to the management of risk. Then I describe and discuss a project at Praxis (where I was employed until recently) where the Spiral Model has been tried. In the following section, the New Spiral Model is presented. It is derived from the Spiral Model and includes a notation, called 'Project SP', for tracking the status of a project from start to finish. The article concludes with a discussion of some related issues.

2. MODELS OF SYSTEM DEVELOPMENT

In order to manage any kind of system development, including small projects, it is necessary to have some kind of model of the development process, preferably one which is explicit and precise. In this section, I will first briefly review some of the more popular models and then I will describe and discuss Boehm's Spiral Model at more length.

- *The Waterfall Model.* This model of system development (see, for example, Buckle (1982)) is one of the oldest and is still popular. In this model, a project proceeds in an essentially fixed sequence of 'stages'. A typical sequence is:

  (1) Project inception: defining objectives and constraints on the project.
  (2) Planning.

(3) Specification of requirements for the system.
(4) Design meaning definition of the software at some high level of abstraction.
(5) Coding, meaning the production of an executable program.
(6) Testing and integration.
(7) Release of the system to the client.

At any stage (except the first) it is possible to return to the previous stage and rework it. More radical backtracking is discouraged because of the management problems which that entails. The Waterfall Model marries naturally with the principle of top-down design. In top-down design, there is a more or less fixed progression in the design process from the definition of the largest abstract components of the design to the progressively more detailed elaboration of each part and its component parts. As with the Waterfall Model, some backtracking is accommodated, provided it is not too radical.

- *The Two-Legged Model.* In this model (see, for example, Lehmann (1984)) the process of design and development is divided into two 'legs': 'abstraction' and 'reification'. Abstraction leads from users' requirements to a formal specification of a system while reification is a process of progressively translating a specification into some kind of runnable 'implementation'. This translation process is sometimes called 'refinement'.

Associated with the concepts of abstraction and reification are the concepts of 'validation' and 'verification'. The former means establishing that the specification conforms to the users' requirements while the latter means proving that the implementation conforms to the specification. There has been a marked tendency in discussions of this model and in its applications for abstraction and validation to receive much less attention than refinement and verification.

- *The Prototyping Model.* This model and variants of it are described in Hekmatpour & Ince (1986). One of the main motivations for this model is the recognition that prospective users of a system are rarely able to define their requirements fully in one operation. Users also often find it difficult to define what they want in abstract or verbal terms independent of some working system: 'I'll know it when I see it' (IKIWISI). A prototype provides a means for users to say more precisely what they do or do not want. The general idea, then, is to construct a series of prototypes, to allow prospective users to examine each one, and say what changes they want in the next one.

Prototyping can also provide a means for system designers to clarify other aspects of a system: how it should be structured for easy modification or maintenance; how best to optimize the performance of the system; and so on.

In the Throw-it-away variant, all prototypes are discarded; the delivered system is the last system in the sequence. In the Evolutionary and Incremental variants, software is carried forward from stage to stage and the functionality of the system is progressively refined and increased. The Evolutionary Model allows deletion and changes from stage to stage while the Incremental Model allows only additions.

There is a natural affinity between the Evolutionary and Incremental Models and object-oriented design (see, for example, Birtwistle *et al.* (1979) and Cook (1986)). The mechanism of inheritance in such languages as Simula, Smalltalk and

LOOPS provides a streamlined way of integrating new software with old. Because it supports the creation of 'well-structured' designs, object orientation facilitates the process of changing designs.

2.1 Boehm's Spiral Model

Boehm (1986) claims, with some justice, that the Spiral Model embraces most other models as special cases. It is a more general view of the process of design and development than other models and can apparently be applied to a wide range of types of project. But it is not so general as to be vacuous: it provides useful disciplines and constraints on the way development is done.

According to the model, a project should comprise a series of *cycles* or *rounds*. The steps in each cycle are broadly these:

(1) Define *objectives* for the cycle.
(2) Identify *constraints*, e.g. budgetary constraints and time scales.
(3) Identify *alternative* means of meeting objectives (e.g. design A, design B, re-use, buy etc.).
(4) Evaluate alternatives with respect to objectives and constraints and, for each alternative, identify areas of uncertainty and the corresponding *risks*.
(5) Decide how to *resolve* risks (e.g. construct a prototype, consult an expert, do a simulation, administer a user questionnaire, build system) and then do the chosen task.
(6) Gather and review the *results* of the risk resolution exercise.
(7) *Plan* the next cycle.
(8) Review the plan and make a *commitment* to it.

The main differences between this model and the more traditional approaches are these:

- There is explicit recognition for alternative means of meeting the objectives of a project.
- The identification of risks associated with each alternative, and the ways in which those risks may be resolved, are brought centre stage. With traditional approaches, the easy bits of a project may be done early and the areas of uncertainty left till later — and this can give a spurious impression of progress. A risk-driven approach to development more readily avoids this pitfall.
- The division of a project into cycles with a 'commit' step at the end of each cycle, means that there is explicit provision for changes in the direction of a project or the termination of a project, at any stage, in the light of what has been learned since the start of the project. By contrast with 'big bang' approaches to system development, the cyclic approach enables a limit to be placed on the risks which have to be accepted at any time.
- The model accommodates types of activity (e.g. consulting an expert or library research) which are often valuable in reaching the objectives of a project but which have no place in other models.

3. THE PCIS PROJECT

In Praxis we have tried using the Spiral Model in an internal project to develop the 'Praxis Company Information System' (PCIS). The experience that we gained with the Spiral Model seems to be useful and worth reporting.

The development of business information systems is, of course, fairly well understood and the project is not intrinsically risky. Nevertheless we found that the framework provided by the Spiral Model has been valuable and has enabled us to retreat from potential pitfalls before any strong commitment was made.

What has been done maps fairly well to the model although there have been some areas of uncertainty as we learned to interpret and apply the model. As we used the model, some weaknesses became apparent and these are discussed below.

Our application of the Spiral Model included the Evolutionary Model as a subset. We felt that it would be rash to try to gather all requirements before producing any working system because of the IKIWISI phenomenon and because the needs of a company like Praxis, which is growing fast, do change as time goes by. We envisaged that several of the cycles of the Spiral Model would each be largely concerned with the development of a 'prototype' or 'version', to be evaluated by prospective users and, in most cases, carried forward into the next cycle for refinement and enhancement.

3.1 The first cycle

The objective defined for the project at the outset, which applied throughout the project, was to 'develop an information system to meet the needs of Praxis management'.

It seemed necessary to start the project off with a fairly conventional gathering of requirements from prospective users of the system but, because we envisaged evolutionary development, this first gathering of requirements was not done in exhaustive detail. An outline data model was constructed together with an outline description and analysis of the functions to be performed and a description of the 'non-functional' attributes required in the system.

This first gathering of requirements was regarded as part of the process of defining the objectives and constraints on the project. The next four steps in the model were covered by a study called 'Analysis of Options and Risks'. In this study, we identified a set of alternative means of meeting the objectives:

- Sub-contract the work to another systems house. Since we are, ourselves, a systems house, this option did not look very plausible. But we felt it would be useful, nevertheless, to weigh the pros and cons.
- Do the work ourselves. On this basis, we identified four alternative means of developing the system:
  - Use software DBMS 'A' and its 4GL tools.
  - Use software DBMS 'B' and its 4GL tools.
  - Use database machine 'C' and its 4GL tools.
  - Assemble a collection of packages to serve the various functions of the company.

  Criteria for evaluation were derived from the initial study of requirements and the options were investigated and evaluated against them. Examples of criteria for evaluating the proposed vehicles for the system include: cost of the vehicle, ease of use of the development tools (and corresponding cost of development effort), the quality of the user interface, the existence or otherwise of mechanisms to preserve the integrity of data in the face of hardware failures, and so on. The criteria may be seen as 'risks': if an option does not meet one or more of the criteria then the final system is likely to be unsatisfactory. The best option appeared to be to do the work ourselves using the database machine 'C', perhaps after some further investigation of the machine.

However, there were constraints which dictated a slightly different course. We already had a licence for software DBMS 'A' and, for budgetary reasons, there was little prospect of getting the database machine soon. There was also a need to gain experience with DBMS 'A'.

Consequently, we planned to do the first one or two versions of the PCIS with software DBMS 'A', and also do some further investigation of 'C'. If, after further investigation, 'C' was still looking good, we would rewrite the system on it and continue with it in subsequent cycles.

This longer-term plan was the basis of the shorter-term plan prepared for the next cycle: to develop a first version of the PCIS to serve the needs of the company in the areas of marketing and sales.

The plan was reviewed and a commitment made to it.

3.2 The second cycle

The objective of the second cycle was the development of the first version of the PCIS under the constraint that it should use DBMS 'A'.

No significant alternatives presented themselves in this cycle and, with a qualification described below, we did not see significant areas of risk requiring investigation. The cycle constituted a fairly straightforward development of the first version of the PCIS. Detailed requirements were gathered from relevant staff, a running system was developed using the 4GL tools, and the system was carefully evaluated by the prospective users of the system. This evaluation led to the definition of changes required in future versions and new features needed.

The evaluation of the first version of the PCIS and the definition of changes required in future versions may be regarded as the first part of the Third Cycle: these activities are part of the process of defining the next set of objectives in the project.

The idea that there was no apparent risk in this cycle should perhaps be qualified by the thought that the development of the first version of the PCIS may, itself, be seen as an exercise in the reduction of uncertainty and the resolution of risk. Before the development is undertaken, there is a degree of uncertainty about what form the system will take and about how well it will work; this uncertainty is reduced or removed by constructing and evaluating the system. In this spirit, the cycle — and the project — were reviewed.

The main conclusion of the review of 'results' was that DBMS 'A' is much less satisfactory than we had anticipated. Its main defect is unacceptably slow response times on our equipment even with very little data in it and few users. A new and bigger machine could, of course, be bought for it but this option needs to be set against the apparently preferable option of buying dedicated hardware — the database machine.

The slow response times with DBMS 'A' could, of course, have been discovered without actually developing a version of the PCIS. In retrospect, it might have been wiser to conduct some tests on the DBMS as a risk-resolution exercise prior to building the first version of the system. However, the development of the first version of the PCIS was not wasted effort because it sharpened our understanding of users' requirements in several other areas, especially the user interface.

On the strength of the review, the Third Cycle was planned to take in a further short investigation of the database machine and its tools, and a decision on its purchase. In this Third Cycle, a new version of the PCIS is to be developed using the new system, drawing on the knowledge gained in developing and evaluating the first version. The definition of these objectives, like the definition of changes required in future versions of the PCIS, may be regarded as the first stage in the Third Cycle.

3.3 Discussion

To date, the Spiral Model seems to have been a reasonably good framework for the PCIS project. But there is a need for more clarity in some areas, or changes in the model. These will now be described:

(1) There is a need to define more clearly how longer-term objectives and plans may be carried forward from cycle to cycle and integrated with the shorter-term objectives and plans. An example of a long-term intention which needed to be carried forward into later cycles is our early decision in the PCIS project to migrate to database machine 'C' after one or two versions of the PCIS produced using software DBMS 'A', provided that further evaluation of the database machine was satisfactory.

(2) There seems to be a need to provide for hierarchical relationships and for 'spirals within spirals':

- Within a cycle, the process of resolving risks may be regarded as a spiral in its own right: there should be objectives and there is likely to be alternative means of meeting the objectives, each with risks which may need to be resolved. The model needs to be applied recursively.
- Similar remarks apply to the planning activity within each cycle. That planning may itself be modelled on a spiral model has been noted and discussed by Boehm & Belz (1986). Other points about how planning relates to the Spiral Model are made below.
- Alternatives may easily demand a hierarchical structure. The alternatives shown in the section on 'The first cycle' are one example. As another example, one of the alternative means of resolving risks — 'consult an expert' — may itself be broken down into a set of alternatives: 'consult Susan', 'consult Joe' etc.

(3) As we saw in the section on 'The second cycle', there may not be obvious major alternatives in a cycle. And it is not very obvious that developing a version of a system is 'risk resolution' in quite the same sense as investigating alternative vehicles for the system.

(4) Not only may the planning activity within each cycle of the Spiral Model be modelled on a spiral model but several of the other activities in each cycle — defining objectives, identifying constraints, identifying alternative ways of meeting objectives, identifying risks and deciding how to resolve risks — may themselves be regarded as planning activities. Moreover, the Spiral Model may itself be regarded as a skeleton plan for a project. There is, in general, a need to define more clearly how any planning done within the model relates to the model itself.

4. 'PROJECT SP' AND THE 'NEW SPIRAL MODEL'

In this section a notation and a new version of the Spiral Model are described. They seem to meet most of the problems with the Spiral Model which were noted above.

4.1 'Project SP': a notation for project management

This section introduces a simple notation called 'Project SP' which is an informal variant of the SP computer language, described elsewhere (Wolff, 1990).

Project SP, which is similar to BNF, may be used for recording the progressively growing knowledge base for a project. This includes the objectives of the project, constraints on the project, alternative means of meeting objectives, the areas of risk and uncertainty, planned activities on the project and the information gathered to reduce uncertainty and resolve risks. The last-mentioned category includes information about the design of the system being developed. Boehm & Belz (1988) have also proposed using a data store in conjunction with the Spiral Model.

Here is the notation:

- (...) — A sequence of items or 'ordered AND object' (OAO). This includes the normal sequencing of words in English sentences.
- [...] — An 'unordered AND object' (UAO): a group of items where order is not defined.
- {...} — An 'OR object' (ORO): the items between the curly brackets represent alternatives.

Each option may be marked with a 'per cent' ('%') or 'weight' showing the apparent strength of the case for choosing that option: 0% means that the option should never be chosen while 100% means that it should always be chosen.

If the weights in an ORO total to 100% then it represents an exclusive OR relation. If weights within an ORO total more than 100% then it represents an inclusive OR relation. If all the weights within an ORO are, individually, 100% then the structure is equivalent to a UAO.

- * — A star placed after an item shows that the item may be repeated.
- ? — Question marks show where more information appears to be needed, the strength of the need being shown by the number of question marks.
- Indentation may be used to improve readability.

4.2 An example

As an example to introduce the uses of Project SP, Fig. 7.1. shows how the notation may be used to describe the knowledge base for the PCIS project at the time of

Ch. 7] THE SP LANGUAGE IN PROJECT MANAGEMENT 181

writing. This and other examples are discussed in the following sections. In Fig. 7.1 sets of three dots ('...') are used to show where information has been left out to save space.

[(The PCIS Project)
    [(project management)
        [(The Spiral Model)
            [cycle ((step-1 ...)(step-2 ...) ...)]*]
        [(project plan)
            (
                [(the first cycle)
                    [define [objectives-1]]
                    [identify [constraints-1]]
                    [2.1–1.0]
                    ...]
                [(the second cycle)
                    [define [objectives-2]]
                    [identify [constraints-2]]
                    [2.2–1.0]
                    ...]
                [(the third cycle)
                    [define [objectives-3]]
                    [identify [constraints-3]]
                    ???]
)]]
    [(requirements for the PCIS)
        [objectives-1
            [(overall objective for the project) ...]
            [("Preliminary Specification of Requirements for the PCIS")
                [41.1–1.0]]]
        [objectives-2
            [("Requirements Statement for the PCIS, Version 1")
                [42.2–1.0]]]
        [objectives-3
            [("Requirements Statement for the PCIS, Version 2")
                [42.3–1.0]]]]
    [(constraints on the development of the PCIS)
        [constraints-1 [time ...][cost ...]]
        [constraints-2 [time ...][cost ...](use DBMS "A")]
        [constraints-3 [time ...][cost ...](use database machine "C")]]]
    [(mode of development)
        {
        [(sub-contract the work) 20% [90.1–1.0]]
        [(do the work in house) 80%
            [(vehicle for the PCIS)
                [(evaluation criteria) [90.1–1.0]
                    [(available from any one terminal) ...]

            [(high level of integration) ...]
            [(access control) ...]
            [(preservation of integrity) ...]
            [(accessibility of information) ...]
            [(user interface) UI [42.3–1.0]
                [(bandwidth of visual display)
                    (size of screen)
                    (windowing)
                    (efficient scrolling)]
                [(flexibility in production of hard copy)
            (landscape printing)
            (printing of screens and reports
            'on the fly')]]
            [(capital and recurrent costs) ...]
            [(development facilities) DF ...]
            [(performance, response times) PF ...]
            [(distributed working) ...]
            [(adaptability to changing needs) ...]
            [(documentation and training) ...]
            [(maturity of system) ...]
            [(other considerations) ...]]
    {
    [DBMS-A 15%
        [90.1–1.0]
        [(experience of second cycle)
            [[PF] poor]
            [[UI] (poor; there are limitations on
                the production of hardcopy and in
                the formatting of forms and reports)]
            [[DF] (not easy to learn but tolerably
                easy to use once learned; X's
                help-line is poor)]
            (other aspects of DBMS-A appear
            to be acceptable)]]
    [DBMS-B 25%
        [90.1–1.0]
        (experience on project xxxx)]
    [(a collection of packages)[90.1–1.0] 10%]
    [(database machine) 50%
            {
            [(database-machine-C) ??? 80%
                [90.1–1.0]
                [(XX's experience) ...]
                [(meeting at Praxis, 22/2/88)[24.6]]
                [[UI] ???]
                [[PF] ??]
                [[DF] ???]]

```
                         [other ?? 20%]}]
                       }]]}]
    [PCIS
      {
          [PCIS-1
             (for marketing and sales)
             [DBMS-A]
             (executable specification)
             [("High level design for the PCIS, version 1")
                [42.1–1.0]]
             [("User guide for the PCIS, version 1")
                [42.2–1.0]]]
          [PCIS-2 ???]
      }]
]
```

Fig. 7.1 — A representation in Project SP of the knowledge base of the PCIS project at the time of writing.

4.3 The uses of Project SP
The ways in which Project SP may be used are described here with illustrations from Fig. 7.1 and other examples.

4.3.1 Groupings of objects
OAOs and UAOs both serve to group their constituent objects. UAOs are used where there is no spatial or temporal ordering of the constituents. One example in Fig. 7.1 is the evaluation criteria for the vehicle for the PCIS. Another is the grouping of any object with its label or identifier (see below).

OAOs are used where there is some kind of spatial or temporal ordering of constituents. Examples in Fig. 7.1 are the ordering of activities in a project plan and the order of words in English text. The relevance of Project SP to planning is discussed more fully below.

4.3.2 Identifiers and references
The notion of 'identifier' has no formal significance in Project SP. Indeed, any object may be identified by any of its constituents which is sufficiently distinctive. However, as a matter of psychology, it is often convenient to regard one of the constituents of an object as being primarily an identifier or label for that object.

The relationship between an identifier or label and what it identifies seems to be best represented as an unordered AND relationship. In Project SP, any object may be labelled by bracketing it with its label within a UAO, e.g. [**Fred** (...)]. If the object being labelled is itself a UAO then the inner brackets may be dropped.

Since the identifier and what it identifies are constituents of a UAO, they may be written in any order. However, for the sake of readability and easy comprehension, it is convenient to put the identifier first. Examples in Fig. 7.1 of the labelling of objects in this way include [**DBMS-A** ...] and [**objectives-1** ...].

A reference to any object may be created by using its identifier as a constituent by itself within a UAO. Examples in Fig. 7.1 include [**objectives-1**] and [**UI**]. The latter example is a reference to the user interface, one of the criteria for evaluation listed elsewhere in the structure.

References may be used to avoid recording a structure more than once when it appears in more than one context. The examples in the last paragraph illustrate this use in Fig. 7.1. References may also be used when incorporation of a large data object at a given point would be cumbersome and would make the organization of the whole structure less easy to see. Examples of this second use of references are the numbers in square brackets, e.g. [42.1–1.0], which are reference numbers for Praxis documents. The text of any such document is not incorporated directly in the main structure.

4.3.3 Uncertainty in the knowledge base

OROs in Project SP provide a means of representing uncertainty in a project. As described earlier, the weights on items within a ORO (figures with '%') show the apparent strength of the case for choosing that option. Whenever weights are less than 100% and more than 0% there is a corresponding uncertainty in choosing.

An example in Fig. 7.1 of the use of an ORO in this way is the choice between doing the development work in-house and contracting it out to another systems house. In this example, the in-house option is itself broken down into a number of subsidiary options.

Question marks in Project SP provide a second means of representing uncertainty or ignorance within a knowledge base. Of course, we can never be sure that our knowledge of any one thing is complete: there is a metaphorical question mark attaching to every object in every knowledge base. The use of question marks in Project SP is intended to show the perceived strength of the need to find out more in this or that part of the knowledge base. Exactly how one makes such judgements is itself a significant question mark in our understanding of system development.

4.3.4 'Deletion' or 'replacement' of objects

The intention with Project SP is that information should never be destroyed within the structure — unless it is a simple error in editing the structure or if it is redundant. In the latter case, where an object has been replicated in more than one context, all instances except one 'master' copy may be replaced by references to that master copy.

If one object supersedes another in the knowledge base then the two objects should be formed into an ORO, with the later item marked as 100% and the superseded item marked as 0%. If, at some later stage in the project, the old item seems useful again, then the weights may be adjusted to show this.

If an object is to be 'deleted' and nothing put in its place then it should be formed into a selection where its alternative is a UAO which is empty except for its 100% weight, e.g. [... {[0% Fred (...)], [100%]} ...]. An acceptable shorthand is simply adding a 0% weight to the object which is to be demoted — without incorporating it in an ORO.

To preserve all information in the knowledge base even when it is out of date may seem cumbersome but it is no different from what has been normal practice for many years with conventional, paper-based filing systems. Of course, many computerized databases are designed for the deletion and overwriting of information but this is likely to change as storage technology improves and the advantages of non-overwriting systems like ADAM (Peeling *et al.*, 1984) are seen.

A main reason for never destroying information in the knowledge base is that one can always backtrack if necessary. Another important reason is that one can always construct an 'audit trail' for a project. This can be useful in project debriefing and in case of dispute if that unfortunate contingency arises.

4.3.5 Representing the structure of software systems

Project SP is an informal version of the SP computer language, described in Wolff (1990). The SP language is intended as a 'broad spectrum' language with a wide range of uses including data storage and retrieval, software specification and design, representation of rules for expert systems, logic programming and others. If the potential of SP is realized — and a research programme is needed to establish how and how far one simple language can serve such a wide range of applications — it may be possible to represent the whole structure of a developing software system with one notation which is the same as is used for other parts of a project knowledge base.

Fig. 7.1 shows information about the PCIS in only the barest outline, with references out to Praxis documents where the real meat of the information about the structure of the system is stored. It would take us too far afield to discuss fully how SP or Project SP could be used more directly to represent the structure of the PCIS (there is relevant discussion in Wolff (1990)) but some brief indication of the possibilities is warranted here:

- Project SP embraces the concepts of 'sequence' (OAO), 'selection' (ORO) and 'iteration' ('*') which are widely recognized as basic organizing principles in software (see, for example, Jackson (1975)). Iteration does not feature in SP but an equivalent effect may be achieved by using recursion. The UAO construct may provide a means of representing 'concurrency' in software systems.
- SP and Project SP apparently lend themselves to the efficient representation of versions or variants of software systems. In other words, they have potential to facilitate configuration management. The mechanisms which will serve the 'object-oriented' concepts of classes, sub-classes and inheritance of attributes (see Wolff, 1990) will also serve to keep track of the several versions of a software system which usually arise in system development. A simple example appears in Fig. 7.1 where the versions of the PCIS are represented as constituents of an ORO — alternative realizations of the PCIS.

4.3.6 Representation of plans

In keeping with the 'wide spectrum' remarks in the last section, there is potential in Project SP to represent plans directly in the knowledge base. The main constructs recognized in project planning also appear in the notation:

- A sequence of activities in a plan may be represented using an OAO.
- A UAO may be used to represent activities which are independent of each other in much the same way that it may be used to represent concurrency in software. Independence of activities corresponds to the slightly inaccurate use of the term *parallel* in project planning. 'Parallel' activities may be performed in parallel or

they may be performed in some arbitrary sequence, depending on the resources available and the required time scales.
- An ORO may be used to represent activities which are *alternatives* in a plan. This is not very common in ordinary projects but the concept is recognized in the term 'contingency planning'. Where there are alternatives in a plan there is a need to know how to choose between the options. This can be achieved by associating each option with a condition which must be satisfied before that option can be chosen. In Project SP, each alternative course of action should be enclosed within an OAO together with its corresponding condition or conditions:

```
{
    (condition-1 action-1)
    (condition-2 action-2)
    (condition-3 action-3)
    ...
}
```

The similarity between the organizing principles recognized in project planning and those recognized in software design is interesting in its own right. It also reinforces Osterweil's (1987) argument that 'Software processes are software too'. If project planning is to be seen as 'process programming' then it will be convenient and elegant if the notation used to describe a software product can also be used to describe the process by which that product is created. Whether or not that can be achieved with SP or Project SP remains to be seen.

4.4 The New Spiral Model
Given the use of Project SP to record the growing knowledge base of a project, Boehm's model may be recast in a modified form.

In the New Spiral Model (NSM), there are two fundamental operations or activities: (1) gathering new knowledge and adding it to the knowledge base; (2) reviewing, analyzing and rationalising what is in the knowledge base. There will usually also be the execution of plans described within the knowledge base. Here is a fuller description:

(1) Gather new knowledge and add it to the knowledge base.
   'New knowledge' in this context can mean any or all of the following kinds of knowledge:
   - Knowledge about the objectives of a project or activity.
   - Knowledge about ignorance and corresponding risks. This is not as paradoxical as it sounds. For example, anyone with experience with computers and similar technology knows that, for any proposed new piece of equipment, one ought to find out how reliable it is, the call-out time for maintenance, the cost of maintenance, the availability of spares, and so on. Knowing what one needs to find out is part of the skill of system development.
     Defining gaps in one's knowledge is closely related to the definition of objectives for an activity or project. A requirement to 'support the production and maintenance of company accounts' is a gap waiting to be filled by a suitable system. The gaps in one's knowledge about any proposed new piece

of equipment are objectives for corresponding activities to plug those gaps: 'find out about reliability', 'find out about call out times', etc.
- Knowledge gleaned from various sources about constraints on a project or subsidiary activity, e.g. budgets and time scales.
- Knowledge about methods of meeting objectives within the given constraints; where there is more than one method for an objective these represent the kind of alternatives which feature in Boehm's Spiral Model.

  A method, together with such information as start and end dates and staff assignments, is the kind of information which is normally represented in some kind of network of activities or PERT chart. As indicated above, SP or Project SP may also provide a means of representing this kind of knowledge, including sequences of activities (OAOs), independent or 'parallel' activities (UAOs) and alternatives or contingencies (OROs).

  Gathering information about methods and corresponding activities, incorporating it in the knowledge base, reviewing, analysing and rationalizing it (see below) is what is normally meant by planning.

  Knowledge about methods includes such humdrum things as how to make a journey to visit a client, how to obtain information from libraries, and so on. Knowledge about methods also includes knowledge about the several models of system development — including the NSM itself!

  If knowledge about methods is supplied from the experience of members of the project team, as it often will be, it is not, in that sense, 'new'. However, in terms of the project's knowledge base it is new knowledge. Unless it is trivial, everyday knowledge, it needs to be recorded explicitly regardless of whether it comes from some external 'expert' or from within the team.
- Knowledge about the developing system. For most projects this is the main 'deliverable' of the project. It includes such things as high-level design, low-level design, source code, maintenance documentation, user guides and so on.
- Records of any commitments made to project plans.

(2) Review, analyse and rationalize the knowledge base. This activity includes any or all of the following kinds of activity:

- Look for redundancy in the knowledge base and reduce it where possible. Where objects are replicated, references may be used to reduce redundancy, as described earlier. Examples of searching for redundancy in a knowledge base and reducing it include the process of 'normalizing' data models and the processes needed to achieve 'good structure' in the design of software (see Wolff, 1990).
- Review objectives against the results of system development to see whether the objectives have been met.
- In the light of any new knowledge gained since the previous cycle, review the weights attaching to the constituents of OROs.
- Identify areas of uncertainty, ignorance and risk and decide where further investigation is needed.

(3) Execute any plans which are ready to go. A plan is ready to go if it has been created and reviewed, if a commitment has been made to it and if all pre-

188 THE SP LANGUAGE IN PROJECT MANAGEMENT [Ch. 7

conditions attaching to it are satisfied. Pre-conditions include such things as the completion of previous activities on which the plan depends (e.g. the delivery of equipment), the availability of relevant staff, reaching the start date, and so on. 'Execute' in this context is analogous to 'eval' in Lisp.

Fig. 7.2 represents the main points in foregoing description of the NSM using the Project SP notation.

```
[NSM
    [activities
        (
        [(gather new knowledge)
            {
            [define [objectives]]
            [identify [constraints]]
            [define [activities]]
            [record [commitments]]
            [create [deliverables]]
            }]
        [(review, analyse and rationalise the knowledge base)
            {
            (look for redundancy and remove where possible)
            (review objectives against deliverables)
            (review and adjust weights on the constituents of OROs)
            (identify areas of uncertainty and risk)
            }]
        (execute planned activities which are ready to go)
        )*
        [constraints ?]
        [commitments ?]
    ]
    [deliverables
        [objectives ?]
        {
        [report ?]
        [(high level design) ?]
        [(low level design) ?]
        [(source code) ?]
        ...
        }]
]
```

Fig. 7.2. — The New Spiral Model represented using Project SP.

The 'activities' object in Fig. 7.2 describes the two basic operations in each cycle of gathering new knowledge and then reviewing, analyzing and rationalizing it. Under each heading there is an ORO describing the options. One or more of these options may be chosen on each cycle.

The [define [activities]] object is the 'planning' or 'process programming' operation. It means fleshing out the bare bones of the basic [activities ...] object in the NSM with the more detailed descriptions of activities needed to make a project go, using any available knowledge about methods.

As already noted, knowledge about methods can include the NSM itself. Thus the NSM may reappear within itself as, for example, when a major project has been planned to contain one or more sub-projects. The model can be applied at any level.

Notice that the application of the NSM within itself means that it can be used in the creation of project plans. In other words, it can be included within the [define[activities]] object. Boehm & Belz (1988) have, in a similar way, proposed using the Spiral Model in the development of project plans.

With or without this kind of recursive application of the model, Project SP accommodates an hierarchical structuring of activities within activities, with sequence, selection, concurrency and iteration at any level.

4.5 Discussion

To quote a well-known phrase, 'forewarned is forearmed': the reduction of risk is closely related to the reduction of ignorance or the building of knowledge.

The idea behind the use of Project SP and the NSM is to treat a development project as a progression from relative ignorance to relative knowledge. The design of a computing system (or anything else) is a form of knowledge and the process of creating a design may be seen as a process of knowledge accretion. Likewise, all the other aspects of a development project — the model of development, objectives, constraints, user's requirements, project plans, and knowledge about equipment and facilities — are forms of knowledge which typically grow as the project proceeds.

Areas of uncertainty in a development project take two forms in Project SP: alternatives in a selection, or straightforward gaps in knowledge (represented by question marks). Uncertainty is reduced when an alternative is chosen or when a gap in the structure is plugged.

Project SP and the NSM together meet the points made in the 'Discussion' section of 'The PCIS project' above:

(1) Short- and long-term objectives and plans may be recorded in the knowledge base and carried forward from cycle to cycle.
(2) Hierarchical relationships are naturally accommodated in the notation. Selections within selections are shown in Fig. 7.1. The NSM is itself one of the candidate 'methods' which may be used in any part of a structure of planned activities and at any level. In other words, the NSM can be applied recursively to create 'spirals within spirals'.
(3) Risk reduction may be achieved by any kind of gain in relevant knowledge. Sometimes this relates to alternatives but it may equally well be the plugging of gaps in knowledge — and that includes gaining knowledge by building a system.
(4) The relationship between 'planning' and the NSM is this:
    - The NSM is itself a skeleton plan.
    - The NSM replaces three activities in Boehm's model with a single 'process programming' activity for fleshing out the skeleton with the more detailed

descriptions of activities needed to make the plan practical. The three activities which are replaced are: the identification of alternative means of meeting objectives, deciding how to resolve risks, and 'planning'.

5. RELATED ISSUES

In this section, I pick up some loose ends from what I have said and discuss them briefly.

5.1 The spiral models and iteration in design

As we have seen, the idea of iteration features not only in the spiral models but in the prototyping model as well. In the spiral models iteration serves a management need to limit the risk to which a project is exposed at any time. In the prototyping model, iteration is probably serving the rather different needs of the design process:

- Iteration seems to suit end-users best. A major reason is IKIWISI but there is the related reason that potential users of a system naturally examine and re-examine their requirements in the process of thinking them out.
- In a similar way, it is psychologically natural for designers to iterate in the process of thinking out the best organization for a design. Drafting and re-drafting has always been required in all kinds of design — from graphic art to the writing of articles and books.

Whatever the reasons for iteration, it is accommodated very well within the spiral models.

5.2 Should one always concentrate on high-risk areas first?

As we have seen, there are good reasons why a project should focus on areas of ignorance and risk. However, in the design process, it sometimes seems better to design the best understood parts first. For example, in object-oriented design it is recognized (see Birtwistle *et al.*, 1979) that one should first identify and define the most salient classes in the system and should later add the less salient classes, whether they be at higher or lower levels of abstraction.

I believe this contradiction is more apparent than real. There is a difference between recording things which you already know and working out something new. As a result of discussions with users, a designer will know things about the form which the system must take and these things need to be recorded. Recording them explicitly in a partial design is quite consistent with the principle of seeking out areas of uncertainty. One cannot see the areas of uncertainty clearly unless one has recorded what one already knows.

5.3 The design of other kinds of system

The ideas which have been presented seem to have a fairly wide scope and should prove useful in the development of systems where there are significant components which are not software.

The main difference between hardware and software is that hardware systems are usually less 'malleable' than software systems. A significant commitment of resources is often required in the construction of hardware systems.

This feature has been a reason for the traditional notion that 'design' always precedes 'construction'. When the software industry first developed, it was natural to borrow this idea. And it flourished because, until recently, significant resources were required in the creation of software systems and there was a consequent need to get the 'design' right before embarking on 'implementation'.

Modern tools and the increasing performance of computers for a given price is progressively reducing the resources required in the creation of a working software system. There is, consequently, more scope to adopt new methods of working which take advantage of this new flexibility.

Of course, it was never entirely true in the hardware world that design necessarily preceded construction. The creation of prototypes has been a part of engineering methodology from the earliest days. Brunel built prototypes where there was uncertainty about design. And the construction of any one bridge, for example, may be regarded as a trial run for the design and construction of bridges which come later. The eighteenth century bridge at Pontypridd, which at the time was the longest single span in the world, fell down three times during construction before a successful design was found.

These observations confirm the validity of the iterative principle in the world of hardware development and suggest that the spiral models can indeed apply to the development of systems other than software.

6. CONCLUSION

In this article, I have tried to identify key concepts in the management of system development which will reduce risks, reduce the cost of failure and thus reduce the overall cost of developing complex systems.

I hope that other people will try out the ideas which have I described and report their experiences and new thinking in the future.

7. ACKNOWLEDGEMENTS

I am grateful to all those involved in the PCIS project, in development work, reviewing, or as prospective users of the system — Dave Allen, David Bean, Tim Huckvale, George May, Jane Northcote, Martyn Ould, Stephen Robertson, Tony Voss — for cooperation in the application of a new management model and for constructive comments on the model and earlier drafts of this article. I am also grateful for very useful comments and suggestions from an anonymous referee.

8. REFERENCES

Birtwistle, G. M., Dahl, O.-J., Myhrhaug, B., & Nygaard, K. (1979). *Simula Begin*. New York: Van Nostrand Reinhold.

Boehm, B. W. (1986). A spiral model of software development and enhancement. *ACM Sigsoft Software Engineering Notes*, **11**(4), 14–24.

Boehm, B. W., & Belz, F. (1988). Applying process programming to the Spiral Model. Proceedings of the IEEE Fourth Software Process Workshop, Devon, England, May 1988.

Buckle, J. K. (1982) *Software Configuration Management*. London: Macmillan.

Cook, S. (1986). Languages and object-oriented programming. *Software Engineering Journal*, 1(2), 73–80.

Hekmatpour, S., & Ince, D. (1986). Rapid software prototyping. Open University Technical Report 86/4. Milton Keynes: The Open University.

Jackson, M. A. (1975). *Principles of Program Design*. London: Academic Press.

Lehman, M. M. (1984). A further model of coherent programming processes. Proceedings of the IEEE Software Process Workshop, February 1984, pp. 27–33.

Osterwell, L. (1987). Software processes are software too. Proceedings of the Ninth International Conference on Software Engineering, Monterey, 1987.

Peeling, N. E., Morison, J. D., & Whiting, E. V. (1984). ADAM: an abstract database machine. RSRE Report No. 84007, Royal Signals and Radar Establishment.

Wingrove, A. (1986). The problems of managing software projects. *Software Engineering Journal*, 1(1), 3–6.

Wolff, J. G. (1990). Simplicity and power: some unifying ideas in computing. *Computer Journal* 33(6), 518–534.

Index

automatic programming, *see* machine learning

cluster analysis, 25–26, 102
concept formation, *see* language learning semantics
connectionist computing, *see* neural computing
content addressable memory, *see* data storage and retrieval
computer models, 11–12, 15, 19–20, 68

database, *see* data storage and retrieval
data compression, *see* information efficiency in *and* information redundancy
data storage and retrieval, 23, 102, 131–132, 133, 140, 153–155, 164–165

entity-relationship models, 126-127
expert system, 131, 155, *see also* data storage and retrieval

information
    efficiency in, 16–18, 22, 31, 38–41, 71–76, 84–86, 104–107, 108–111, 135, 136–139, 140–142, 145–147
    meaning of, 27, 142
    redundancy, 17, 28, 102–103, 110–111, 140–142, 145–146, 170, *see also* information, efficiency in
    theory, 26, 140
IPSE, 20–21, 23, 102, 133, 167, 180–190

Jackson's Structured Programming, 110

knowledge management, *see* data storage and retrieval

language
    grammars and linguistic theory, 14–15, 18–19, 21, 66, 68–70, 127–128
        Context-Free Phrase-Structure Grammar, 18, 31, 66, 68–70
        context sensitive power, 127–128
        Definite Clause Grammar, 14, 19, 21, 22–23, 128
        inference, grammatical, *see* machine learning
        SP and, 119–120, 141–142
        taxonomic linguistics, 14, 66
        Transformational Grammar, 18
    learning, 10–20, 31–65, 66–99, 148–151
        cumulative complexity, Brown's Law, 52
        empiricist arguments, 32
        episodic-semantic shift, 46, 53–54, 95
        generalizations and correction of overgeneralizations, 15–16, 18, 31, 35–38, 48–49, 54, 66, 76–78, 92
        nativist arguments, 58–59
        order of acquisition, 50–52, 93–95
        parts of speech, 26, 46–48, 66, 148–149
        phrases, 45–46, 47, 149–150
        rate of acquisition, 49–50, 54–56
        segmentation, 10, 26, 43–46, 92, 148–150
        semantics, 12–14, 33, 56–58
        S-P shift, *see* episodic–semantic shift
        syntax, 14–15, 148–150
        theory, 32–33, 40–41, 58–59
        words, 44–45, 49–52, 148–149
    parsing, 119, 139
    processing, 24, 127–128, 159, 171, *see also* parsing
    semantics, 27, *see also* language learning semantics
    word frequency effect, 59
logic, *see* reasoning

machine learning, 24, 101, 103–104, 129–130, 148–151, 165, 169, 171
means-ends analysis, *see* plans and automatic planning

neural computing, 25–26, 101, 102, 139

object-oriented design, 21, 22, 23, 101, 123–126
    class, sub-class and inheritance, 21, 22, 101, 124–125, 126, 127, 150–151, 156–157, 168
    instance, 126
    meta-class, 126
    methods and messages, 125–126
    part-whole relations, 123–125

pattern recognition, 24, 101, 129–130, 157, 171

plans and automatic planning, 24, 102, 131, 157–158, 172, 185–186
polythetic class, 56–58, 127
power, see information efficiency
problem solving, see plans and automatic planning
project management, 173–191
    Boehm's Spiral Model, 173, 176, 177–180, 189–190
    New Spiral Model, 186–190
    Prototyping Model, 167, 175–176
    Two-Legged Model, 175
    Waterfall Model, 174–175
Prolog, 20, 101, 114, 140

reasoning
    deductive, 24, 120–123, 151–153, 171
    inductive and probabilistic, 24, 28–29, 102–103, 131, 153–155, 171
relaxation, see search, hill-climbing

search, hill-climbing, 22, 24, 109, 111–112, 137–139, 145–146, 147

simplicity, see information efficiency
software
    configuration management, 24, 102, 130, 168–169
    change, 24, 169–170
    formal methods, 23, 101, 132, 166, 167–168
    porting of software, 132–133
    prototyping, see project management Prototyping Model
    re-use, 24, 102, 130, 168
    systems analysis, 23
    translation between computer languages, 132–133
SNPR, 15, 31, 33-38, 66, 79–95
SP
    applications, 23–24, 119–133, 147–159, 180–186
    system, 21–25, 114–119, 142–147
    theory, 33–43, 100–114, 136–142

unification, 20, 22, 24, 102, 109–110, 111, 113–114, 117–119, 140, 146–147
user interface, 24, 133, 144–145, 170

STAFFORD LIBRARY COLUMBIA
006.3 W833t c.1
Wolff, J. Gerard
Towards a theory of cognition and comput

3 3891 00031 0576

STAFFORD LIBRARY
COLUMBIA COLLEGE
1001 ROGERS STREET
COLUMBIA, MO 65216